Student Companion to
John
STEINBECK

Recent Titles in
Student Companions to Classic Writers

Student Companion to
John
STEINBECK

Cynthia Burkhead

Student Companions to Classic Writers

Greenwood Press
Westport, Connecticut • London

Library of Congress Cataloging-in-Publication Data

Burkhead, Cynthia.
    Student companion to John Steinbeck / Cynthia Burkhead.
        p.   cm.—(Student companions to classic writers, ISSN 1522-7979)
    Includes bibliographical references and index.
    ISBN 0-313-31457-8 (alk. paper)
        1. Steinbeck, John, 1902-1968—Criticism and interpretation—Handbooks, manuals, etc.
    I. Title   II. Series.
    PS3537.T3234 Z6195   2002
    813'.52—dc21   2002017134

British Library Cataloguing in Publication Data is available.

Library of Congress Catalog Card Number: 2002017134
ISBN: 0-313-31457-8
ISSN: 1522-7979

First published in 2002

Greenwood Press, 88 Post Road West, Westport, CT 06881
An imprint of Greenwood Publishing Group, Inc.
www.greenwood.com

Printed in the United States of America

The paper used in this book complies with the
Permanent Paper Standard issued by the National
Information Standards Organization (Z39.48-1984).

P

Contents

Series Foreword

This series has been designed to meet the needs of students and general readers for accessible literary criticism on the American and world writers most frequently studied and read in the secondary school, community college, and four-year college classrooms. Unlike other works of literary criticism that are written for the specialist and graduate student, or that feature a variety of reprinted scholarly essays on sometimes obscure aspects of the writer's work, the Student Companions to Classic Writers series is carefully crafted to examine each writer's major works fully and in a systematic way, at the level of the nonspecialist and general reader. The objective is to enable the reader to gain a deeper understanding of the work and to apply critical thinking skills to the act of reading. The proven format for the volumes in this series was developed by an advisory board of teachers and librarians for a successful series published by Greenwood Press, Critical Companions to Popular Contemporary Writers. Responding to their request for easy-to-use and yet challenging literary criticism for students and adult library patrons, Greenwood Press developed a systematic format that is not intimidating but helps the reader to develop the ability to analyze literature.

How does this work? Each volume in the Student Companions to Classic Writers series is written by a subject specialist, an academic who understands students' needs for a basic and yet challenging examination of the writer's canon. Each volume begins with a biographical chapter, drawn from published sources, biographies, and autobiographies, that relates the writer's life to his or her work. The next chapter examines the writer's literary heritage, tracing the literary influences of other writers on that writer and explaining and discussing the literary genres into which the writer's work falls. Each of the following chapters examines a major work by the writer, those works most frequently read and studied by high school and college students. Depending on the writer's canon, generally between four and eight major works are examined, each in an individual chapter. The discussion of each work is organized into separate sections on plot development, character development, and major themes. Literary devices and style, narrative point of view, and historical setting are also discussed in turn if pertinent to the work. Each chapter concludes with an alternate critical perspective from which to read the work, such as a psychological or feminist criticism. The critical theory is defined briefly in easy, comprehensible language for the student. Looking at the literature from the point of view of a particular critical approach will help the reader to understand and apply critical theory to the act of reading and analyzing literature.

Of particular value in each volume is the bibliography, which includes a complete bibliography of the writer's works, a selected bibliography of biographical and critical works suitable for students, and lists of reviews of each work examined in the companion, both from the time the literature was originally published and from contemporary sources, all of which will be helpful to readers, teachers, and librarians who would like to consult additional sources.

As a source of literary criticism for the student or for the general reader, this series will help the reader to gain an understanding of the writer's work and skill in critical reading.

The Life of
John Steinbeck

Following his death on December 20, 1968, John Steinbeck's ashes were carried by his third wife, Elaine, from the couple's home in New York to their permanent burial spot beside his parents' graves in a cemetery in the city of Salinas, California. Sixty-six years earlier, on February 27, 1902, Steinbeck was born in his parents' home on Central Avenue in Salinas. Steinbeck had come full circle. The life that filled the moments between beginning and end was one of struggle and success, elation and despair, love and loss; in short, Steinbeck's life was not the stuff of fantasy. His were the real experiences of a man facing life in twentieth-century America.

In many ways, John Steinbeck's story begins before his birth. In Steinbeck's family history are found the seeds of Steinbeck's literary themes. A part of this history Steinbeck knew only second hand through stories and records. Those were the stories passed to him by his father, John Ernst Steinbeck. John Ernst was the son of John Adolph Grossteinbeck, a strongly religious Lutheran and adventure lover who was born in Düsseldorf, Germany. As a young man, John Adolph traveled to Palestine with his brother and sister-in-law on a mission to convert the Jews. While there, his brother was stabbed to death and his sister-in-law was violently raped by desert tribesmen. Some good did result from the trip, however; John Adolph met Almira Dickson and the two were soon married. The couple settled down in Almira's Massachusetts hometown where John Adolph worked as a wood carver, a skill later practiced by his grandson. They eventually settled in California, but not before yet another misadventure.

John Adolph moved his young family to Florida at an inopportune time, just before the onset of the Civil War. He was conscripted into the Confederate Army, from which he soon deserted. By luck or by fate, Almira and the children were allowed by Confederate authorities to follow John Adolph. The family soon migrated to California where they bought ten acres of land north of Salinas, establishing a dairy farm and orchard and later opening a flour mill.

While less adventure filled, the family of Olive Steinbeck, John's mother, also had stories to offer the future author. Samuel Hamilton, Olive's father, was born in Ballykelly, Northern Ireland. As a young man he moved to New York, where he met and married Elizabeth Fagen, also from Ireland, in 1849. In 1871, the family moved to California, eventually living in Salinas where Samuel became one of the town's founding members. Samuel soon moved his family to a ranch near King City, which Steinbeck re-created in many of his fictional works, including *The Long Valley* stories and *East of Eden*.

Olive Hamilton, a teacher, and John Ernst Steinbeck, a flour mill manager, met at a church in King City. They soon married and moved to Salinas where they established a middle-class life in the middle-class home on Central Avenue where John was born the only son, and the third of four children. The family seemed to be secure and happy. But there was, using one of Steinbeck's favorite descriptors, a grayness within the home. John Ernst was restless and often depressed, conditions that resulted from his losing his job at the Sperry flour mill, which closed partly because of his mismanagement. Olive Hamilton prevailed upon a family friend to arrange an accounting position for her husband at the Spreckels sugar plant, a company where young John also later worked. This same friend later arranged for John Ernst to fill the vacant position of treasurer of Monterey County, a position John Ernst kept for the remainder of his life. Even though he was now able to provide for his family, John Ernst remained distant from them, never completely regaining the self-assurance lost when the flour mill collapsed. In contrast, Olive was a confident woman whose interest in social justice made her an active member of the Salinas community. She also had high expectations of those around her and pushed her son to live up to the potential she saw in him. As an adult, Steinbeck would establish similar high standards for himself, the pressure from which would result in a low self-image manifesting itself as a lifelong fear of failure, "grey" periods, and trouble with alcohol.

There were many distractions to ease the emotional tension in the Steinbeck home. At the age of ten, Steinbeck was introduced to Thomas Malory's Arthurian legends by his aunt. Thus began a lifelong fascination with Malory's themes and structures, on which John would build in his own work. By this time John was already an advanced reader thanks to his mother's diligent instruction and to the availability of reading material in the Steinbeck home. John also established close childhood friendships, some of which were maintained until his death. There were also breaks from the Salinas home, mostly seaside vacations at a small holiday home John Ernst built for his family in Pacific Grove, near Monterey, a location Steinbeck would return to many times both in his life and in his literature. During high school, John was active in sports and other school activities. While he was popular enough among his classmates to be elected president of his senior class, John's real interest, as early as his first year of high school, was writing. He received little support in this from his family but found encouragement from teachers and friends. His desire to write continued as he entered Stanford University in 1919.

Steinbeck attended Stanford on and off for the next six years but left without ever earning a degree. During those semesters when he was enrolled, Steinbeck missed classes frequently and, when in attendance, failed to apply himself to those courses that held no interest for him. Consequently, much of his college career was spent on academic probation. Steinbeck did devote himself completely to celebrating his freedom from the restriction of home by attending too many parties and drinking far too much, a habit that would be a problem for Steinbeck throughout his life. But the social distractions were not the ultimate causes of Steinbeck's academic problems at Stanford. Steinbeck wanted to be a writer and would not apply himself to anything but writing, although his attempts at being a student would continue for six years.

Summers and other breaks from the university offered exposure to people and experiences that Steinbeck filed in his memory for later use in his writing. During his first summer break from Stanford, Steinbeck worked for two weeks as a surveyor but found the work too physically trying. He then began working as a maintenance man at the Spreckles plant in Salinas. There he met men and heard stories that found a place in his later fiction. Some of his breaks from school were spent working as an itinerant ranch hand, or bindlestiff. This exposure to the life of the bindlestiffs was written into the story *Of Mice and Men.* During a subsequent break from Stanford, Steinbeck worked as a foreman over a crew of migrant workers at another Spreckles ranch. This job lasted only four months, however; then Steinbeck returned to Salinas, where he moved from job to job before being readmitted at Stanford in 1923.

Steinbeck found more success as a student during this period at the university. He made new friends, some who were English Club members with whom Steinbeck read and debated the merits of various works of literature. Steinbeck also met two Stanford professors who had an impact on his writing. Margery Bailey, a Yale Ph.D. who taught literature and set high standards for her students, admired Steinbeck's drive and gumption, and she became both his mentor and his friend. Another teacher who took the young writer under her wing was Edith Mirrieless, a published writer teaching creative writing. The support Steinbeck finally found for his work paid off with the 1924 publication of two short stories, his first real publications, in the *Stanford Spectator*. In the summer of 1923, Steinbeck had another experience that contributed to the eventual course of his writing. Steinbeck attended a summer course with his sister Mary at the Hopkins Marine Station near Monterey. This marked the beginning of his interest in ecology and the scientific nature of life, which remained a driving interest and later found firmer development through conversations with a man whom Steinbeck met seven years later in a dentist's office.

Steinbeck left Stanford for good after a final attempt at his education in the winter and spring of 1925. He earned no degree but had accumulated volumes of lessons, both about writing and about life. The time seemed right to pursue a writing career. The Roaring Twenties, the decade following World War I and before the Great Depression, was characterized by optimism and prosperity. It was also a time when seasoned authors, such as Sinclair Lewis, Theodore Dreiser, and Willa Cather, as well as new writers, such as F. Scott Fitzgerald and Ernest Hemingway, were finding success in literature. John Steinbeck believed he, too, could make a career as an author. The realities of life, however, necessitated a need for steady work.

This need for steady employment took Steinbeck first to a resort in Lake Tahoe, where he worked as a maintenance man for the summer and fall months of 1925. Leaving Tahoe in November, Steinbeck went to San Francisco, where he found work on a ship going to New York via the Panama Canal. Steinbeck had a romantic image of himself as a struggling artist in the Big Apple; however, the reality of his time there soon stripped away all of the romance. For a time Steinbeck lived with his sister, Beth, and her husband, from whom Steinbeck was forced to accept help almost as soon as he got off the boat. He found a job with a construction company, but the work was grueling and long and left little time for writing. With help from his uncle, Joe Hamilton, Steinbeck was hired as a reporter for the *New York American*, a newspaper owned by the publisher William Randolph Hearst. While he wrote very compelling journalism later in his career, this first journey away from fiction was a failure. What he wrote was far too figurative for the news. He was eventually fired. Unable to find a publisher for his collection of short stories, Steinbeck returned to California as he had come, earning his passage on a ship bound for San Francisco via the Panama Canal.

Steinbeck returned to Salinas to visit his family, but the stay there was short. His failures in New York reinforced his parents' conviction that Steinbeck should give up the idea of making a profession of writing and that he should instead find steady work with a secure future. Leaving Salinas, Steinbeck visited friends at Stanford and then returned to Lake Tahoe, where he lived and worked for the next two years, and where he completed his first novel, *Cup of Gold*.

In June 1928, while he was working at a fish hatchery in Lake Tahoe, Steinbeck met Carol Henning, who was visiting Lake Tahoe with her sister. Steinbeck fell in love with Carol within a week. When she returned to San Francisco in July, Steinbeck fell into a deep depression. He was insecure about his manhood and his looks, which conflicted violently with his sense that he was destined to become a great author and a great man. By the end of that summer, Steinbeck was on his way to San Francisco.

In San Francisco, Steinbeck and Carol spent a lot of time getting to know one another, but John also worked in the daytime at another manual labor job, and at night on a new novel titled *To a God Unknown*, a story taken from a play abandoned by his friend Toby Street. Also, Carol introduced him to new people, including a group of socialists. Steinbeck never joined this group and never joined the Communist Party, but after the publication of *In Dubious Battle* in 1936, and *The Grapes of Wrath* three years later, his passing association with these people was used as ammunition by some for the charges that he was a communist.

His time in San Francisco was happy, but Steinbeck still found too little time for writing, so he moved to the family vacation home in Pacific Grove. While John Ernst was still doubtful about his son's prospects for earning a living as a writer, he began paying Steinbeck an allowance of $25 a month, enough at that time to provide for his basic needs. Pacific Grove was close enough to San Francisco that Carol could make frequent visits. These visits were kept secret because of perceived impropriety, although the two were very nearly found together in bed by Steinbeck's parents arriving for a surprise visit with their son. It seemed Steinbeck finally had the time and security to pursue his vocation full time. His life was good. As if to verify this, *Cup of Gold* was accepted in January 1929 for publication by McBride and Company, a firm that refused to read his short stories when John was living in New York. Steinbeck received a $250 advance, his first real income from writing.

In January 1930, after temporarily moving to Los Angeles, John and Carol were married. In many ways, Carol heavily influenced Steinbeck's literature for the next ten years. She was self-assured, independent, and assertive, but she was also very supportive of her husband's work. Carol typed his manuscripts, and, the most taxing job of all, she corrected his grammar and spelling. She was also an informed advocate of social justice; this seems to be the area where she most influenced Steinbeck's work, which previously is marked by themes focusing on the individual. Steinbeck wrote his greatest social and political works while married to Carol, including *In Dubious Battle*, *Of Mice and Men*, and *The Grapes of Wrath*.

For most of their marriage, the Steinbecks lived in the Pacific Grove home. Carol worked, John wrote, and even during the lean depression years that marked most of their marriage, the couple was happy and secure. Unlike many, the Steinbecks paid no rent on the house in Pacific Grove, and their garden and the nearby ocean provided an abundance of food. They also made good friends during this time. In the fall of 1930 John Steinbeck met Ed Ricketts in a dentist's waiting room in Monterey. This meeting produced the closest and most influential friendship of Steinbeck's life.

Ricketts was a man who, like Steinbeck, had left college with no degree but with a passion; his was a passion for ecology. After he left the University of Chicago, Ricketts moved to Pacific Grove and opened Pacific Biologicals, a company that supplied marine specimens to schools and researchers. Steinbeck began to spend time daily at Ricketts's lab, and the two men would talk for hours about science and philosophy and nature. Along the way, ideas that had been growing shapelessly for Steinbeck, ideas about humans and their existence, began to take on definition. One idea given form through these often late-night discussions—usually accompanied by much drinking—was that of the phalanx. This idea holds that groups consisting of individuals are connected to a larger drive or spirit with a separate will and that, functioning as part of a group, individuals will work to fulfill the will of the larger entity. This process causes a shift from "I" thinking to "we" thinking. Problems occur when the "I" thinking, or the individual will, asserts itself. The phalanx would become a major theme in Steinbeck's work, most notably in *The Grapes of Wrath*. Steinbeck's other major theme that can be directly traced to Ricketts was that of nonteleological thinking, the philosophy Ricketts attempted to foster in his own life. Teleology is the idea that there is an ultimate design or purpose in nature. Nonteleological thinking restricts all answers to questions about the world to what can be demonstrated through natural explanations. It is scientific thinking that does not allow unverifiable possibilities, such as God, to answer questions of cause or effect. In *Of Mice and Men*, the reasons for the tragedies of Lennie's life and his death are not offered as mysteries to be solved. The narrative focus is restricted to the events occurring in the story. What might have been or what could be must not, for the scientist, for Ed Ricketts and, subsequently, for John Steinbeck, stand in the way of a clear observation of what is.

The friendship with Ricketts was much more than academic. The lab became a place for the men to drink and to listen to Ricketts's large collection of music and to share their most personal joys and pains. The depth of their relationship gave Steinbeck the material with which to model six of his characters after his closest friend. Even after Steinbeck eventually moved to New York, the friendship continued to be strong, and remained so until Ricketts's car was hit by a train, killing him in the spring of 1948. Steinbeck never completely recovered from this loss.

Life in Pacific Grove remained good for John and Carol Steinbeck until John began to find success as an author. Money and fame became problems for the writer and for his marriage. In 1935, *Tortilla Flat* became the first work for which Steinbeck earned more than a publisher's advance. His first royalty check was $300, a considerable sum during the depression years, and the film rights to the book were soon sold for $4,000. This income frightened Steinbeck, who had never had money and worried that having it now might change who he was and, consequently, change his work. After the publication of *Of Mice and Men* and *The Grapes of Wrath* over the next four years, both followed by the sale of film rights, the problems of financial success would be compounded by pressure from people, mostly strangers, who began to bombard Steinbeck with requests for loans, investments, and outright gifts of money. His new-found fame made him a sizable target, but the difficulties caused by fame had much deeper roots for the writer. Steinbeck was torn between his desire for success and his fears about the public recognition such success would necessarily bring. This fear had many facets. Similar to his wariness of the financial rewards for his work, Steinbeck was concerned about what the effects of fame would be on him. Again, he did not want it to alter who he was. Also, the more Steinbeck was noted for his success, the more he felt an obligation to continue that success. Even when he assailed the critics who continually compared subsequent works to *The Grapes of Wrath*, only to claim these works did not measure up, Steinbeck was himself guilty of privately doubting the quality of his work, of feeling like it was not good enough to be the work of a famous author. Steinbeck's struggle with his success never completely disappeared.

Steinbeck's success also placed new pressures on his marriage. Since his most popular works of the 1930s were all made into films, the Steinbecks were introduced to many people in the film industry and their social circle grew to include a faster, more socially active set of friends, such as actors Spencer Tracy, Charlie Chaplin, and Anthony Quinn. At first, Carol liked the new social opportunities John's fame had created, while John felt ill at ease and wanted the comfort of his old friends. Eventually, Carol, too, found it impossible to keep up with the pace of the Hollywood crowd. The problems in their marriage that were building at a steady rate along with Steinbeck's success eventually became irreparable.

During this time, the Steinbecks had moved from the house in Pacific Grove to a home they built in Los Gatos, north of Monterey. Feeling the need for even more seclusion from the public that was increasingly seeking Steinbeck out, the couple then moved to a small ranch outside of Los Gatos, where in 1939 John finished *The Grapes of Wrath*. It seemed they now had everything they could ever want. But both were drinking heavily, and John was becoming more difficult to live with. By 1940, he was having an affair with

Gwyn Conger, a singer from Los Angeles introduced to John by his childhood friend Max Wagner. Carol eventually learned of the affair; this was not difficult since John and Gwyn often were seen together publicly. Carol filed for divorce on the grounds of mental cruelty, and it became final in the spring of 1943. Eleven days later, Steinbeck married Gwyn Conger.

Soon after his breakup with Carol, Steinbeck had moved with Gwen to New York City. Not long after their move, the Japanese bombed the American bases at Pearl Harbor, and the United States entered the Second World War. Two months before the December 7, 1941, bombing, President Franklin D. Roosevelt had asked Steinbeck to help in fighting German propaganda. He collaborated with the newly formed Foreign Information Service (FIS), and through his experiences with that organization learned of the groups in Europe organizing and carrying out resistance against their Nazi occupiers. This experience provided the material for *The Moon Is Down*, Steinbeck's anti-occupation novel and play. In 1943, almost immediately following his marriage to Gwyn, Steinbeck left for Europe as a war correspondent for the *New York Herald Tribune*. His columns from England, North Africa, and the Italian front were syndicated in England, much of South America, and were printed in newspapers in most of the United States, except Oklahoma, which was still punishing Steinbeck for his representation of the state in *The Grapes of Wrath*. The forty-one-year-old Steinbeck spent five months covering the war and returned to New York in October 1943, tired and deeply affected by what he had encountered.

Steinbeck had spent a great deal of time arranging the necessary clearances as a war correspondent, so Gwyn both knew about and had time to prepare for his absence, but she was still resentful of his leaving so soon after their marriage. Upon his return, her further resentments toward her famous husband became an undercurrent to their marriage, which seemed to fluctuate between highs and lows until its end. One of the high points was the birth of Steinbeck's first child, Thom, on August 2, 1944. Another should have been the family's move back to Monterey in October 1944. John missed his friends and the town that had been home for so much of his life. The Steinbecks bought a house, intent on making Monterey their permanent home, but soon found they were not welcome there. After the January 1945 publication of *Cannery Row*, the people of Monterey began to shun the Steinbecks, believing the author had created a negative image of the town as a place defined by drunkenness and prostitution. Escaping the painful treatment of his neighbors, Steinbeck went to Mexico to work on the film version of *The Pearl*, and in the fall of 1945, the couple left California and returned to New York. Soon, Gwyn was pregnant again, and on June 12, 1946, John Steinbeck IV, called Catbird by his father, was born.

Gwyn's resentments toward Steinbeck continued to increase. With two children, a home, and Steinbeck's busy career, she saw her own chances of a singing career slipping away while her husband's star grew brighter. She traveled with Steinbeck to Europe but was jealous of all the attention he received there. The problems continued after the couple returned to New York. Happy for a break from the tensions of his marriage, Steinbeck traveled to Russia in July 1947 with photographer Robert Capa, collecting material for *A Russian Journal.* He spent part of the winter of 1948 in California, conducting research for the novel that would become *East of Eden.* In May, immediately upon his return from Ed Ricketts' funeral, with Steinbeck experiencing one of the lowest emotional periods of his life, Gwyn hit him with her request for a divorce.

Emotionally and physically weakened, John returned to California to the family home in Pacific Grove. He tried to work, traveling to Mexico to work on the film script for *Viva Zapata!*, but he had difficulty concentrating. The breakup with Gwyn had left him with little money, and she refused to return his books and notebooks, which contributed to his problems with work. She was also making it hard for him to see his children.

Steinbeck's life began to improve in the spring of 1949. He began dating such women as Ann Sothern and the actress, Paulette Goddard, who was the ex-wife of his friend Burgess Meredith. Ann brought a friend with her on a weekend visit with Steinbeck in Pacific Grove, and that friend, Elaine Scott, would become John Steinbeck's third and final wife. Elaine was an independent, self-assured daughter of a Texas oilman. While pursuing her own aspirations as an actress, Elaine had met and married the actor Zachary Scott. By the time she met Steinbeck in 1949, her marriage to Scott was all but over. Because both she and Steinbeck were still legally married, however, they dated secretly.

By the summer of 1949, Gwyn had allowed the boys to visit John in Pacific Grove. This was a very happy time for Steinbeck. He was getting to know his young sons. There would be later tensions between the boys and their father, but Steinbeck was always aware of the importance of forming a strong relationship with his sons even though this was often made difficult because of Steinbeck's work and Gwyn's interference. Also, Elaine and Zachary Scott had decided to divorce. After her divorce hearing in December, she and her daughter, Waverly, moved to New York, and Steinbeck, wanting to be close to his children and Elaine, soon followed. They rented separate apartments in the same building. The move turned out to be opportune for Steinbeck. Elaine introduced him to many of her friends in the theater business, including the team of Rodgers and Hammerstein, who later produced two of Steinbeck's plays.

On December 28, 1951, John Steinbeck and Elaine Scott were married. They had purchased a house in New York and Steinbeck settled down there to write *East of Eden.* The book had been in various stages of development since

Steinbeck had traveled to California to begin research in 1948. But now he could focus on the book, partly because Elaine was very supportive of his work and took care of the house and Steibeck's sons when they visited. He was not totally consumed by the work, however. In the summer after their marriage, they rented a house in Nantucket and Steinbeck bought a small boat. The couple cut back on their drinking and enjoyed life quietly with their children. At the end of the summer, they returned to New York, where Steinbeck finished *East of Eden* in November.

The manuscript for Steinbeck's sweeping California novel was delivered to his editor, Pascal Covici, in a wooden box carved by the author. The box also included a letter to Pascal, or "Pat," that would become the book's dedication. That Steinbeck dedicated the novel that was perhaps for him the most personally and emotionally important of his career to his editor attests to the bond between these two men, a bond that began as a business relationship and grew into one of the most important friendships of Steinbeck's life.

Pascal Covici owned his own publishing company when he was introduced to the work of the still fairly unknown Steinbeck by a Chicago bookstore owner in 1934. Steinbeck had by then published his first three books with three different publishing firms and was having difficulty finding a publisher for *Tortilla Flat*. Covici published the novel, which earned Steinbeck his first real income and critical attention. After the publication of *In Dubious Battle*, Covici's firm went out of business, but the editor took Steinbeck as a client with him to Viking, which would continue to publish Steinbeck's work even after both he and his editor were dead.

The friendship between the two men was based in part on Covici's understanding that Steinbeck needed encouragement—he often had to verbally pull Steinbeck out of slumps caused by depression or personal crisis—and an advocate, especially against the strong attacks of the critics. But there was also genuine affection and admiration between these two men. Many of the letters from Steinbeck to Covici outline the author's daily activities; he wrote of home repairs and gardening and even his perpetual search for the perfect pencils with which to write. Covici's responses often indicated a desire to be by his friend's side planting flowers or painting a room. When Steinbeck found the perfect pencil, it was Covici who kept him amply supplied. Like any friendship, theirs had moments of tension, especially toward the end. But this did not lessen the pain Steinbeck felt over the loss of his friend on October 14, 1964, just one month after Covici had traveled to the White House to witness his friend receiving the Presidential Medal of Freedom.

What remained of the 1950s after Steinbeck completed *East of Eden* in 1952 were years of relative calm and stability for Steinbeck. There was, however, creative struggle—after the critical failure of *Sweet Thursday*, his 1954 sequel to

Cannery Row, Steinbeck wanted to abandon the novel form entirely and focus his energies on drama. But he had trouble getting words on paper, and *Pipe Dream*, the Rodgers and Hammerstein musical based on *Sweet Thursday*, found little more success in the theater than had Burning Bright, his 1950 play that closed almost as soon as it opened. Steinbeck returned to fiction with *The Short Reign of Pippin IV* in 1957, but the focused energy with which he had written through the 1930s and 1940s seemed to be fading. There were diversions, though, that kept the author busy and engaged.

One of those diversions was politics. Steinbeck had always been a patriot with strong political ideas. He had throughout his career expressed his ideas in literature, either challenging American policies, as with *The Grapes of Wrath*, or supporting them, as with the propaganda novel *The Moon Is Down*. His World War II journalism is a further indication of his support and real hopes for America as a nation. But it was not until the 1950s that Steinbeck participated in the political process. Motivated by a sincere belief that a great man could rise to lead the nation out of its decline, Steinbeck campaigned in 1952 for Adlai Stevenson, a New Deal Democrat like himself who was running for president against Dwight D. Eisenhower. Steinbeck was greatly saddened by Stevenson's loss but found hope again four years later when Stevenson challenged Eisenhower a second time. Steinbeck's participation grew in the 1956 election. He covered both the Democratic and Republican conventions for the Louisville *Courier-Journal*, which syndicated his pieces nationally. At the Democratic convention, he met Adlai Stevenson for the first time, and the meeting only bolstered his support for the candidate. After the conventions, Steinbeck was asked to write a speech for Estes Kefauver, Stevenson's vice-presidential running mate. The Democrats were impressed and asked Steinbeck to write speeches for Stevenson, which he did but with some dissatisfaction. He felt the Democrats were not being assertive enough in their campaign, and he wanted to write a more aggressive and challenging speech, which never happened.

The Steinbecks also spent a great deal of time traveling in the 1950s, with yearly trips during the New Year season to the Caribbean and a number of longer trips to Europe. Traveling in Europe was always emotionally positive for Steinbeck, who was a favorite American author in many countries, perhaps second only to Hemingway. In Russia, his books were passed from reader to reader underground; the people liked his literary support of the common man, but the government found his work anti-Communist. This must have delighted the author, who at home was still resented for his presentation of the downtrodden and was labeled by some as a Communist. In 1957, Steinbeck traveled first to Italy and then to England conducting research for his rewriting of Malory's Arthurian tales in modern English. Steinbeck worked on this project for the remainder of his life. *The Acts of King Arthur and His Noble Knights* would be published in 1976, eight years after Steinbeck's death. The project in many ways completed a circle for the author, returning him to the literary roots planted in his childhood by his aunt.

It was also during the 1950s, when he was feeling a new sense of self-assurance, that Steinbeck's health began to decline. In October 1953, he suffered the first of what much later would be diagnosed as a series of small strokes. Steinbeck's reaction to his illness was to succumb to it emotionally and physically; he refused to see beyond the condition and do anything for himself to overcome it. Steinbeck had always relied upon women to care for him, and it took the strongest woman of his life, Elaine, to convince him to do something for himself. He began to think of things other than his illness, and he also sought help from a psychologist who helped him through this period of illness and emotional instability.

The last decade of Steinbeck's life was bittersweet professionally and personally. By 1962, he had published his last piece of fiction, *The Winter of Our Discontent*, and his last full-length work, *Travels with Charley*. Although he would work on his Malory project off and on until his death, the translation was never completed and the portions Steinbeck did finish were never quite satisfactory either to the author or to his editor. Ill health contributed greatly to Steinbeck's inability to focus his energies on writing in the 1960s, but other major detractors were the critical attacks that began with a late 1958 review by Alfred Kazin of a book of critical work on Steinbeck. Much of Kazin's fire was directed toward Steinbeck rather than the volume of criticism under review. In many ways *The Winter of Our Discontent* and *Travels with Charley* were written on the defensive as Steinbeck attempted to prove Kazin wrong.

There was a brief period of respite from the critical attacks. Steinbeck was invited to receive a number of honorary degrees but turned each down believing that his own failure to earn a real college degree prevented him from accepting false ones. His books continued to be popular with readers, which was perhaps Steinbeck's greatest defense against the critics. But the attacks resumed again when it was announced in October 1962, during the height of the Cuban missile crisis, that Steinbeck had been awarded the Nobel Prize for Literature. The *New York Times* initiated the assault with an editorial claiming Steinbeck's award was undeserved because he had produced no major work since *The Grapes of Wrath* and because he had made no profound influence on literature. Most American publications followed the tone set by the *Times* in their own editorials. Along with his anger over these attacks, which Steinbeck vented in his Nobel acceptance speech by confirming his allegiance with the common man, the reader, Steinbeck must have felt a great sense of disbelief and betrayal. Even in the case of an internationally competitive prize, his own countrymen did not have enough patriotism to support one of their own.

Steinbeck's own patriotism never wavered. In 1963 he traveled on a cultural exchange to the Soviet bloc countries where, although he was watched closely by the KGB, he was able to meet with the people who, like Western Europeans, still counted Steinbeck as one of their favorites. He stirred up a satisfactory amount of trouble, as he had promised President John F. Kennedy he would, mostly over the Soviets' refusal to pay Steinbeck royalties for the Russian publications of his work. Back in the United States, a month after President Kennedy's assassination, the Steinbecks were invited by President Lyndon B. Johnson to dinner at the White House, beginning a close friendship between the Steinbecks and the Johnsons. His friendship with and loyalty to Johnson would be tested during the intensifying Vietnam conflict.

The years after the publication of *Travels with Charley* were ones of frequent travel for the Steinbecks. It was also a time when Steinbeck tried to establish a close relationship with his sons, who had run away from Gwyn and lived with their father and Elaine for a time before returning to live with their mother, which Steinbeck took as a sign of problems in their relationship. In the spring of 1966, John IV enlisted in the armed forces, presenting an opportunity for John to show support for his son and for his country. John and Elaine traveled to Vietnam in December 1966, where John served for the next three months as a correspondent for *Newsday*. There the sixty-four-year-old author went directly to the fighting, often traveling in helicopters with the First Cavalry. In his columns, Steinbeck stayed away from policy debates and directly addressed the experiences of American fighting men. Privately, he felt a successful outcome to the war was impossible, but he did not allow his doubts to become public. This was Steinbeck's way of remaining loyal to president, country, and, perhaps most consistent with his focus throughout his career, to the thousands of American men who were risking their lives.

Steinbeck's health, slowly failing for almost fifteen years, went into a rapid decline in the eighteen months following his return from Vietnam. In the spring of 1968, he suffered another "spell," which left him temporarily without feeling in his hands and briefly unconscious. He had a small heart attack the following July, and by November, he was having trouble breathing due to emphysema. By this time, Steinbeck was confined to his apartment in New York, and Elaine had to hire a nurse to help care for him. On December 20, 1968, after spending the day with friends and his beloved Elaine, Steinbeck quietly slipped into a coma and soon stopped breathing.

Unlike his contemporary Ernest Hemingway, Steinbeck's death was not dramatic. But in a complete analysis, neither was his life. He had a full career, working hard to earn his living. He suffered personal pain and had to learn to accept many losses, including two marriages and a number of close friends. He had a precarious relationship with his sons. He was never quite sure of his own

worth either as a man or as a writer. In short, while more public and perhaps more intense, Steinbeck's life was very much like the lives of the common people he spent his own life honoring and defending with his writing.

2

Steinbeck's Career and Contributions

The year 1929 ended bleakly for most of America. The Wall Street crash of October 24 ushered in the ten-year misery that was the Great Depression, creating paupers out of millionaires, and for those with less to lose, the future offered little more hope.

While the economy during this period in America came to a near halt, American literature was thriving. F. Scott Fitzgerald had published *The Great Gatsby* in 1925, and Ernest Hemingway's second novel, *A Farewell to Arms*, appeared in 1929, the same year that Thomas Wolfe and William Faulkner published their first novels. Also in 1929, John Steinbeck joined these young American authors with the publication of his first novel, *Cup of Gold*.

STEINBECK'S CAREER

While the 1929 publication of *Cup of Gold* served as the public literary introduction of John Steinbeck, it proved to be both critically and artistically rocky, and this tenuousness in his career continued until the publication of *Tortilla Flat* six years later. Yet, *Cup of Gold* served Steinbeck well by allowing him to find and establish the conditions in which he would need to write for the rest of his career. These conditions came to him more by necessity than experiment. Having left Stanford without a degree, and then spending time working in San Francisco and New York, Steinbeck found employment as a caretaker on an estate on the south shore of Lake Tahoe, where he remained for two years. While he later handwrote his work in pencil on yellow legal pads, he produced this first novel on a small Corona typewriter, surrounded by the nature that seemed always an important element of Steinbeck's environment. At Tahoe, too, he lived in the isolation that, finally, became a painful and yet necessary element to Steinbeck's work.

It is difficult to find much of the John Steinbeck of *Tortilla Flat* and *The Grapes of Wrath* in *Cup of Gold*. Having discovered the practical necessities of writing, Steinbeck had yet to find the natural and poetic style that defined his greatest work. *Cup of Gold* is the story of Henry Morgan, a young boy from Wales in the seventeenth century, who, after a consultation with Merlin, goes on a failed quest for two prizes, a cup of gold and a virgin saint. He learns his saint is married, and the resulting attitudes about his failed quest lead to the failure of his symbolic quest, the cup of gold. Unsuccessful in both quests, Henry returns to England to face charges of piracy. Charles II decides not only to drop the piracy charges, but also to knight Henry Morgan. He is sent to Jamaica as governor, where he punishes two of his fellow pirates with death and later dies himself from a mysterious disease. His own death is punishment for not staying true to those original dreams that took him from Britain to the tropical regions of the world in the first place. After his death, Henry's sins continue to haunt him in a final vision.

Steinbeck's own assessment of his first novel was grim. He confessed to a friend that he felt the book was bad, but he believed the experience would help him create better work. While self-criticism was typical for Steinbeck, the assessment was not without merit in the case of *Cup of Gold*. The language of the novel is inflated, the style is inconsistent, and the adjectives are overused. The novel's reception was mixed. A number of books were sold, although not enough to earn the author more than his small advance. Additionally, there was an absence of reviews, mostly because his publisher, Robert M. McBride and Company, failed to send out review copies of the novel. Whatever its problems, *Cup of Gold* did earn Steinbeck the advance of $250, the first real income from his writing, and an introduction to American readers.

It was three years before John Steinbeck published another book. He finished the novel *To a God Unknown*, but the book required a complete revision. During this period, Steinbeck published *The Pastures of Heaven*. One of the difficulties Steinbeck encountered at this early point of his career was maintaining a publisher for his work. McBride had rejected the earlier version of *To a God Unknown*, so Steinbeck's agent sent *The Pastures of Heaven* out to other publishers after its completion in December 1931. In February 1932, Robert Ballou of Cape and Smith accepted the manuscript. Before the book went into production, however, Ballou left Cape and Smith, fearing the publisher was about to go under, and he took Steinbeck's book with him to Brewer, Warren, and Putnam, who would publish *The Pastures of Heaven* in November 1932.

Like *Cup of Gold, The Pastures of Heaven* brought few reviews and no critical response, and Steinbeck again earned no more initial income from its publication than the advance. While the book is rarely read today, scholars realize its literary value and its value to Steinbeck scholarship. *The Pastures of Heaven* is not a novel; it is a series of stories, each complete in itself, about a family or an individual living in a hill valley not far from Monterey, California. Nor is the book a short story collection; each story is tied together by the place and by the associations between these valley residents and the members of the Munroe family, who move into the peaceful and established agricultural community.

In *The Pastures of Heaven*, readers first see the natural and poetic use of language familiar in Steinbeck's greatest works. Steinbeck forsakes the foreignness of distant places seen in *Cup of Gold* for a California landscape that is imbedded in his own psyche. In this familiar place with familiar language, Steinbeck also begins to develop his lifelong themes. When the Munroes move to the valley, they carry with them an unconscious, unintentional quality of evil, and the people with whom they come into contact begin to suffer injury as a result. The violence that comes to the valley, the evil events that begin to touch the lives of the people, is presented by Steinbeck not as a moral issue, but as a random, scientific occurrence, and the author adopts the tone of a scientific observer that, while consistent with literary naturalism, is uniquely Steinbeck's. More specifically, the presentation of the evil events in the stories signals the initial development of Steinbeck's theme of nonteleological existence, the scientific focus on what is rather than what might be.

In 1933, Steinbeck's editor, Robert Ballou, discovered that Brewer, Warren, and Putnam was also experiencing financial difficulty, so he left the company to start his own publishing house. His initial promise to Steinbeck was to publish two books, and Ballou kept this agreement by publishing *To a God Unknown* just one year after the appearance of *The Pastures of Heaven*. Steinbeck borrowed the original title of the novel, *The Green Lady*, and the general story from a play written and then abandoned by his college friend Toby Street. Steinbeck revised the novel after its original rejection by Steinbeck's first publisher, and the new version included new ideas that resulted from new influences on the author, including archetypal images and characters.

At the novel's publication, reviewers once again ignored Steinbeck, resulting in his third financial failure. But the novel shows the continuing growth of the author as well as the influence of the mythologist Joseph Campbell, with whom Steinbeck had become friends. *To a God Unknown* is the story of four Wayne brothers who, led by Joseph after he receives his father's blessing, make the westward move from Vermont to California. Three of the brothers, including Joseph, are married, and each possesses a different spiritual orientation; thus, each has a different conception of God or the gods. Only Burton, with no wife and a life of continued degeneration, has no religion and, thus, no relationship to the gods at all.

The Waynes' arrival in California is followed by a drought, which Joseph feels he is ultimately responsible for and only he can stop. Here the connection to the mythological Fisher King illustrates one influence of Joseph Campbell on the revised version of *To a God Unknown*. As the drought continues, Joseph Wayne begins to follow pagan rituals, including ancestor worship, and he develops an increasing sense that his responsibility to the land is as great as it is to his family. His primitive behavior eventually causes Joseph to become a negative force. After their child is born, Joseph insists his wife and child climb with him to a sacred rock, and his wife falls and is immediately killed. The rain begins falling at the time of her death. But the drought is not eased—indeed it continues to worsen—and Joseph returns to the rock, this time sacrificing himself by cutting his wrists. As the blood flows out of his veins, the rain begins, and Joseph's dying words signal a final epiphany for the protagonist: "I should have known. . . . I am the rain."

With three major publications and the appearance of short stories in various magazines, Steinbeck found himself little better off financially or influentially than when he began. His work had already been through three publishers, and he had earned less than $1,000. In 1935, Steinbeck's literary fortunes, both financial and critical, turned around. The shift in Steinbeck's career began when a Chicago bookstore owner introduced New York publisher Pascal Covici to Steinbeck's work in the winter of 1934. He immediately contacted Steinbeck's literary agents, who sent him the recently completed manuscript of *Tortilla Flat*. Covici agreed to publish the novel, as well as to republish past works and to publish all of Steinbeck's future work. *Tortilla Flat* was a success; for the first time Steinbeck's work was publicized and reviewed, and the reviews were good. Steinbeck received the first royalty check of his career and the public attention that would ensure that Steinbeck's work would never again be ignored.

Later that same year, Covici published *In Dubious Battle*. This novel represented new subject territory for Steinbeck. Steinbeck wrote his first political fiction using layers of the Bible, Milton, and Malory, and further developing the phalanx idea, the study of group man found thematically in *Tortilla Flat*. The Depression and resulting voices representing workers' causes brought a renewed attention to political writing that followed closely on the heels of earlier authors such as Upton Sinclair and Sherwood Anderson. Steinbeck's interest in the issues facing the common man is not surprising. While he was the product of a middle-class family, Steinbeck had spent much time working among and forming camaraderie with the laborers at the sugar factory and ranches where he worked during his college years. These were a people Steinbeck knew and liked, as evidenced by his presentation of the paisanos in *Tortilla Flat.*

In Dubious Battle is the story of what happens when agricultural workers unite under Marxist leaders to challenge the establishment of The Torgas Valley Growers Association, which is backed by all the town's authorities. Jim Nolan, the novel's protagonist, becomes one of the labor organizers after deciding his life is empty and meaningless. He ends up in the Torgas Valley with Mac, a seasoned Communist Party organizer, where they will recruit apple pickers for a strike. Steinbeck exposes the violent undersides of both the association and the labor group. Rather than attempting to create a romance that would stir reader sympathy for the working people, sympathy that did result from reading the novel, Steinbeck was interested in portraying what can result from the group, or phalanx, getting out of control. One result is the death of Jim Nolan, who is shot and dies in Christ-like symbolism, and who will be held up by Mac as a martyr to fuel the cause.

In Dubious Battle helped to show those critics who had dismissed *Tortilla Flat* as trite that Steinbeck was a serious writer. Indeed, two of his most serious and most studied works appeared soon after *In Dubious Battle*, with both maintaining the focus on the common man. *Of Mice and Men* was published a year after *In Dubious Battle*, in 1937, and *The Grapes of Wrath* in 1939. *In Dubious Battle* also prompted Steinbeck to see his art beyond the written page. Broadway interest in producing the strike story for the stage made Steinbeck consider expanding his craft to include other media, and the experimentation began immediately. *Of Mice and Men* was written as a playable novel, able to move from the novel page to the stage with little or no adaptation. Two film versions of the story were later produced. *The Pearl*, published ten years later, was written with the knowledge that it would become a film, and the influence of the screen is evident in Steinbeck's descriptions and characterizations. Other films would be made of Steinbeck's work, including *The Grapes of Wrath* and *The Red Pony*, and in 1950, Steinbeck would write the screenplay for *Viva Zapata!*, a film about Mexican revolutionary Emiliano Zapata starring Marlon Brando and Anthony Quinn.

While the works on which the remainder of this book focuses are those that today are the most read and studied, they in no way fully represent Steinbeck's impact on American literature. The second half of the 1930s gave Steinbeck an opportunity to deal with issues concerning the downtrodden in America, not only in fiction, but also in nonfiction. He wrote "The Harvest Gypsies," a series of articles for the *San Francisco News* about the California migrant camps; these articles were later published with other journalism pieces as *Their Blood Is Strong.* This investigative reporting not only contributed to *The Grapes of*

Wrath, but it also helped raise public awareness of the migrant situation. The first half of the next decade allowed Steinbeck to shift his focus and express his deep patriotism in both fiction and nonfiction. In 1942, he wrote *The Moon Is Down*, a novel and play about the invasion of a small town by a conquering army and the town's efforts at resistance, with the moral message that free men will always win in such struggles. While the propaganda piece is widely believed to have little literary merit and was harshly attacked by literary critics, its effects on the public in both America and besieged Europe were positive. Because of its value as an inspiring piece of wartime propaganda, the novel sold a million copies in its first year and continued to be popular worldwide, going through seventy-six editions between 1945 and 1989.

Steinbeck earned $300,000 for the film rights to *The Moon Is Down*, but he felt guilty over profiting so greatly from a work he knew was not a good product, and one that concerned war and the suffering of others. He avoided this guilt with his next war work. The more lasting difficulty for Steinbeck was his fear of being changed by the money he was making as a writer. Much of Steinbeck's ability to capture the experiences of common or downtrodden characters came from his sense that he was one of them. He did not want to lose this and would continue to struggle with the effects of financial success for the remainder of his career.

Steinbeck's work as a journalist increased during the World War II years. From June to December 1943, he served as a special correspondent to the *New York Herald Tribune*. He traveled to England, North Africa, and Italy, where he covered the Allied invasion. He wrote about what he saw, maintaining the required journalistic objectivity, but presenting the scenes of war in poetic language that made his reports almost sentimental but popular. When he returned to New York, visibly affected by the war he had encountered, he wanted to return to his own subjects and to his fiction. In 1958, his World War II columns, along with other material, were collected and published as *Once There Was a War*.

In the same year as *The Moon Is Down* was published, Steinbeck was approached to write a nonfiction book about American bomber crews. He spent a month, accompanied by a photographer, visiting a number of airfields across the nation. *Bombs Away* allowed Steinbeck to further explore his phalanx theory, the characteristics of the group under which individuals are united for the benefit of its members. Hollywood purchased his "story" for $250,000, which Steinbeck donated to the Air Force Aid Society Trust Fund.

The travelogue was one of the nonfiction genres that Steinbeck worked in for the rest of his career, even after he stopped publishing fiction. In 1947, he toured Russia and returned to publish *A Russian Journal*, a poetic travel narrative of early Cold War Russia. In the summer of 1960, immediately after completing his final novel, *The Winter of Our Discontent*, Steinbeck, accompanied by his dog, Charley, embarked upon a trip across America in a specially made apartment on wheels named Rocinante, after Don Quixote's horse. Steinbeck wanted to rediscover his own country from which he felt he had gotten too distant. *Travels with Charley in Search of America* is Steinbeck's catalogue of impressions of this trip. Steinbeck maintains an objective voice in his travelogue, and his snapshots of America are mostly positive, but the author began to feel disillusioned during this trip. Even though they were open and friendly, the people he met during the trip did not possess the depth of opinion about the issues facing America that Steinbeck had hoped to find. Steinbeck felt the country was in a rapid decline, and he wanted to find that other people were concerned and searching for answers. He did not. Steinbeck did finally encounter deep opinion in New Orleans at a school where black children had just been enrolled for the first time. At this school, the white mothers stood waiting to heckle and spit on the children as they entered the school each day. The hatred he witnessed in New Orleans and the similar sentiments he found in Alabama sickened Steinbeck, who lost the energy for his project and returned home quickly. *Travels with Charley*, published in the summer of 1962, was Steinbeck's most critically acclaimed work since *The Grapes of Wrath*.

In November 1965, Steinbeck began publishing a column in *Newsday*, the Long Island newspaper owned by Harry Guggenheim. The column took the form of letters to the publisher's wife, Alicia. The columns allowed Steinbeck to write about whatever subject interested him. Many of the columns were written from foreign locations visited by Steinbeck and his third wife, Elaine. In 1966, the columns began to address the Vietnam War, expressing Steinbeck's support for President Johnson. He also expressed disagreement with the antiwar protests increasing throughout the nation. The loyal and patriotic author would not voice his growing belief that America could not possibly win the war, although many believe that had he done so, it would have added substantial weight to the antiwar efforts.

The final full-length work of Steinbeck's career was published before he went to Vietnam. *America and Americans* contains essays about American life, accompanied by photographs. Much of the objectivity maintained in *Travels with Charley* is lost in *America and Americans*, where Steinbeck, now aging and suffering the effects of a heart condition, felt free to express his observations of America as a country steadily losing all moral imperative, in part because it had lost sight of its founding myths. The book ends with Steinbeck's claim that America embraced "no new path to take, no duty to carry out, no purpose to fulfill."

Although Steinbeck's last works were nonfiction, it is fiction for which he is ultimately known and judged. Many claim that *The Grapes of Wrath* was the artistic pinnacle of Steinbeck's career and that his work was never quite as good after his epic story of Oklahoma migrants. Certainly, no later work would arouse as great a reaction as *The Grapes of Wrath*, and none would have so great a political focus, but Steinbeck was not an author interested in repeating himself, either in subject or in form. If never quite sure of himself as a writer, after the success brought by *Tortilla Flat*, Steinbeck could be sure that he could live off of his writing. This allowed him the artistic freedom to follow his subject and thematic interests.

While Steinbeck was enjoying relative success with his nonfiction, he continued to write fiction, publishing *The Wayward Bus* in 1947. Those critics still looking for the social message of *The Grapes of Wrath* were disappointed. Many claimed the novel was a failed allegory when, in fact, it is not allegory. *The Wayward Bus* is the story of an old, broken down bus driven by Irish/Mexican Juan Chicory along a route ignored by major bus companies. The passengers on the bus represent the various types, both personal and social, that make up America. The novel focuses on one trip, during which the bus comes to a washed out bridge. Juan decides to detour onto a long unused stagecoach route where the bus becomes stuck in the mud. Juan has hoped this would happen so he could escape his bus and his life and run to Mexico, which Juan envisions as freedom. One of the passengers chases and then seduces Juan, while back at the bus the other passengers are taking the same opportunity for sexual encounters, both consensual and otherwise. Now satisfied with life, Juan returns to the bus, frees it from the mud, and delivers his passengers to their destination.

As he did many times with other characters, Steinbeck presents Juan Chicory as a Christ figure, addressing the needs of the ignored, facing temptation, and finally acting as a savior to his people. One interesting aspect of Steinbeck's development of Juan as a Christ figure is the mixture of both male and female qualities he gives to the character. While other characters, including Juan's wife, are disturbed by this, Steinbeck has presented the conflicting traits as positive. Also noticeably new is the characterization of women in *The Wayward Bus*. The female characters are presented as strong and independent, unlike the majority of Steinbeck's depictions of women in earlier works, and the overall presentation is sympathetic toward women.

If *The Wayward Bus* was misunderstood by the critics, Steinbeck's next work of fiction dumbfounded them. The playable novel *Burning Bright* was published and produced on the stage by Rodgers and Hammerstein in 1950. Intended as a morality piece, the play, although eliciting more critical attention than the novel, was experimental, impressionistic, and abstract; it was also a failure. *Burning Bright* is the story of Joe Saul. Joe is married to Mordeen, who, realizing that her husband is sterile, decides to become pregnant by another man. Joe learns that he is sterile, that Mordeen's child is not his, but comes to realize that the human species is important, not bloodlines, and the species must continue. Thus, he professes his love for the child and claims him as his son.

The theme is a variation of a familiar one for Steinbeck; survival can only be achieved when individuals recognize they belong to a single, human family. Neither theme nor character presented the major difficulty for the critics. Mostly, the problems stemmed from the fact that there was little or no realism to grasp onto in the play. The dialogue was too formal and was composed of a language Steinbeck had created consisting of difficult compound phrases. Even the time sequences were confusing. The play closed after only thirteen performances.

Over the next two years Steinbeck concentrated on *East of Eden*. Two years after its publication, he resurrected the setting and characters of *Cannery Row* in *Sweet Thursday*, which was released on June 10, 1954. The novel opens with Doc returning from the war, no longer excited or satisfied by science; the search for new knowledge no longer fulfills his needs. Seeing that Doc is unhappy, his old friends find him a woman, Suzy, one of the town whores with whom he falls in love. Even though Doc's return begins to show promise, he chooses to ignore his professional responsibilities and give his attention to Suzy, who has left prostitution. The story ends as a typical romance, with love conquering all worldly trouble.

Sweet Thursday mirrors the theme of discontent Steinbeck was exploring in his nonfiction at the time. It is also evidence of a change occurring in Steinbeck's philosophy. Doc, older and more seasoned than in *Cannery Row*, begins to focus on the end of his life and to view the present moments of his life against that end. This indicates a change from, or at least a deep consideration by Steinbeck of the non-teleological ideas found in his earlier literature and based in part on conversations with Ed Ricketts, Steinbeck's friend and the model for the character of Doc.

The reviews of *Sweet Thursday* were mixed. Some critics felt Steinbeck was taking the easy way in bringing the old story back in sequel form. Others noted the promise indicated by the shift in Steinbeck's theme. Steinbeck angrily defended his work as he usually did even when he was not happy with it himself. Steinbeck had little time to devote to worrying about the critics because Rodgers and Hammerstein were producing a musical version of *Sweet Thursday*, titled *Pipe Dream*, which opened in 1955. The novel was written for easy transition to the stage, a technique at which Steinbeck was well versed by this time. While *Pipe Dream* did not suffer the brutal reception faced by his play *Burning Bright*, the musical did not find the audience support its producers had hoped for and it closed after one season. *Pipe Dream* was to be Steinbeck's final theatrical experience.

Steinbeck's growing concern with the moral decline that he felt was spreading throughout America claimed the thematic focus of his final two full-length works of fiction, although the two novels are dramatically different in form and presentation. In 1957, Steinbeck published a short, political satire set in France titled *The Short Reign of Pippin IV*. With no true plot, the futuristic novel is episodic, covering a wide variety of subjects and crossing national boundaries, both of which allowed Steinbeck to make his spoof universal. The novel's main character is Pippin, a novice astronomer and a descendant of Charlemagne. He is beckoned by his country to re-establish France's monarchy. Pippin represents the moral rebirth of a nation and a world. The political spoof was well received by the public at the time but never sustained lasting attention by either readers or scholars.

By the time Steinbeck began his final novel in 1960, shortly followed by his cross-country trip with his dog Charley, his health had begun to deteriorate. Like *Pippin*, *The Winter of Our Discontent* takes as its subject moral decline, but unlike *Pippin*, the presentation is tragic rather than comedic. The novel is set in Sag Harbor, New York, where Steinbeck and his wife were living, and significantly opens on Good Friday, 1960. The story's themes are presented through the main character, Ethan Allen Hawley. Ethan works as a clerk in a store he once owned but lost through poor management. Like Steinbeck, Ethan feels contempt for America's moral decay, but Ethan has difficulty holding on to his own greatest possession, his integrity. He succumbs to financial temptation and robs the town bank, which allows him to buy back his store. Looking beyond the surface contempt Ethan feels for the moral decay around him, a direct result of America's desire for material wealth, it is clear Ethan is as seduced by materialism as are his fellow Americans. Ethan's own moral decline causes him to turn his back on his boyhood friend, Danny Taylor, rather than helping him out of the moral and psychological depths he had sunk to and from which he could not escape. Losing his only true and worthy possession, his integrity, Ethan attempts suicide, but fails even in this. The discontent survives and grows and infects, as shown in one of the story's subplots. Ethan's son, Ethan, Jr., wins a national contest with an essay he has plagiarized by piecing together lines from a variety of famous speeches. Even after the essay committee identifies his crime, Ethan, Jr. cannot see that he has done anything wrong. Ethan, Jr.'s, ignorance expressed Steinbeck's vision of a continuing legacy of degradation in America. That he is not alone in his moral mire is further supported by the title, which by its use of the word *our* indicates a universal discontent.

The language of *The Winter of Our Discontent* is concise and concrete, and its social themes are as forceful as those taken up by the author in the 1930s and 1940s. Many saw the quality and importance of this novel, but many, as they had done for years, were still searching for another version of *The Grapes of Wrath*. Almost as if he were unwilling to face the critics again, Steinbeck never wrote another novel.

The critics, however, still did not leave Steinbeck alone. In 1962, during the height of the Cuban missile crisis, Steinbeck was awarded the Nobel Prize for Literature. The celebration was marred by criticism, led by the *New York Times*, claiming Steinbeck's work had not made a significant enough impact on literature to merit the award. While any writer, including Steinbeck, would be grateful for a positive critical reception of his work, in the end it was clear Steinbeck never allowed such a desire to alter his own purpose in fulfilling that human need for answers about human existence to which he alluded in his Nobel acceptance speech. Unlike Ethan Allen Hawley, John Steinbeck never traded away his own integrity.

STEINBECK'S CONTRIBUTIONS TO THE SHORT STORY

Ironically, the difficulty in categorizing Steinbeck's work, of determining whether a work is short story, novel, or drama, points to one of the author's major contributions to American literature. As he did with his characters and his themes, Steinbeck placed form itself under the microscope to determine its qualities and its limits. Based on what he observed, Steinbeck allowed each form within which he worked to expand to its limits as he believed it was defined.

One of the ways Steinbeck pushed the limits of the short story was to create loose connections between stories in a collection. The results of this are Steinbeck's story cycles. In these collections, much like *Winesburg, Ohio* by Sherwood Anderson, each story may stand alone; each carries its own meaning but additional meaning is found when the stories are read together as a unit. *The Pastures of Heaven* is the first example of Steinbeck's work with the story cycle. It is also, significantly, Steinbeck's first California fiction and his first thematic focus on the experiences of everyday people. The stories of *The Pastures of Heaven* present the separate experiences of the residents of a California valley. The element connecting the stories is the Munroe family. Each story separately invites the reader to consider the misfortune caused by the Munroes in the incident the chapter presents. When reading the book as a unit of stories, the reader is forced into a deeper consideration of cause and is forced to analyze the nature of each unfortunate consequence of the Munroes' actions, weighing them against each other. The order in which Steinbeck places the stories also indicates the author's own assessment of the Munroes' various acts of destruction upon their neighbors.

Critics and scholars often debate the formal place of *The Pastures of Heaven*. Many discussions of the book use the term "novel" when discussing the entire collection and "short story" when focusing on one of the collection's episodes. This identification difficulty is intensified when discussing *The Red Pony*. The setting becomes smaller in this story cycle, effectively limited to one family farm, and the number of characters is reduced to the three members of the Tiflin family and their farm hand, Billy Buck, with outsiders occasionally introduced for thematic importance. The connection between the stories is the development of Jody Tiflin, the young son whose experiences on his parents' farm are the focus of the stories. In each story, Jody is faced with some challenge that he must adapt to or overcome, and with each he grows closer to adulthood. Each story in the cycle offers a valuable lesson, but in its completeness the cycle presents the development into manhood that must include each of the lessons.

His use of the story cycle is not the only reason for which Steinbeck's short stories are admired. The stories of *The Pastures of Heaven* and *The Long Valley*, in which *The Red Pony* stories were first included, were written during the period when Steinbeck's presentation of characters suffering under the uncontrollable forces of nature, literary naturalism, had not begun to include the individual's ability to adapt to natural forces as a means of survival, a shift that occurs in *The Grapes of Wrath*. "Flight," a story appearing in *The Long Valley*, is considered by many to be an example of classic literary naturalism. While most authors writing in the tradition of naturalism present society as a determinant of human happiness, Steinbeck's settings, in contrast to the urban settings in the novels of Theodore Dreiser and others, squarely present the natural environment as a force over which humans have little control. Additionally, the symbols found in Steinbeck's short stories are found to carry multiple layers of meaning, enhancing the economy of the stories and contributing to the poetic quality of his work. The short stories, most written early in his career, possess the objectivity of narration that allows the reader to exercise judgment without influence by the author, a quality that became one of the most recognized of Steinbeck's fiction. While they remain an often ignored element of the body of Steinbeck literature, his short stories have earned an important place in the history of American short fiction.

STEINBECK'S CONTRIBUTIONS TO THE NOVEL

Steinbeck's experiments with literature produced their most significant results in his novels. As he did with the short story, Steinbeck questioned contemporary definitions of form and style and found them too limiting. Just like his characters, Steinbeck faced an environment to which he would have to find a means to adapt or he would have to surrender to traditional terms of fiction, something the author was unwilling to do.

His experiments with form resulted in one of the most notable of Steinbeck's contributions to the novel. A novel is broadly defined as a story that creates a sense of actual life in book length. Chapters of the novel traditionally present the chronological action of the story but are not themselves independent stories. Together the chapters present the novel's major action and theme. Interruptions in the action are generally considered intrusive, resulting in an inconsistent flow of the action.

Steinbeck's novels frequently defy this definition of the form. In *Tortilla Flat*, his first successful full-length work, Steinbeck adopts the episodic style of Thomas Malory, creating a novel consisting of connected episodes, each that can be read independently, and each carrying a separate theme or lesson. But like his other story cycles, when read as a unified whole, *Tortilla Flat* presents a separate and overriding theme that is indiscernible in any single episode. Indeed, *Tortilla Flat* falls into the category of story cycle but is referred to as a novel because of its length and because, unlike *The Pastures of Heaven* and *The Red Pony*, its episodes or stories together move toward a final climactic action, Danny's death.

With *The Grapes of Wrath*, Steinbeck continued to test the limits of the novel form with his use of interchapters to provide a universal context to the experiences of his main characters, the Joads. The interchapters do temporarily pause the main action of the story, but they do not intrude upon it, which may account for Steinbeck's success with this device. He also used the interchapters to provide necessary historical context without having to break the flow of the narrative in the chapters presenting the main action of the novel. Later, Steinbeck reversed the purpose of the interchapters when he used them again in *Cannery Row*. Rather than utilizing them for universal context, he narrowed his lens in the interchapters to present single, concrete examples of the ideas presented more abstractly by the main chapters of the novel.

In 1937, Steinbeck began testing the limits of form in a new way. In writing *Of Mice and Men*, Steinbeck's desire was to write a novel, or novelette, that could be moved onto the theatrical stage with little or no adaptation. This required him to apply limits to characters, setting, and chapters. These limits do not prevent *Of Mice and Men* from fulfilling the definition of novel. Once again, they force an economy on the narrative that results in the poetic qualities of the story. In writing *The Pearl*, Steinbeck began with another dual purpose: to write a novel that could easily be adapted to the film screen. While he had to write the novel with an eye to its second purpose and again be somewhat restricted by that second purpose, the result is a narrative filled with gloriously visual descriptions of settings and action. In stretching the boundaries of literature beyond the page, Steinbeck enriched rather than diluted the fiction.

Experiment with form makes Steinbeck one of the most versatile authors of the twentieth century. His contributions, however, extend beyond formal innovations to elements of theme and style. One such example is his treatment of literary naturalism. Naturalism is based on the idea that natural forces, such as biology and social inheritance, control or limit human experience; humans can control neither their natural instincts not the social forces acting upon them. The Alaskan novels of Jack London, and *Sister Carrie* by Theodore Dreiser are examples of literary naturalism. True naturalism is bleakly deterministic, offering no salvation for the humans suffering under the unconquerable forces of heredity and environment. Few writers created fiction that was truly naturalistic; most went only so far as to allow their characters to escape the environmental forces with their lives. Steinbeck went further, however, adding hope to the lives of his characters. This hope was based on the idea that humans have the ability to adapt to their circumstances. Sometimes they adapt through group initiative, but mostly their power comes from one source—compassion—that can only be located in the individual.

Steinbeck also deviates from traditional naturalism by weaving humor into his stories. The homelessness and alcoholism that characterize the lives of the *paisanos* living on Tortilla Flat are classic representations of a world where nature has no concern for people. But Steinbeck chose to present these realities of the *paisanos'* lives through a series of comic stories. While he was often accused of trivializing the dark realities of American life with this humor, Steinbeck knew that humor survives in even the most depressed circumstances; indeed, it is one thing people use to bear those circumstances. As he later clearly expressed in his Nobel Prize acceptance speech, he did not write for the critics but for the common people, those who truly needed it.

Steinbeck has been cited as a contributor to changes in twentieth-century journalism. In his news stories during World War II, Steinbeck is accused of entering into the story rather than maintaining journalistic distance. Ironically, at the time of its publication, *The Grapes of Wrath* was discussed not on the basis of its literary merit but on the basis of its accuracy in fact, as a piece of social documentation. The dismissal of *The Grapes of Wrath* as mere journalism attests to Steinbeck's importance as a social realist, but it was his literary genius that accounts for the popularity of *The Grapes of Wrath*, as well as his other novels written in the style of social realism, with today's reader, so distanced in time and circumstance from America's Depression years.

Sadly, Steinbeck's attention to social issues in *The Grapes of Wrath* was so fine that critics refused to accept any other approach from the author who exemplified so many styles in the complete body of his work and who contributed so much to each style within which he worked. Each time Steinbeck finished a piece of literature he moved on to new forms, styles, and techniques and, in the end, left American literature greater in scope and richness.

STEINBECK'S INFLUENCE

John Steinbeck's place in the literary canon is under continual debate. Many argue that an author who has made such a lasting impact on American social consciousness cannot be dismissed in critical discussions of the literature, and others claim that Steinbeck was never more than a writer of popular fiction. Those who today voice the latter opinion are echoing the words of critic Alfred Kazin in his 1958 review of a volume of criticism on Steinbeck's work. Kazin wrote that except for *The Grapes of Wrath* Steinbeck's work was trivial and overly sentimental. Kazin had a great deal of power in American culture, and his words stuck with critics and scholars, many of whom began to speak of Steinbeck as a popular novelist. Steinbeck's social and political positions as they were represented in his fiction also made him vulnerable to those, like Kazin, who wielded cultural authority. The liberals, who were in the majority among critics and scholars, felt Steinbeck did not go far enough in demanding social change, and the conservatives believed he went too far. In many ways, Steinbeck was banished to the realm of popular fiction because of the agendas of a few powerful critics rather than on the basis of actual merit.

Popular fiction rarely outlasts the era in which it was produced, so one test of literature is its endurance. Large numbers of Americans today continue to buy and read Steinbeck's work. Steinbeck's fiction continues to be a major offering in high school and college literature courses, and his power is proven by the number of public schools that still ban *Of Mice and Men* and by those who still seek to locate factual errors in *The Grapes of Wrath*. Steinbeck's popularity has never wavered in Europe; *The Grapes of Wrath* is listed as one of the most popular books in Great Britain. His literature is translated throughout the world. People are independent, as Steinbeck knew, and seldom yield their choices to the critics.

The legacy of Kazin and his contemporaries is found in graduate and upper class university courses in the American novel where Steinbeck is rarely included on a syllabus. The authors studying at American colleges and universities, consequently, have had little exposure to Steinbeck, making it difficult to find evidence of direct influence by Steinbeck on the authors who followed him. Steinbeck's California literature of disillusionment is recalled when reading Shirley Jackson's California novel *The Road Through the Wall*. Ruth Comfort Mitchell has made allusion to situations in *Of Mice and Men* in her fiction. Writers of young adult fiction often turn to Steinbeck for examples of form and theme, both of which endure. But for the most part, Steinbeck's influence is ironically and fittingly found most among those he cared most about influencing—everyday people. The popular culture has honored Steinbeck's vision since the early stages of his career. Steinbeck has inspired music ranging from folk, most notably Woody Guthrie's *Dust Bowl Ballads*, to jazz, with Duke Ellington's "Suite Thursday" as example. Many of his works were made into films following their publication, and many of those remain popular today, including *The Grapes of Wrath*; *East of Eden*, the movie that made James Dean famous; and *Of Mice and Men*, which was recently remade. The 1980s film *Raising Arizona* was strongly influenced by Steinbeck's characterizations in *Of Mice and Men*. Even the idea of taking to the road to find the real America can be directly traced to Steinbeck's *Travels with Charley*.

Steinbeck's writing is literature and it is popular. Among other things, sympathetic critics point to Steinbeck's innovation in structure and method in his fiction and his multiple layered symbolism when defending the literary merit of Steinbeck's literature. These criteria, along with the enduring and universal themes that touch the everyday reader, ensure that Steinbeck will continue to be read and studied, and he will continue to influence the readers, those whose needs literature exists to fulfill.

3

Tortilla Flat
(1935)

Tortilla Flat was Steinbeck's first critical and commercial success. In his reaction to the change in his fortunes, Steinbeck was very much like Danny, the main character of *Tortilla Flat*, who comes suddenly upon property and responds by getting drunk and vandalizing the town of Monterey, a crime for which he is sent to jail, a place where he could not benefit from his new fortune. Success, like money, made Steinbeck uncomfortable, and for this reason he did not personally accept the award for Best Novel of 1935 given by the Commonwealth Club of California for *Tortilla Flat*. The novel's publication also proved bittersweet for Steinbeck. Steinbeck's father, John Ernst, died five days before *Tortilla Flat* appeared in print. His mother, Olive, had died the previous year, so John Ernst's death meant that neither parent was able to witness Steinbeck's success.

SETTING, PLOT, AND STRUCTURE

The town of Monterey, California, begins where the water of the bay meets the beach. From there, the town spreads out, along Cannery Row and Alvarado Street, up to the hills surrounding Monterey Bay. In one area of these hills a shanty town once existed called Tortilla Flat, "although it isn't flat at all" (2).

Steinbeck begins his story of Monterey *paisanos*, longtime California residents of mixed descent, shortly after the end of World War I. Danny, the story's central character, has returned from the army, having never made it to the war, to a town bustling with the canning of sardines and squid and suffering from the restraint of Prohibition, which forbade the making or sale of alcoholic beverages. These two elements, work and law, define the world outside of Danny and the other *paisanos*' experience, but exist only as inconveniences to these men. Daily life for the *paisanos* focuses on getting around these encumbrances.

Steinbeck relates these daily exploits in episodes, or chapters, that are complete in themselves but that contribute to the novel's overall plot and theme. This is one way that Steinbeck borrows from Thomas Malory's Arthurian legends. Another is his use of chapter headings, which Steinbeck added to clarify the novel's theme and structure. While the episodic structure may cause the reader to believe there is no true plot to the novel, rather that it is a series of unconnected events, the episodes taken together present thematic conflict, action that leads to a climax and a resolution of the conflict.

Since the *paisanos*' story does not really begin until Danny comes home from the army and learns he has inherited property, Steinbeck begins the novel with a preface that provides the reader with background information necessary to understand the main action of the story, as well as introduces Steinbeck's major theme, foreshadows the eventual breakup of the *paisanos* and avows to the authenticity of the story. This prefacing allows the narrator to introduce the setting and historical context of Danny's circumstances before the action begins, preventing a later ungraceful intrusion into the narrative. It also makes explicit comparison of the story to the Arthurian legends, setting up the structure of the story to follow. The effect is, interestingly, to challenge the reader to accept the truth the story presents, just as those who take the most from Malory's stories are those who accept the truth they present.

The chapters of *Tortilla Flat* combine to present a highly structured novel. The first eight chapters are concerned with establishing the group of *paisanos* and creating the special unity of this group about which the story is thematically concerned. Chapter 1 begins with Danny, who, after learning he has inherited two houses from his grandfather consequently gets drunk, tears up the town, and goes to and escapes from jail. During these escapades, Danny happens upon his old friend Pilon. As they drink and lament their lost friends and their own homelessness, Danny remembers he owns the two houses and swears to share whatever he has with Pilon. Pilon accepts Danny's invitation mostly because he does not believe Danny. Pilon also realizes that Danny's new position as a property owner signals the end of Danny. He understands that the good *paisano* life is now over: "Thy friends will mourn, but nothing will come of their mourning" (10). This is Steinbeck's second foreshadowing of the story's tragic ending.

Danny takes possession of his properties and realizes his life has changed. Pilon worries, too; he is concerned about getting into debt to Danny and losing his freedom to this debt. The debt is actually increased when Pilon agrees to rent Danny's second house for fifteen dollars a month, which he knows he will never be able to pay. Indeed, Pilon does attempt to give Danny a few dollars toward the rent on a number of occasions, but the money is never applied to the debt. Always there is the temptation of Mr. Torrelli's wine, which is bought and then sometimes shared with Danny, a gesture Pilon uses to rationalize as payment of his debt to his generous friend.

One method Pilon uses to acquire the money for his rent is to lure other *paisanos* into the house he is "renting" from Danny, and then to charge them the same rent he has agreed to pay. The first friend he comes upon is Pablo, who has just been paroled from jail. Pablo agrees to sublet part of Pilon's house for fifteen dollars a month. In Chapter 4, Pilon and Pablo find Jesus Maria Corcoran passed out in a ditch with a half-full bottle of wine, which they try unsuccessfully to steal from him. Jesus Maria is a humanitarian and gives them the wine to drink, telling them how he got it. While he was sleeping on the beach, a rowboat washed onto the shore. He sold the boat for seven dollars, bought two gallons of wine and silk underwear and whiskey for a girl named Arabella, who took his gifts and ran off with some soldiers. He still has three dollars and a dime left, with which he intends to purchase a bra to give to the same girl. Pilon convinces him he is sick from sleeping in the night air, and he and Pablo take Jesus Maria home and nurse him as if he is truly ill, at the same time convincing him of the health and joy that comes from living in a house. After this sales job, Jesus Maria agrees to rent part of the house for fifteen dollars a month and to pay two dollars on account, which they use to buy the wine they intend to give to Danny. Pilon tells Jesus Maria he can still buy Arabella the bra with the dollar he has left.

These attempts to acquire rent money and Pilon's subletting to others the house he is renting from Danny, are examples of the plot repetition that is an important element of *Tortilla Flat*. Illustrated at a larger level by the daily routine of the group, which includes waking, telling stories, procuring wine and food, singing, fighting, and sleeping, this repetition of events is what makes Danny so depressed at the end of the novel, eventually leading to his death and the breaking up of the group. The plot repetition is also one of the formal elements Steinbeck borrows from Malory's stories of the Knights of the Round Table. In Malory, the knights feast, fight and quest, and then recount their experiences in storytelling. In *Tortilla Flat*, the *paisanos* do the same, feasting on the spoils of their begging and thievery; fighting to reinforce their manhood;

questing, initially for the beloved gallon of wine but later for more valiant rewards; and storytelling, sometimes about their own exploits, but mostly about
the people in their community.

With Danny living in one house and Pilon, Pablo, and Jesus Maria living in
the other, the unity of this group has not yet been established. In Chapter 5,
however, unity occurs through the divine intervention of St. Francis. Pablo and
Pilon buy two gallons of wine with Jesus Maria's two-dollar rent deposit, but
then drink one gallon, rationalizing their action by considering that two gallons of wine would be unhealthy for Danny. They head back to their house,
taking with them a candle Pablo has bought and had blessed for San Francisco.
When Jesus Maria returns, once again beaten by soldiers after another ill-fated
rendezvous with Arabella, the three *paisanos* fall asleep and the blessed candle
starts a fire, burning the house to the ground. The result is the unification of
the group because the three, homeless once again, move into Danny's house.

Moving into Danny's house allows the other *paisanos* to act as Danny's pro-
tector, which they feel a responsibility to do since he has taken such good care
of them by giving them a roof over their heads. One concern they have about
Danny's welfare is Mrs. Morales, his neighbor, with whom Danny has begun to
spend his nights. The *paisanos* believe no woman can be trusted into their fraternity. They drink together on their first evening as guests in Danny's home,
and Jesus Maria swears for himself as well as Pilon and Pablo to "see that there is
always food in the house for Danny" (46). This is the oath the *paisanos* swear to
their leader, just as Arthur's knights swore an oath to their king.

The *paisanos* are distracted from their focus on drinking and revelry when
Pirate joins the group. Pirate, a "huge, broad man with a tremendous black and
bushy beard," is a Monterey local whose mental abilities never fully developed
(48). Pirate's family consists of five dogs of various sizes and pedigrees who follow him on his daily routine of begging food, cutting kindling wood from the
forests which he sells to earn twenty-five cents per day, and retiring to an old
chicken house where the six sleep together. Pilon, observing Pirate's daily routine, reasons that he must have a great deal of money hidden somewhere. The
paisanos convince Pirate to come live with them, telling him they are concerned for his welfare. Pirate eventually believes them; their concern and
friendship are almost too much for the man/child, and he is overwhelmed with
happiness. Although the group has less than honorable motives, they do have
empathy for Pirate because each has experienced this sudden realization that
he, too, had someone who cared about his welfare.

Friendship with Pirate is quite a separate matter from finding his treasure,
however, and the *paisanos* continue to watch and follow Pirate. Finally, they
make him afraid that his money will be stolen, and Pirate decides that only his
new friends can ensure his money's safety. This trust produces a guilty rage in

the *paisanos* and exemplifies the continual conflict between the *paisanos'* desires and the moral code of the group. The conflict, in this case, is resolved by the story Pirate tells about his promise to buy a golden candlestick for San Francisco de Assisi if the saint would heal his sick dog. The dog was healed only to be run over by a truck a short time later; the miracle was delivered, however, and Pirate must keep his promise. Helping Pirate protect his treasure is a sacred quest the *paisanos* cannot refuse. The earlier generosity of the men, the sharing of home and wine, hints at something deeper than pleasure seeking, but through guilt feelings about their manipulations of Pirate, and their inability to steal Pirate's money—even that they must help him protect it until the candlestick can be bought—the paisanos are shown to possess the goodness that attracted Steinbeck to such men and compelled him to share some of that goodness with his readers.

The final *paisano* to join the group is Big Joe Portagee, who has just returned from the army. The misbehavior that landed him in jail for most of his time in the army continues once he joins the other *paisanos* at Danny's house, where he breaks both of the sacred rules established by the group. He attempts to sleep in Danny's bed, and, later, he steals the Pirate's candlestick money, although the others soon find it after they have beaten its location out of Big Joe.

The narration begins to change in Chapter 8, after the coming of Big Joe. The chapters become more episodic, and more storylike, with less telling of the *paisanos'* routine and more telling of specific, legendary experiences. The first of these stories is that of the treasure hunt on St. Andrew's Eve when, by local custom, the people take to the woods to hunt for buried Spanish treasure. Pilon, partnered with Big Joe and aided by a crudely constructed cross, locates an almost indiscernible glow coming from the forest floor that must surely be the treasure sought after by so many for so long. When Big Joe digs up the treasure the next morning, it turns out to be a U.S. Geodetic survey marker. Selling the marker would constitute a federal crime and an imprisonment that even these men were not willing to risk. Taking bags of gold to Danny would fulfill both the pledge to feed Danny forever and the particularly American dream of rising above circumstances to find wealth and security. However, Pilon finally concedes that "Happiness is better than riches. . . . If we try to make Danny happy, it will be better than to give him money" (77).

The next five chapters are more self-contained and mostly present stories that continue to illustrate the character of the group. Chapter 9 is the story of the vacuum cleaner Danny buys for Sweets Ramirez to gain her affections and a place in her bed. The effect that this relationship has on Danny begins to worry his friends. He has grown weak from the time and physical energy required by the relationship. Pilon, acting as leader once again, steals the vacuum cleaner and trades it to Torelli for wine. The complete uselessness of the gift becomes known, and a reinforcement of Pilon's earlier statement about happiness is accomplished when Torrelli discovers the vacuum has no motor.

The story of the Mexican corporal in Chapter 10 is different from the novel's other episodes in many ways. It is the novel's only presentation of the *paisanos* interacting personally with someone from outside their Monterey community. The corporal has run away from the Mexican army with his baby son after his wife leaves them for his captain. The corporal comes to Monterey for work but finds none; instead, he has a baby who has become very ill, no job, and a policeman giving him a hard time about loitering. This is when the humanitarian Jesus Maria comes along and rescues the young corporal, taking him to Danny's house for shelter and food. The *paisanos* learn that the corporal tells his son every day he will grow up to be a general, believing that the telling makes it so. The *paisanos* believe this is so the child, grown into a general, can take revenge on the captain. After the baby dies in Danny's home, the *paisanos* tell the corporal he should take the revenge himself. The corporal informs the friends that his intent was not for revenge but, rather, to give Manuel, the baby, a better life than his father had lived. The lesson is not lost on the *paisanos* or on the reader. The friends admire the corporal for the values that run contrary to the codes dictated by their machismo and for the purity of his concern for his child. The reader cannot help but compare the corporal's story to the group, where Danny is the surrogate father who wants his friends to have a good life, no matter what it is costing him in terms of his freedom.

Chapter 11 tells the story of Big Joe's sexual encounter with Tia Ignacia. At first the inclusion of Big Joe's chance meeting with Tia Ignacia seems like a formal mistake on Steinbeck's part, but in reality it is a necessary element to an overall understanding of Steinbeck's characters and the history he is telling. These men are mythic, but myth concerns truth, and physical desire is part of the *paisanos*' truth, just as it was with Arthur and his knights and with the heroes of Homer's epics, and just as it is with the human beings all of these characters at some level represent. Steinbeck reminds the reader that the need for sex, wine, and battle does not cancel out the goodness these men possess. It is part of who these good men are.

Chapters 12 and 13 most fully illustrate the group's potential for goodness, and it is important to understand that each episode, each good deed carried out, would not be possible for any of the paisanos individually. In Chapter 12, Pirate is finally able to keep his promise to St. Francis, but not until after his money is almost lost. Big Joe steals the bag of money from its hiding place in Danny's bed; the other *paisanos* know Big Joe is guilty and beat him until he tells them the money's location. After counting the money to verify that Big Joe has taken no more than the four quarters he confessed to, they learn Pirate has met his goal of a thousand quarters for the candlestick, with seven left over. After determining that Pirate must take the money to the priest and tell him the story of his sick dog and his promise to San Francisco, they must decide how to make Pirate presentable for the church service that will dedicate the candle. They give Pirate the extra seven quarters to buy new clothes, but instead he spends the money on a colorful handkerchief and a glass studded belt, so the others must loan him their clothes for the service. This is a great sacrifice by Pirate's friends; they have given him the shirts off their backs, and it means they now cannot attend the dedication service. But they celebrate nonetheless. They buy real food from money they gained by selling salvage found earlier that day. They drink quietly, putting off the profane singing that is usually part of their revelry.

Although the other *paisanos* do not get to experience this miraculous day, Pirate's experience at the dedication service and what happens afterward strengthen the idea that what this group has done is special. Pirate goes to church and sees his beautiful golden candlestick and hears the priest tell the audience the story of St. Francis of Assisi. The service is interrupted by Pirate's five dogs, which have broken away from the other *paisanos* and followed their leader to church. The dogs are led outside to wait for Pirate and, after the service, he takes them to the woods so he can re-create the service for them so they, too, can feel the joy Pirate felt during the priest's sermon. "That day his memory was inspired" (118). This is a miracle for the man whose brain never developed with the rest of his body. Another seeming miracle occurs when the forest becomes "silent and enchanted" (118), and the dogs see something Pirate believes to be St. Francis. This story may have the quality of a fairy tale—its tone is different from the other chapters in the novel—but it is a marrying of the sacred experience with the profanity that appears to define these *paisanos*. Just as the daily activities of Arthur's knights are interrupted by the higher purpose of Christian pursuits, the *paisanos'* lives also become a synthesis when their purpose is greater than procuring a gallon of wine.

Chapter 13 illustrates the growing altruism that follows from the proud experience of the candlestick. In this chapter, the *paisanos* expand their goodness beyond the group to feed the family of Teresina Cortez after the bean harvest fails, threatening to starve the family whose sole diet is beans. Jesus Maria learns of the family's plight and returns to Danny's house to tell his friends. They vow to make sure the children do not starve. At first it seems to be a good deed gone bad. They collect great quantities and types of food that the children are not used to eating, leading to rotting food and sick children. To correct their mistake, they steal beans, also in great quantities, and deliver them in the night to Teresina's home. The abundance created by the *paisanos* goes beyond food, as the narrator informs the reader that one of the *paisanos* has also left Teresina the gift of another pregnancy.

The final four chapters of the novel chronicle Danny's slow decline and eventual death, which cause the division of the group. Chapter 14 begins to set the tone of the monotony of daily life in Tortilla Flat that eventually will cause Danny to flee. It explains how the *paisanos* measured time by the sun, how they slept, how they awoke, and how they began their morning with rituals. "Life took shape about them, the shape of yesterday and of tomorrow" (130). Their lives were becoming so repetitive, however, that yesterday and tomorrow were much the same picture. The idea that times stands still in Tortilla Flat is repeated in Chapter 15, and Danny feels this particularly. He becomes angry and remembers what life was like before he had a house. There was no responsibility, he slept in a different place every night, and there were good fights then. Danny runs away even as his friends are trying to think of ways to bring him out of his depression. The friends foreshadow Danny's end when they say, "Danny is running to his death" (146). They know he needs help but there is nothing they can do. The pain of helplessness is felt by all the *paisanos*. Only Danny is outside of the group now, working in his own direction, going toward his own needs. He sneaks into the house and steals Pilon's shoes while the *paisanos* are sleeping. He sells his house to Torrelli, which the *paisanos* manage to reclaim by stealing the bill of sale from the wine dealer. Danny eventually returns to the house with food and with the jailer, Tito Ralph, who himself has been sent to jail.

The *paisanos* are happy to have Danny home, but it is soon clear that Danny is still depressed. Pilon notes that Danny has changed, that he is old. "His eyes had no light of desire nor displeasure nor joy nor pain" (156). It is a condition from which Danny does not recover. He cannot be happy as a property owner who has taken on a group of grown men to shelter because this does not allow the freedom and the diversity his life held before. But he cannot return to his earlier life either; he has felt what it is to belong to something bigger than the self and has seen what this group can accomplish that is bigger than himself. Life has become a trap for Danny.

Pilon's plan to give Danny a party draws all of Monterey into the *paisanos'* desire to bring Danny out of his depression. The *paisanos* concede to their ultimate enemy for a day and they go to work packing squids for money to finance the celebration. The other citizens prepare food and take out their fancy clothes, seldom worn because there is seldom need. While the community plans, Danny wanders the town. Danny can sense that real life is over, and he is just waiting for his body to go also. After Pilon hunts Danny down and brings him to the party, Danny joins with the others in celebration.

Danny seizes the party passionately, almost like a last breath. He spends the evening in violent fighting and violent loving. After this evening, the narrator suggests, Danny will be a god, and like other gods, the accounts of his deeds will be inflated. For Danny himself, he already is a god. He begins to transform, to become fearsome, and challenges others to fight, but now no one will. Danny responds by announcing, "Then I will go out to The One who can fight. I will find the Enemy who is worthy of Danny!" (164). He goes to the gulch roaring, and the people of Tortilla Flat hear a frightful answer to Danny's call, and then they hear a cry, a thump, and the silence that testifies to Danny's death.

The remaining *paisanos* cannot join in the public good-bye to Danny; they cannot go to the funeral because their clothing was destroyed in the party. Instead, they spend the morning telling stories of Danny while all the rest of Monterey prepares to attend Danny's funeral. They witness his funeral from the same vantage point they have watched the outside world all of their lives. They stand outside the church, and then follow the procession at some distance to the cemetery. They are ashamed and miserable; they are Danny's real family, so they return to Danny's home to mourn, just as was foreshadowed in Chapter 1 of the novel. The fire Pilon was stoking when he prophesied this mourning also takes on meaning as Danny's house burns to the ground during their mourning, started by a match Tito Ralph discards after lighting a cigar. Their leader is gone, the symbol of their brotherhood is gone, and there is nothing left to hold these remaining *paisanos* together. Each leaves the place where the house once stood, each walking alone to find, once again, a lonely life.

CHARACTERS

Steinbeck's reliance on Malory in *Tortilla Flat* goes beyond form and theme and into characterization. Studies of medieval literature include no real character analysis. The medieval worldview did not include the concept of the individual but, instead, the concept of community. Because of this, medieval literature does not include characters who develop over the course of a story. The characters' relationship to the group is of sole importance. This is true for Malory in his Arthurian tales, and it is true for Steinbeck in *Tortilla Flat*.

Most characters in the novel have distinguishing elements. Pilon is the logician. His ability to see reason through the haze of Torrelli's wine allows him to identify and forecast the eventual and tragic outcome of the *paisanos* regularly sleeping with a roof over their heads. But the temptation of shelter is as great as the temptation of drink, and all Pilon can do is prophesy—he hasn't the will or the strength to resist. Pablo is the philosopher. He can discern the existence of meaning in the *paisanos'* experience, but the effort to uncover or interpret that meaning is too great for a man who, like his fellow paisanos, avoids all effort that does not produce immediate, sensory satisfaction. Jesus Maria is the humanitarian. Unlike his fellow *paisanos*, whose chief characteristics remain abstract qualities, Jesus Maria acts on humanitarianism and rallies his friends to help. Big Joe continually tests the rules of the group. Pirate, being naive, brings purity to the group. And Danny is the leader. All of these are qualities that manifest themselves within the group. The description of the *paisanos* before they come together does not serve to differentiate the men in any way. They were all homeless. They all ran from any kind of work and ran to whatever physical pleasure they could find. Danny, Pilon, and Big Joe went in the army and all stayed home from the war.

Because of the importance placed on the characters' relationship to the group, tracing character development in *Tortilla Flat* is difficult. Character development requires that the character undergo some type of growth during the course of the story. There is much change for the *paisanos*, but there is no indication that any of them has experienced growth. Once Danny is gone and the house in which they found their unity is gone, these *paisanos* revert back to the individuals they were before Danny came home to Monterey to find he owned two houses.

Because he is placed at the center of the novel's action and because he suffers such an extreme crisis of self at the end of the story, readers might be tempted to analyze Danny in terms of development, but Danny is not a developing character. He experiences the same changes as the other *paisanos*; he goes from a solitary state to belonging to a group in which he experiences a life of unity. Danny does not make a choice to enter into this group. The houses come to him through inheritance, and the friends come to him because they want to share in that inheritance. After the first house burns leaving Pablo and Pilon homeless once again, Danny invites them into his home because he is lonely and, as an owner of property, he does not have the same resources for addressing that loneliness he once had. He has been thrust into a position he neither asks for nor knows how to handle. Although Danny leaves this position in the end, taking once again to the streets and to the forests, he learns it is futile to try to go back in time. His life has changed, and rather than adapting to that change, rather than growing into that change, Danny tries "one last glorious hopeless assault on the gods" (173) who changed his world to include houses and the responsibility of friends.

THEMES

In *Tortilla Flat*, Steinbeck introduces a theme he will continue to include in his work of the 1930s and 1940s, one that will be most fully developed in *The*

Grapes of Wrath. This is Steinbeck's idea of the phalanx, a term often used in science to describe the behavior of animals or other organisms. Steinbeck believed that when individuals become part of a group, the self-focus that causes the individual to think in terms of "I" transforms to a group focus, where thinking is in terms of "we." The change is not arbitrary; the individual, once choosing to belong to the group, cannot ultimately choose to deny this group drive, or phalanx, and still belong to the group. Individual behavior is largely inconsistent with the rules established by the group since those rules are established to protect the group and carry it toward a group goal. A person within the group who does not give over to a real belonging in the group, who maintains the "I," will threaten the unity of the group.

Big Joe Portagee is the clearest example of the conflict between an individual and the phalanx. There is already evidence that his inclusion in the *paisano* brotherhood will be a problem. Big Joe spent most of his military enlistment in jail, failing to experience full inclusion in one of the largest groups of men there is. When he returns to Monterey and comes to live in Danny's house, he continues to resist inclusion. Within the *paisano* group there are two explicit rules or codes. No one must sleep in Danny's bed, and no one must steal from Pirate's candlestick fund. From the beginning, Big Joe ignores the first rule, an offense for which the other *paisanos* must beat him. When he later steals Pirate's sack of quarters that was hidden in Danny's bed, the beating is much more severe, with salt administered to his wounds to insure the lesson of the beating sticks. Yet, even Big Joe's resistance does not prevent the group from continuing to do what the phalanx does by nature, to protect its size and thus its power. After teaching Big Joe his lesson, he is not banished from Danny's home. Rather, he is nursed back to health, in Danny's bed, so he can be welcomed back to the group.

Initially less clear is Danny's resistance to the group, and there is early evidence that Danny's inclusion into the group is never quite complete. The original relationship between Danny as landlord and Pilon and Pablo as tenants prevents the group from forming in the first place, at least a group that could include Danny. As landlord, he felt it was his responsibility to collect the tribute owed him, the rent he was charging for the second house, and this established a division between Danny and his friends that prevented any unity or bond. Compounding this problem was his relationship with Mrs. Morales. Pilon and Pablo talk about how no woman can be trusted into the fraternity of *paisanos*, and when Danny suggests they pay their rent so that he can buy Mrs. Morales a gift, Danny is forming an allegiance with an outsider, and with a woman, no less, thus threatening the friendship, at the least, if not the possibility of the larger unity that later develops.

By inviting his friends to live with him as guests rather than as tenants after the first house burns down, Danny removes the first obstacle to the formation of a unified group. When he decides he really does not want to give Mrs. Morales a gift, and instead talks to Pilon and Pablo about the importance of having friends, he is ready to make the shift from "I" to "we."

Later, the pressure of the group and the longing for his old life of responsibility only for the self becomes too much for Danny and he leaves. The friends' observation that, in running away, Danny was "running to his death" (146), supports the idea that the group is powerful, whereas the individual is weak. Danny discovers this; he becomes old before his friends' eyes and is no longer able to feel either pleasure or pain. Unable to live in either human state, the individual or the group, Danny challenges the gods, or the fates, which give him no other options but death.

The unity of the group is destroyed because Danny turns his back on it to seek the personal freedom he feels he has lost to the group. While Danny never truly acted as the group's leader, Danny was the member who provided the opportunity for both the group's existence and its purpose. His home drew this group together, and the *paisanos'* pledge to feed Danny in return for his gift of a home was the driving force behind the group. With Danny gone, the purpose no longer existed; thus, the house no longer had any usefulness. This is why the *paisanos* saw no tragedy as they watched the house burn down. Without its purpose, the group must also dissolve, so each of its members returns to individual lives.

Although connections between Steinbeck's paisanos and Malory's stories of King Arthur and his knights are clear, *Tortilla Flat* is an American story, and Steinbeck made changes that reflect a particular American theme, that of the American Dream. To do this, Steinbeck had to create a complete reversal of class structure. Malory's characters are at the highest levels of society; indeed, the socioeconomic and political realities of historical England allow for no other group to become the focus of such legend. But America has no such restraint. In America, peasants can become kings and knights, which is exactly what occurs in *Tortilla Flat*. In their own limited way, the *paisanos* fulfill the American Dream of property and status.

Steinbeck qualifies this American Dream, however, which ultimately poses questions about its possibility at all. He infers through his idea of the group that the dream is not attainable by the one acting alone. The power of the group is what gives the dream any possibility of becoming reality. Steinbeck will continue to support this idea in later work, including *Of Mice and Men* and *The Grapes of Wrath*. Additionally, nature is a force continually threatening the group's drive toward any purpose, including the American Dream. In *Tortilla Flat*, human nature threatens the long-term fulfillment of the *paisanos'* American Dream, that need for individual freedom and fulfillment that will always stand in conflict with the group.

ALTERNATIVE READING: NEW HISTORICISM

Before the 1980s, postmodern critical approaches to literature were predominantly characterized by removal of the contexts of time, culture, and authorship in literary works. New Historicism seeks to restore these contexts, arguing not only that they are necessary for interpretation, but also that they are inseparable from the works themselves. New Historicism holds that literature is an action rather than simply a conveyor of actions. Literature is created by a society or culture, but it is, conversely, part of the creation of that society or culture. The New Historical critic searches for the connections between the literature and the culture within which it produces and is produced. To do so, the New Historicist examines texts and documents from within the culture to learn about matters affecting the lives of the people, issues of everyday concern as well as larger issues of politics and power. Two major influences on New Historicism are French philosopher Michel Foucault, who argues that the norms of a culture are shaped by those holding power and are manifested by the experiences of those within the culture, and Russian theorist Michail Bakhtin, who expands on Foucault's assertions about cultural subjection to claim that every history will include resistances to the dominate power.

Steinbeck's *Tortilla Flat* is set in a period of rapid change in America, of which the author was himself an observer and participant. The country had just experienced its first world war, which demonstrated that it could not remain happily isolated from the rest of the world. This forced a reconsideration of its national identity. Prohibition was enacted by constitutional amendment in 1919, indicating a shift in national values. Productivity was rising due to increasing industrialization. A New Historical reading of *Tortilla Flat* finds John Steinbeck concerned with these issues facing America, and with the resistance to the dominant American values expressed through Prohibition and industrial progress.

One of Steinbeck's concerns about early twentieth-century American culture is the place of citizens who are not descended from white European ancestry. As was the case in much of America, the expansion of the United States to include California was accomplished only by the forced submission of the indigenous peoples. Driven by a belief in manifest destiny, that their rights as conquerors were divinely ordained, the newcomers to California relegated the native peoples to the lowest social classes where they served, through manual labor, the financial interests of those bringing railroads and industry to the state. Ironically, California was admitted to the union as a free state, but its native citizens as well as those people of more exotic heritage, such as the Chinese, who were often imported to increase the labor force, were placed in virtual servitude by the whites in power.

Steinbeck is clearly troubled by the treatment of the *paisanos* by the dominant powers in Monterey. His definition of *paisano* includes the claim that a portion of their ancestors had lived in California for almost two hundred years, which the *paisanos* felt granted them a certain nobility. But the nobility of *paisano* ancestry is not of importance to the Americans in control; only the *paisanos'* color matters, which is why, according to Steinbeck, the *paisanos* publicly insist on a pure Spanish heritage and show the color of their skin on the inside of the arm, untouched by the sun, to prove this descendancy. This is the *paisanos'* response to the dominant belief in European supremacy; they attempt to show membership in the dominant group. The response is ignored or unnoticed, however, and the *paisanos* remain separated from the larger culture by attitude as well as place. They are relegated to the shantytown located in the most inconvenient area of Monterey, at the top of a steep hill, away from the view of the town's leaders.

The *paisanos'* employment opportunities in Monterey are limited to the most laborious and disgusting jobs in the city, the cleaning and packing of fish. The reaction of Danny and the boys to this reality is to resist work entirely and, instead, to survive through the more creative means of stealing or scavenging for what they need. The seeming aversion to work presented in the novel stands in direct conflict with the American cultural value of a good work ethic. While the inclination is to blame the boys' perpetual unemployment on laziness, the condition actually indicates a clash or conflict between two distinct cultures. The first is the dominant American culture for which progress was a driving idea at the early part of the century, with industrialization a key to that progress. The growth of the fish cannery business in Monterey is an example of that progress. Thanks to modern methods of canning and the abundant supply of fish in the local waters, canned sardines and fish meal, a by-product of the canning, could be produced at a fast and steady rate. Canned foods, requiring no refrigeration, were in great demand. The Monterey industry clearly illustrates capitalism at its best.

But the *paisanos* are not capitalists; they do not derive from a capitalist background. Their hereditary culture is agrarian, rooted in the idea of taking what is needed for daily survival from the natural environment. The essence of industrialism conflicts directly with this natural environment on which the *paisanos'* ancestors relied and on which the *paisanos* also rely as indicated by their sleeping in the woods before acquiring a home. There is no capitalistic drive in the *paisano* culture. The accumulation of property or wealth is a foreign idea to these men, making regular employment, the means to such accumulation, equally foreign. Therefore, the *paisanos'* lack of a work ethic is not only indicative of resistance to dominant values, but is also representative of an outright clash of cultures.

Steinbeck also expresses concern for what happens when the dominated, and thus separated, attempt to fit in to the larger culture. While they resist the American work ethic, Danny and the boys do make an attempt to belong to the larger culture, an action that consequently shows evidence of the division within the culture. At the onset of World War I, Danny, Pilon, and Big Joe Portagee are, with a little help from the wine bottle, consumed with the same patriotism that sweeps the entire nation, a patriotism evidenced by the many historical documents of the period. Like so many Americans, the *paisanos* volunteer for duty in the war. The conscription of men into the military services was a policy at the time of World War I; that the *paisanos* do not wait for the government to draft them is proof of their desire to participate. Ironically, none of the three for whom fighting is a cultural norm is sent to fight America's enemies. Danny tells the recruiter he is a mule skinner and is sent to Texas to break mules, which were still used at that time by the military as pack animals; Pilon is sent to Oregon to learn to be an infantryman, but never gets beyond the practice stage; and Big Joe Portagee goes to jail. Why Danny and Pilon remain on American soil while over four million American men were sent to the fighting is not made clear in the novel. However, as late as the 1950s, to a lesser or greater degree minorities were treated differently than whites in the U.S. Armed Forces, either by outright segregation or by job assignment. Even when attempting to become a part of the larger culture, as weak as their attempt may have been, the *paisanos* still face the conflict caused by their difference.

A final element that troubled Steinbeck about America was the prevailing attitude about the consumption of alcohol. The United States had attempted to discourage the use of hard spirits from the early days of its history and, based on the belief that drunkenness was the cause of increasing crime and poverty, many states began to pass their own Prohibition laws in 1851. After the Civil War, however, the increase in the number of saloons in America, considered to be hotbeds of vice and violence, led to a grass-roots movement of women who marched from local churches to local saloons where they demanded the closing of the establishments, sometimes using their own violent methods. This movement later led to the organization of the Anti-Saloon League of America (ASL). The ASL gained political force and endorsed political candidates who would demand state elections to stop the issuance of saloon licenses. The anti-saloon movement grew so large that the 18th Amendment to the United States Constitution was ratified, prohibiting the "manufacture, sale, or transportation of intoxicating liquors."

Prohibition did not have the desired effects upon American culture. Much literature of the time, and later literature such as *Tortilla Flat*, presents Prohibition as a cause of increased moral decay and disorder. Many claimed that it was causing more people to drink as well as to disrespect the law. Literature focused on the illegal sale of alcohol by bootleggers at speakeasies, highlighting what was felt to be the adverse effects of the law. In *Tortilla Flat*, Mr. Torrelli's sale of wine from his home is not as glamorous a portrait of the problem as those presented by other authors such as F. Scott Fitzgerald, but it does show the inability of the law to control the personal choices of Americans. The extent to which the *paisanos* would beg, borrow, and steal in order to get a gallon of Mr. Torrelli's wine indicates even more fully the ineffectual nature of Prohibition. Steinbeck's mention of the women meeting at the Methodist Church in Pacific Grove to plan a new attack against the vice in Monterey attests to the continuing efforts by those in power to control American values and morals. The efforts failed, at least as far as alcohol was concerned, and the 18th Amendment was repealed at about the same time Steinbeck was completing *Tortilla Flat*.

For Steinbeck, issues of culture are inseparable from issues of the individual. Consistently, his themes are concerned with the behavior of the individual within the group. A New Historicist reading of Steinbeck's work produces a clear picture of the prevailing cultural ideology as well as Steinbeck's own questions and concerns about those controlling ideas.

4

Of Mice and Men
(1937)

When he was writing *Of Mice and Men* in early 1936, and even during the period between the novel's completion and its publication, John Steinbeck's expectations for the book were low. It was typical of Steinbeck to doubt the quality of his work after it was finished. Additionally, Steinbeck had experimented with novel form in *Of Mice and Men* and he was unsure about how readers would react to this. The book's positive reception was, then, a surprise for the author, who seemed to put such little stock in his product. *Of Mice and Men* was selected as a Book-of-the-Month Club main selection in January 1937. In less than a month after its February debut, 117,000 copies were sold, and the reviews were, for the most part, encouraging. The novella was and still is a success, both commercially and critically, and has a somewhat interesting history. Initially titled *Something That Happened*, Steinbeck claimed he was writing the book for children. But the action and themes of the finished novel show a clear change from this original purpose. Also, early in the spring of 1936, Steinbeck's setter puppy tore up half of the novel's manuscript. A second writing was completed in mid-August 1936. The history behind its production attests to the appropriateness of the novel's final title, taken from Scottish Poet Robert Burns's "To a Mouse," advising that "the best-laid schemes o' mice an' men/Gang aft a-gley," or "go oft awry." Regardless of what might have occurred during production, *Of Mice and Men* has become one of Steinbeck's most read, most studied, and most beloved works. Ironically, this story originally intended for children has also become one of the ten most frequently banned books in America.

SETTING, PLOT, AND STRUCTURE

The setting Steinbeck chose for *Of Mice and Men* was a familiar one for the author. The novel recreates the landscape of his maternal grandfather Samuel Hamilton's ranch in King City, California, where Steinbeck spent time as a youth, and a place to where Steinbeck would again return his readers in the stories of *The Long Valley* and in *East of Eden*. The ranch to which George and Lennie go for work is more specifically modeled after the ranches in the California Salinas Valley owned by the Spreckles Sugar Company where Steinbeck worked during breaks and absences from Stanford University. The descriptions of the work and of the workers, the stable hands, and the roving bindlestiffs come from Steinbeck's recollections of his own experiences as a ranch worker.

The plot structure of *Of Mice and Men* reflects Steinbeck's intention of writing a novel that could be played on stage without extensive adaptation. Only three settings are created for the six chapters of the novel, with each chapter confining its action to a single setting or scene, and each setting used for only two chapters. The story is framed by Chapters 1 and 6, both set in a closed-in area around a "narrow" pool where the river "drops in close to the hillside bank" and where branches from the sycamore trees "arch over the pool" (3). The pool and its surrounding area are secluded and motionless, creating a scene of security reinforced by George telling Lennie, in Chapter 1, that if there is any trouble at the new job to which they are traveling, Lennie is to make his way back to this pool where George will find him. These instructions foreshadow the final scene of the novel. The four interior chapters equally divide the action between the ranch's bunkhouse in Chapters 2 and 3, and the barn in Chapters 4 and 5. It is when George and Lennie must interact with other characters that the most conflict occurs and, thus, the novel's main conflict occurs in these four interior chapters.

In addition to introducing the story and setting up the plot's frame, Chapter 1 establishes the objective, dispassionate narration that Steinbeck continues to use through the final pages of the story. In describing the physical setting, Steinbeck writes of "leaf junctures" and "recumbent limbs" (3), terms not unfamiliar to the author who spent a great deal of time studying the natural sciences. Those readers who can discern the naturalism resulting from this language in these early pages will forsee a bleak ending for the novel.

The story's main characters, George and Lennie, are introduced as they walk to the pool in the opening scene. The path they follow is heavily traveled. Lennie drops to his knees to drink from the pool and is quickly chastised by George, who warns him that the stagnant water may be bad. This immediately establishes George's paternal relationship with Lennie, who is mentally challenged. The remainder of Chapter 1 reinforces the roles of each character. George decides they will finish their walk to the ranch the next morning after sleeping under the stars; he tells Lennie to get rid of the dead mouse he's been carrying around in his pocket because it is old; he prepares their meal, warns Lennie about what to do if they face trouble at their new job, and prepares Lennie for sleep by sharing with him, once again, their dream of the little house they will someday own, complete with cows, pigs, rabbits, and a garden. Steinbeck's intentions of making this novel a play are evident as this opening scene comes to an end, with two sleeping bindlestiffs next to a fire from which "the blaze dropped down" and "the sphere of light grew smaller" (17).

Chapter 2 introduces the other characters in the story and further prepares the reader for later action in the novel. George and Lennie arrive at the ranch and are taken to the bunkhouse by Candy, an old, lame maintenance man who is followed around by an even older, lamer dog. The unnamed ranch boss enters wearing "high heeled boots and spurs to prove he was not a laboring man" (21). He is angry because George and Lennie arrived too late to put in a morning's work, and according to Candy, he has already taken out his anger on the black stable hand. The two are next confronted by Curley, the boss's bitter son, who positions his small body in a fighter's stance as he surveys the new workers. George and Lennie learn from Candy that Curley is newly married, and that his wife's "got the eye" (28). This information, coupled with the fact that George and Lennie left their previous work because Lennie had been accused of assaulting a woman there, foreshadows Lennie's later trouble with Curley's wife. George quickly anticipates the potential for trouble and warns Lennie to stay away from Curley. At the same time, he tells Lennie to defend himself if Curley attacks him, but reminds him of their prearranged meeting spot if trouble does occur. As if instinctively able to predict inevitable danger, Lennie tells George, "This ain't no good place. I wanna get outta here" (32).

The tension of George and Lennie's introduction to the ranch is eased somewhat by the appearance of Slim, the ranch foreman, who appears in the novel as the kindly leader with kingly characteristics. After speaking with George, he offers his approval of George and Lennie traveling together and, at the same time, offers a philosophy that punctuates for the reader the atmosphere at this ranch, and in retrospect, at the places George and Lennie have already worked and lived. Slim comments on the rarity of bindlestiffs traveling together and contemplates the reason. "Maybe ever'body in the whole damn world is scared of each other" (34). The comment points to a general condition of humanity but perhaps more specifically to a specific condition created by the circumstances of 1930s America, where jobs were scarce because of the depression, and even scarcer in California where, following empty promises, a large migrant force fleeing the drought and decay of middle America has congregated in search of livelihood.

The next two characters to enter the bunkhouse present an opposition to the kindliness displayed by Slim. Carlson highlights the rarity of Slim's concern for human feelings, especially among these itinerant workers. Carlson asks about Slim's dog, which has just had nine puppies, and suggests they give Candy one of the puppies and convince him to shoot the old, lame dog that stinks up the bunkhouse. As Chapter 2 closes, Curley comes angrily to the bunkhouse looking for his wife, and he and George size each other up as George tells him she had been there earlier looking for Curley. Slim's theory about humans basing their actions on fear is represented in this encounter and in George's statement to Lennie that "I'm scared I'm gonna tangle with that bastard myself. I hate his guts" (37).

The bunkhouse is again the setting in Chapter 3. The conflict continues to mount between the possibility of George and Lennie fulfilling the dream of their own home, on the one hand, and the potential for trouble on the other. In the beginning of the chapter, Lennie is in the barn with a puppy Slim has given him, and George and Slim again are discussing the relationship between George and Lennie, a conversation that adds to the mounting sympathy for Lennie. George tells Slim, who is now described as having "Godlike eyes" (40), that Lennie is dumb, but he is not crazy. Slim offers that Lennie is "nice" (40) and tells George that intelligence is not necessary to be pleasant. Indeed, according to Slim, intelligence is often a prerequisite for meanness. Slim's understanding compels George to confess what led him and Lennie to leave their last job. Because of Slim's approval, there is a sense that George and Lennie may have a chance of fulfilling the better life defined by their dream. The comfort of such a possibility, however, is quickly upset by the next occurence in the bunkhouse.

Carlson and Candy enter the bunkhouse with Candy's dog. Carlson tells Candy he should shoot the dog because it suffers all the time, because it has no fun, and because it stinks. There is no indication that Carlson is intellectually capable of connecting those conditions to the many men around him, including Lennie, who fit his requirements for destruction. Candy agrees to allow Carlson to shoot the dog. After doing so, Carlson comes into the bunkhouse to clean his gun. There is no discussion from the other bunkmates about the discomfort that this display may cause Candy, nor is there any indication that such feelings would matter in the natural course of events. The dog's death illustrates the naturalism in the novel. It is just "something that happened." The reader begins to understand that the same could happen to any of the other suffering characters in the novel.

Juxtaposed with the killing of Candy's dog and its interpretive significance is the building of the hope represented by George and Lennie's dream. Candy hears the two discussing their plans and expresses his interest in participating. This is when the reader learns that there is substance to the dream; George has already located a property, and its owners are desperate to sell for the price of $600. With Candy's announcement that he contribute his savings of $350, the dream is transformed into real possibility.

The fulfillment of any plan requires some control by the planners, and Steinbeck quickly points out that people like George and Lennie have little power to control their environment and thus the outcome of their lives. Earlier, Curley had come into the bunkhouse once again looking for his wife and was suspicious that Slim was in the barn. As they later re-enter the bunkhouse, Curley is apologizing to Slim for being suspicious, and Carlson calls Curley a coward. Lennie is still smiling about plans for the farm, and Curley mistakes his smile for ridicule, attacking Lennie. Lennie is afraid to fight back until George tells him to, and then Lennie quickly and uncontrollably gets the better of Curley, whose hand is crushed in the fight. To protect Lennie, Slim tells Curley to tell everyone he got his hand caught in a machine; otherwise, they will tell the truth and embarrass him. Slim is able to control this situation because of his status and because of his wisdom, but it is clear that none of the others, including George, has any power to control the hostile environment.

In Chapter 4, the setting of *Of Mice and Men* moves to the barn, the home of Crooks the stable hand. Crooks is set apart from the others by place, but also by his color and the permanency of his job at the ranch. The chapter opens and closes with Crooks alone, rubbing liniment on his back. The scene is one of loneliness, emphasized by the books and eyeglasses in Crooks's bunk area. Lennie, also a figure of loneliness since George and the others have gone to town, appears at Crooks's doorway but is told he is not wanted there because Crooks is not wanted in the bunkhouse. Crooks relents, however, because of Lennie's "disarming smile" (68) and goes on to reinforce the importance of friendship earlier introduced by Slim. He tells Lennie that the talking George and Lennie do is important even if Lennie does not understand what George is saying. "It's just bein' with another guy. That's all" (69). He punctuates this idea by telling Lennie how different it would be if he did not have anybody, if he could not play cards in the bunkhouse. It is clear that Crooks is talking about his own isolation, creating a parallel between Crooks and Lennie, both forced into loneliness by the cards that nature has dealt them, one by the hand of color, the other by the hand of mental disability. When Crooks learns about the men's plan to buy the farm, he first dismisses the dream and then asks if he can come work for them in exchange for room and board. His request makes it even clearer that none of these men wants to remain the way he is, lonely and isolated. They all want to participate in a community, even if it is a community of those cast out by the rest of society.

When Curley's wife enters the barn looking for Curley, the other characters' dismissal of her leads her to observe openly that none of them will talk to her if more than one is around. She supports Slim's earlier claim that they are all afraid of each other, and she defines it further by pointing out that each is afraid the others will "get something on you" (75). She refuses to leave when Candy, who has joined Lennie and Crooks in the barn, tells her she is not wanted there. Her description of married life with Curley, along with Curley's rejection, actually serves to include Curley's wife in the building classification of humans to which dreamers belong. She is lonely even with a husband. Candy's claim to her that they have friends, and that is why they will get their own farm, is the one way it is clear she will never be like these men as long as she is on this ranch. She will never have friends. With this realization, the scene closes with Crooks, alone and again lonely, rubbing liniment on his back.

The barn continues as the setting of Chapter 5 and represents a place of loneliness. The chapter opens with Lennie holding his puppy, lifeless because Lennie holding his puppy, lifeless because Lenny has stroked it too roughly. Lennie seems to be more worried about the consequence of the puppy's death—that George will not let him have rabbits to tend—than the actual loss of the puppy, an important indicator of Lennie's mental capabilities. As he is trying to hide the puppy, Curley's wife enters the barn and expresses her own loneliness. She asserts her right to recognition, supporting this by saying she could have been in the movies. Instead, she has married Curley, whom she admits she does not like, and has come to the ranch seemingly to find refuge from a world where no men have been nice to her. With this, the parallels between Lennie and Curley's wife are made evident. When Curley's wife asks Lennie why he thinks so much about rabbits, Steinbeck is able to provide an explanation for Lennie's obsession and to introduce the climactic action of the story. Lennie moves closer to Curley's wife and tells her he likes to "pet nice things" (87), mostly rabbits, but mice when he cannot find rabbits. She invites him to feel her hair, to feel how soft it is, but soon tells him to stop because he is messing it up. She jerks away, but Lennie is unable to process her quickly changing commands and his own desires, so he panics. She screams and he covers her mouth and nose with his hand. He gets angry. "And then she was still, for Lennie had broken her neck" (89).

Just as he did with the puppy, Lennie tries to cover her with hay, confirming the foreshadowing of her death by Lennie's earlier killing of the puppy. He then takes his dead puppy and leaves the barn to hide, as instructed by George, in the brush by the pond. The narrator's description of Curley's wife in death provides a new clue to the coming action. She is described in death as having lost all the pain and manipulation from her face, which is transformed into a picture of peace and beauty. Knowing the consequences of Lennie's actions will be extreme, the reader begins to feel hope that he will find a similar peace in death.

While the action of the story continues to occur chronologically, Steinbeck imposes a modern treatment of time over the events. After describing Curley's dead wife, the narrator reports a stoppage of time. "As happens sometimes, a moment settled and hovered and remained for much more than a moment" (90). Sound and all movements occurring in a moment also stop. The idea that the action has been removed from the limits of human time brings to the story a sense of ancient or sacred time, confirming death as a release from all human limitations. The surreal halting of time is quickly interrupted by Candy's entrance into the barn.

After seeing what has happened in the barn, Candy goes to get George, who says they will have to find Lennie and turn him over to the police; otherwise, he will starve to death, alone and running. At this moment the dream disappears. George tells Candy he knew from the beginning it would never materialize and that now he will just live like the other bindlestiffs, making money, drinking, playing pool, and visiting whorehouses. He tells Candy he will not let Curley and the others hurt Lennie, and asks for some time before Candy tells the others so they will not think he was in on the killing. After a few minutes, the others come in and Curley stirs them to action. Carlson finds that his gun is missing and believes Lennie has stolen it. George convinces them Lennie would have headed south, and they leave, except for Candy who stays behind and continues to express anger at Curley's wife for ruining their dream. The ambiguity of the chapter's final line, Candy's muttering the words "Poor bastard" (96), reinforces the parallel between Curley's wife and Lennie, to either of whom Candy could be referring.

Chapter 6 returns the story's action to the pool where Steinbeck first introduced George and Lennie. The objective and scientific description of the natural setting adds further to anticipation of the events to follow. The pond in the afternoon is still, and a snake glides across the water only to be eaten by a "motionless heron" (97). The description exemplifies the idea of the strong surviving at the expense of the weak. Lennie appears at the pool alone and, because he is alone, left to his own irrational thinking, he is unable to retain his sanity. His dead Aunt Clara appears to him, chasing him and telling him that he always does bad things, that he never thinks about George and all the nice things George has done for him. Aunt Clara disappears, and Lennie immediately sees a huge rabbit speaking in Lennie's voice. The rabbit tells Lennie he is not fit to tend to rabbits, that George is going to beat Lennie and then leave him. As Lennie begins to cry for George, his friend appears, and Lennie's nightmare visions stop. With George, some sanity returns to Lennie's life.

For a few moments George and Lennie return to normal, with George talking about their friendship and about how they are different from the other bindlestiffs who have nobody in the world. When George tells Lennie to take his hat off and look across the river, he tells him again about the house and the rabbits, creating for Lennie once again the impossible dream. The dream transforms into a description of afterlife as George prepares to shoot Lennie. He tells Lennie that everyone will be nice to him and there will be no more problems for him to face. George defines death and what comes after in terms that Lennie will understand. As Lennie begs to go to this place George is describing, George fires Carlson's gun, shooting Lennie in the head.

Steinbeck intends to show that the dream has finally become reality for Lennie, but that it is only possible in death because in life things will always happen, out of human control, to destroy those dreams. As George walks away with Slim, it is clear the manager is the only one who understood the friendship between George and Lennie. That Curley and Carlson cannot understand what is bothering George and Slim, and thus cannot understand the importance of friendship, casts the last element of tragedy on *Of Mice and Men*.

CHARACTERS

In *Of Mice and Men*, Steinbeck manages to present a cast of characters who are vivid and compelling, as well as complicated. Only George Milton develops in the course of the novel, and that development occurs as a result of actions he takes in response to the actions of the other major character, Lennie, who does not develop in the story.

George is a small, single man with no social position and an uncertain employment future, yet he is presented early in Chapter 1 as a man with "sharp, strong features" (4) who displays characteristics of leadership and parental responsibility. As George and Lennie first appear, walking single file to the pool, George is leading, establishing his position in the hierarchy of this twosome. Shortly after reaching the pool, this leadership is reinforced by Lennie's exact mimicking of George's movements and posture as he sits down. George's sense of responsibility for Lennie becomes clear as the two discuss the job to which they are heading. George must remind Lennie where they are going, and he is carrying both of their work tickets. He instructs Lennie to keep his mouth shut once they reach the ranch so that the boss will not deny them work. It is evident here that George is not speaking out of meanness, but out of concern for Lennie. This distinction is reinforced when George takes away the dead mouse Lennie has been carrying in his pocket, again, not out of meanness, but because the mouse "ain't fresh" (11), and additionally when he gives Lennie instructions about what to do if they have trouble at the new job.

George's parental role in his relationship with Lennie is necessary because of Lennie's apparent mental disability. This difference between the two men would naturally lead to an assumption that George will present a rational contrast to Lennie's inability to reason. Yet George's development in the novel occurs with his transformation from dreamer to realist, and his actions result from moral rather than reasoned decisions.

One would not expect bindlestiffs, the men who traveled from one California ranch to another seeking work, to be dreamers, especially during the depression era. The work was hard, compensation was slight, life was lonely, and there was little on which to base any dreams of change. Literary convention, however, creates the expectation of such a character developing from hardened realist to dreamer. Many factors make George different from other bindlestiffs. Even though he is single, George does have responsibility for another human being. Caring for Lennie fulfills a promise George made to Lennie's Aunt Clara before she died. Because he is always with Lennie, George is not a solitary figure. Most bindlestiffs found only temporary companions among the other workers at their temporary jobs. Because he is not alone, George is not completely lonely. Even his need for occasional female company is balanced by his concern about leaving Lennie unsupervised, so he does not regularly visit the whorehouses with the other bindlestiffs.

These traits that make George different from the other roaming ranch workers, as well as his need to make Lennie happy, make it possible, while not necessarily natural, for him to be a dreamer. This characteristic results from his association with Lennie, specifically from his need to appease Lennie. Lennie needs to hear often about the farm George and Lennie will one day own, a place where he will not be singled out and persecuted for his difference. Simply satisfying Lennie's need to envision a better world would not be enough to show that these dreams were real for George also, however. Because of Lennie's belief, the dream becomes a real possibility for George. As long as Lennie is there, as long as there is a reason for the fulfillment of the dream, then for George the dream is possible.

George's development occurs when the dream is erased, and he must come to terms with the inevitable reality that justice is absent from the world, and justice is a requirement for a fulfillment of their dream. George and Lennie's roaming has already illustrated the world's injustice. Lennie is tormented at each place to which they move in hopes of a peaceful working environment, and George, only a bindlestiff, has no authority to claim justice for Lennie. He can continue taking him to new places where the same treatment is bound to occur. Their dream of a farm of their own is created in reaction to these experiences. With a farm, they would be able to build their own small world and, consequently, separate from the unjust society. This world would be larger than just George and Lennie. As the novel progresses, the dream begins to include both Candy and Crooks. Since these men are also lame in the eyes of society, Candy for his age and his broken body and Crooks for his color, their inclusion reinforces the idea that this dream farm would be a place of justice. That George seems to be the character capable of facilitating the dream makes him likable.

When, at the novel's close, George recites to Lennie one last time the dream, it has changed from a dream of a farm to a dream of peace in death. George presents a place of extreme goodness and extreme justice, not just for Lennie, but for everybody. By doing so George makes true justice a possibility only in death, thus eliminating it as something to ever be found in life. This is how the reader knows that, even with Lennie gone, George will never attempt to buy the farm in order to give Crooks and Candy a safe haven from the world. George now knows the justice earlier represented by the farm is impossible in earthly life.

So George performs his own act of justice in reaction to the understanding that Lennie, who has killed Curley's wife, will never be treated justly. Curley would not allow Lennie to go to jail; instead, he would want to kill him, and jail would be a cruel punishment for a person like Lennie. Even letting Lennie escape, George realizes, would be wrong. Lennie would starve or find more trouble without George's protection.

With his final act of shooting Lennie, George becomes a man without dreams. He is a realist, not only about the world, but also about his own life. He will always be a bindlestiff; to be anything more socially would require family and friends, and through his relationship with Lennie he learns that people are no more lasting than dreams. Even his relationship with Slim, bound by shared knowledge of what really happened when George shot Lennie, is temporary. Slim will stay on to run the ranch, but George will have to move on to the next job.

Of Mice and Men requires both George and Lennie because it is a story of friendship, and while these two are an unlikely pair, their relationship is the story's hope; its loss is the story's tragedy. The friendship between George and Lennie is characterized by its balance. George's ability to think and plan balances Lennie's mental disability. George's reason keeps Lennie's passions in check. George's experience in the world is softened by Lennie's innocence. Most importantly, George's sanity keeps Lennie's insanity at bay.

While Lennie is important as the balance to George, and as the force behind George's actions, he is not a developing character in the novel. Indeed, Lennie seems incapable of developing, of changing or growing. Lennie's significance as a character is that he represents the motifs and themes of the novel. Lennie's experiences in the world illustrate the injustice with which George must come to terms. Lennie's fear of losing George enables Steinbeck to present friendship at an unconditional level. Finally, Lennie represents dreams and their importance in a world of unbending realities.

Lennie appears to be characterized by qualities often considered negative: insanity, overwhelming passion, and innocence. Yet, through Lennie, Steinbeck presents these qualities, often associated with the mentally disabled, as positive. Lennie experiences the world with his senses rather than his mind. He is driven to the feel of soft things, of fabrics and women's hair and dead mouse fur. Lennie loves the taste of ketchup. As compelling as these sensations are to Lennie, he is willing to give them up to preserve his relationship with George, perhaps the most satisfying and certainly the safest passion in his life. In this, Lennie's instinct for survival is made clear.

ROLE OF MINOR CHARACTERS

All of the remaining characters in *Of Mice and Men* are minor characters. Their functions vary; some merely represent types and are stock characters, while others carry more symbolic importance.

Curley and Carlson are both stock characters, characters that represent a recognizable type. While many stock characters are routine and predictable, Steinbeck has an interesting way of presenting these characters and the role they serve. Steinbeck presents the character of Curley by showing the reader who Curley is and also by telling who he is, which serves to guide the reader in an evaluation of the character. When he first appears in the novel, Curley's glance at George and Lennie is described as cold and calculating. His body is positioned in a fighter's stance, curled almost as if to explain his name. Curley is characterized before he participates in any action. His treatment of Lennie and of his wife shows the reader further that Curley is a small, weak, and insecure man who uses his position of authority to make others feel smaller than himself, a type widely represented in fiction and in other media.

Carlson's role in *Of Mice and Men* is rather narrow. He is the vehicle through which Steinbeck presents the Darwinian ideas of survival that apply both to

Candy's dog, which Carlson manages to rid the bunkhouse of by substituting a more fit dog in its place, and to the characters who represent weakness through their various differences as contrasted to Carlson's seeming fitness. He is physically and mentally fit, and he belongs to a socially accepted race, making him different from Lennie, Candy, and Crooks, a difference necessary to reinforce the novel's theme.

It is the difference from the norm that Candy and Crooks represent that makes them symbolically important. Their mistreatment by society for their differences, including the abuse by other characters in the novel, forces the reader to consider the experiences of all those who appear to deviate from the accepted standard. The reader is less surprised by the actions taken against Lennie because Steinbeck has already shown how easily a lame old man's dog can be taken from him and how easily a black man can be locked out of a white world. Lennie's story is tragic, but by placing Candy and Crooks into a similar social category, Steinbeck abstracts Lennie's tragedy to a universal level, forcing the reader to consider an even larger tragedy.

Slim, while also representing a type, that of the wise man, is presented in more detail, or more roundly, than the other minor characters. He is important because he is the voice of the author. His understanding and approval of the relationship between George and Lennie creates further sympathy for their circumstances. Because of the description Steinbeck gives Slim, the reader is compelled to accept his observations and philosophies. He is both physically godlike, a more expert jerkline skinner than any other, and spiritually godlike; Slim is ageless and omnipotent. He knows why people live and act the way they do, but his knowledge has not made him sour; he is a kind man. What he sees is what Steinbeck would like the reader to see—his kindness is Steinbeck's hope for a world where the reality is harsh.

THEMES

Much of his work in this period emphasizes the philosophy Steinbeck shared with his closest friend Edward Ricketts. Ricketts was a marine scientist at whose side Steinbeck learned much about objective, scientific observation and natural processes. The philosophy resulting from this collaboration was the non-teleological thought developed in much of Steinbeck's work in the 1930s and 1940s. Non-teleological philosophy stresses what "is," the actual facts of human existence, as opposed to what might be or could be hoped for in a caring universe. The moment is what is important, what can be known, not some potential end or goal. In *Of Mice and Men*, Steinbeck presents this philosophy through the eventual negation of George and Lennie's dream, which is taken away by the events occurring in their life, the things that happen to them to show the dream, or end, to be merely a fantasy. *Of Mice and Men*'s major theme of naturalism, as well as the objective, nonjudgmental narration of the novel, is consistent with the philosophy of the author and the scientist.

Naturalism is the idea that the scientific facts of heredity and environment are the forces controlling human existence, and neither human will nor divine assistance can alter the course determined by heredity and environment. Both forces are clearly functioning in *Of Mice and Men*. George and Lennie are bindlestiffs because that is the class of worker to which they belong by the facts of their birth, their potential, and the socioeconomic circumstances of their environment. Their attempts to change their circumstances are shown to be impossible.

The novel's naturalism is also presented through the reactions of Carlson, one of the ranch workers, toward Candy's dog. Entering the bunkhouse in Chapter 2, Carlson asks about Slim's dog, which has just had nine puppies. Through Carlson, the fear Slim speaks of is put into a naturalist context and can be specifically applied to George and Lennie. When Carlson asks about the puppies, Slim tells him he killed four of the puppies so the mother could feed the other five. Carlson suggests they give Candy one of the puppies and convince him to shoot the old, lame dog that stinks up the bunkhouse. In this exchange about the dogs, Steinbeck introduces the Darwinian idea of selection, where the strong will survive and the weak will perish. Candy's dog, Carlson suggests, should be sacrificed to be replaced by a stronger dog. Lennie, who because of his mental disability and the resulting need to be taken care of by someone else, is a weak member of humanity, and the reader begins to consider the possibility of his being sacrificed because of his weakness.

Another major theme in *Of Mice and Men* is that of friendship. Steinbeck's presentation of this theme is both scientific and sentimental. In later work, Steinbeck develops fully his phalanx idea, the idea of group man and the changes that occur when individuals join groups to accomplish a common goal, specifically the change from "I" thinking to "we" thinking. Steinbeck's phalanx ideas are another result of his own friendship with Ed Ricketts. The idea is introduced in small measure in *Of Mice and Men* with the beginning of the phalanx composed of George and Lennie and the growth of the phalanx that occurs when Candy and then Crooks are admitted into the group. George's selfless behavior throughout the novel indicates the "we" thinking of group man, and this thinking is further supported by Candy's quick offer of his savings for the purchase of the farm, and by Crooks's bold request that he be allowed to work on the farm in exchange for room and board.

The idea that life is improved by friendship is the more sentimental aspect of the friendship theme. For example, Slim reasons that bindlestiffs are loners because people are fearful of one another. When fear is overcome, however, and people form the bonds of friendship, the remaining difficulties of life are easier to bear. Friends overlook the differences for which individuals are singled out and bear discrimination. Lennie's mental disability is forgiven, Candy's lameness is ignored, and Crooks's color is overlooked. Each is made a better human being as a result of giving himself to friendship. Unfortunately, friendship does not create a force strong enough to ultimately restrain natural forces, and so friendship is vulnerable to inevitable loss.

Finally, the farm about which George and Lennie dream respresents the theme of fallen man attempting to find or create a new Eden, a theme that can be identified in much of Steinbeck's fiction. The farm, imagined as a place without fear or injustice, where the men will not be singled out because of differences but will instead live in common, illustrates in specific terms the abstract qualities of the biblical Eden. That it is a woman, Curley's wife, who ultimately destroys any possibility of the men getting their farm, of finding their Eden, creates a direct parallel to the biblical story. In withholding Eden from his characters, Steinbeck confirms that such searching will always be fruitless.

ALTERNATIVE READING: FEMINIST CRITICISM

There are actually many types or branches of feminist criticism, including but not limited to Marxist feminism and psychological feminism. Each type has a different focus, but in each can be found the common purpose of locating in literature, mostly literature written by men, the marginalization and constraint of women in culture and society. One goal of such investigation is to illustrate patriarchal principles, the social and cultural ideas promoted as truths by dominant male literary voices and the bias against women that result from those ideas. Like any political attack, feminism is concerned with effecting social and cultural change by accenting injustice. Two of the specific wrongs feminist critics analyze are the absence of women from meaningful discourse in literature, evident in the small number of works by female authors in the literary canon, and the distortion of female characters resulting in a misrepresentation of femininity as abnormal.

A feminist reading of *Of Mice and Men* might begin with an analysis of Steinbeck's description of Curley's wife. Feminist critics are often concerned with what is missing from the depiction of female characters, and in the case of

Curley's wife, one of the most necessary elements of a defined self, a name, has been omitted. This is significant at two levels. First, without a name, the reader will have less sympathy for the character. Curley's wife does not seem as real a person as a character with a name, an identifying marker. Thus, her death at Lennie's hands is less tragic than if she were named. This leads to the second level of significance: without a name to distinguish her from other women and other wives, Curley's wife automatically becomes respresentative of women. Consequently, what applies to Curley's wife applies to all women. Since Steinbeck's presentation of Curley's wife can be considered negative, there is a resulting association of negativity toward women in general.

The physical description of Curley's wife is a large part of her negative image. Before she even enters the story's action, Candy informs George and Lennie that Curley's wife is a tart, or whore, with an evil eye, distinguishing her as opposite from Slim, with his "Godlike eyes." Curley's wife is otherwise described throughout the novel as heavily made up and always wearing some item of red clothing. The color red is frequently associated with violent passion and disorder. This reinforces the suggestion by Candy that she is a whore and serves to locate her on the outskirts of normal, respectable culture. The description also serves to present Curley's wife as a threat to the society of the ranch and its bindlestiff population. Her evil eye is active. She eyes the workers and thus appears as a corrupting threat to the group.

Other actions by Curley's wife present her as a corrupting force in the novel. She is always moving about where she is not supposed to be, always searching for her husband, ostensibly, in the male territories of the bunkhouse and the barn. Curley's inability to control his wife's movements creates chaos amidst the orderliness of the ranch. Curley's position as the boss's son, coupled with his meanness and jealousy, make the threat of his wife's presence in forbidden places even more dangerous to those confined to those places. Steinbeck has created a male world, and the woman who enters this world is a menace.

Compounding the problem of her mere physical presence is the fact that, as she is quick to remind the other characters, Curley's wife is not a dumb woman. In Chapter 4 she accuses them of ignoring her if more than one of them is around, implying that each is open to talking to her if he is alone. She offers a reason for this: "You're all scared of each other, that's what. Ever' one of you's scared the rest is goin' to get something on you" (75). One aspect of feminist criticism, cultural analysis, focuses on the ways female characters portray the fears and anxieties of males. Curley's wife is able to express openly the way males see others around them as threats to their progress or even to their continued existence. This perceptiveness should be a trait that raises her above the level of dumb whore; however, her truthful pronouncement reinforces the danger of her character. If the men were to acknowledge their fears, their world would be turned on end and become even more chaotic than Curley's wife has already made it.

The traits that elicit sympathy for the male characters, indeed that are associated with sympathy for Lennie, are presented for Curley's wife in a negative light, even in death. Along with losing its "meanness" and "plannings, " her facial expression loses its "discontent" and "ache for attention," leaving her with a face that was "sweet and young" (90). Discontent and a need for attention are universal qualities of the cast of characters in *Of Mice and Men*, yet only when they belong to Curley's wife are they considered harmful detriments to youth and goodness. This treatment by Steinbeck contributes to the prejudice against women that results in the consideration of women as "other."

The reactions of the male characters to her death emphasize in what way women are made objects in this process of othering. George's grief is not for the loss of this woman's life, but instead for the inevitable result of her killing, Lennie's death. George seems to resent Curley's wife for getting herself killed, and thus creating the events that follow. Candy explicitly blames Curley's wife for getting killed. He calls her a "tramp," a "tart" (93), and blames her for messing up George and Lennie's dream, which is now Candy's dream also. Even Curley reacts as if he is angry for losing a piece of property rather than for losing a wife. He does not stop to show sorrow or pity over the body of his dead wife but instead immediately initiates his revenge on Lennie. None of the men seems to be affected by the loss of a human life; each sees her death as an obstacle to his happiness.

John Steinbeck's letters, collected in *Steinbeck: A Life in Letters*, include correspondence with Clare Luce, the actress who played Curley's wife in the stage production of *Of Mice and Men*. Steinbeck provides Luce with a biography of Curley's wife, including much that could only be loosely gathered from the background provided in the novel. In this letter, Steinbeck describes Curley's wife as irrevocably injured by her childhood, persecuted, enslaved, lonely, and "if you could ever break down the thousand little defenses she has built up, you would find a nice person, an honest person, and you would end up by loving her" (154). It is tempting to re-read the character of Curley's wife through the new lens this letter creates. Yet, a feminist reader is not interested in authorial intent. What the author may have hoped to convey is irrelevant in comparison to what is actually presented in the text. How an actress may play the role of Curley's wife on stage does not change the role given to the character in the pages of the novel. Curley's wife, for the feminist reader, is typical of the way male authors represent women: corrupting, dangerous, and "other."

The Grapes of Wrath
(1939)

In May 1938, John Steinbeck began writing, in longhand, the novel that brought both his greatest acclaim and his sharpest criticism. Preparation for *The Grapes of Wrath* began even before Steinbeck's decision to create this epic story of a fictional family's Dust Bowl experiences. Shocked by the exploitation and living conditions of California's migrant workers, Steinbeck wrote a series of news reports, titled "The Harvest Gypsies," for the San Francisco *News* in October 1936. "The Harvest Gypsies" would be reprinted together in a 1938 volume titled *Their Blood Is Strong*.

As the migrants' problems continued, so too did Steinbeck's need to make them the focus of his writing, and in December 1937, he began work on a long novel titled *The Oklahomans*, but he soon discarded this work. From February to May 1938, Steinbeck attempted to address the topic through a satire, "L'Affaire Lettuceberg," which targeted the Salinas, California, citizens whom Steinbeck felt were responsible for the violence that erupted during a lettuce strike there. He found the writing unsatisfactory. Indeed, neither of these projects satisfied Steinbeck's twofold need to create good literature and to inspire his readers to take action against the great injustices created out of America's depression era droughts in what became known as the dust bowl.

On October 26, 1938, Steinbeck wrote the final words of *The Grapes of Wrath*, a title suggested by his first wife, Carol Henning Steinbeck. Officially published on April 14, 1939, the novel was an immediate bestseller, and it retained that status through most of the first year of publication, with hardcover sales of 428,900 copies. The novel's public reception also included angry attacks from private groups such as The Associated Farmers of California and from local and state government representatives from both California and Oklahoma. Based on charges that the novel misrepresented the migrant situation and that it was Communist propaganda, the book was banned from many libraries and became the fuel for bonfires in cities such as East St. Louis, Illinois. If the emotional impact, both favorable and negative, that a political novel inspires is a gauge of its greatness, then *The Grapes of Wrath* was and still is much more than a run-of-the-mill novel.

HISTORICAL CONTEXT

The Grapes of Wrath is set against the historical time period from 1929 to 1939, which was known as the Great Depression in America. The stock market crash of October, 24, 1929, known as Black Thursday, financially ruined millions of people. This led to widespread unemployment and the failure of people to pay their debts. In addition to these hardships, large parts of America were hit by a severe drought in the 1930s. An area extending from the Dakotas to the Texas panhandle became known as the "dust bowl." Lack of rain, heavy winds, and poor soil conservation practices caused topsoil to be blown away. Many farmers sold their farms or lost them to the banks. Others became tenant farmers but, like the Joads, were forced off the land they worked. In 1933, Franklin D. Roosevelt became president and made restoring prosperity to America his first priority. While Roosevelt's economic recovery program, the New Deal, did much to address the hardships of the depression, full relief would not be found until America entered the Second World War.

SETTING, PLOT, AND STRUCTURE

Much of the success of *The Grapes of Wrath* as a piece of literature can be attributed to the author's treatment of setting and plot structure. In many novels, the setting supports or creates a backdrop for the plot. In *The Grapes of Wrath*, however, setting determines the plot. The opening scenes of the novel are the catalyst for the initial and continuing action of the story. When the novel opens, the reader is introduced to the dark and windy barrenness of Oklahoma farm country. It is a country bereft of clouds and rain, leaving "the surface of the earth crusted, a thin hard crust, and as the sky became pale, so the earth became pale, pink in the red country and white in the gray country" (3). Steinbeck's fictional family, the Joads, must go to California because, as far as they are capable of determining, that is the place of color and life.

The way Steinbeck presents setting throughout *The Grapes of Wrath* serves a significant purpose. Beginning with Chapter 1, landscape and people are described in sweeping and poetic language, heavy with alliteration and metaphor and mythic in its largeness. This opening chapter presents the creation story, or cosmogony, of all those who are displaced by drought, industrial progress, and economic depression. Steinbeck does not introduce specific characters of the story in this opening chapter; instead, he presents only those unnamed people whom the Joads will represent. While these people have lives and histories that precede the devastation that drives them from their homes, Steinbeck begins his novel with the new birth of a nation of people for whom the past will serve little useful purpose.

Most of the novel's action occurs in open or nearly open spaces. Forced out of their homes, the Joads and other migrants must live in their cars or trucks or in makeshift tents. They come into contact with each other in camps and in the fields, thus reinforcing the thematically important idea of community or groups. This new life without walls or firm boundaries, however, leaves them with weakened defenses. The Hooverville camp is burned out after migrants there question the authority of the sheriff and the labor contractor. Another enemy, nature, forces the Joads from the boxcar camp when the rains flood their shelter. In their temporary settlements even religion, foreign and oppressive, becomes an enemy of the Joads.

The grandness of description in Chapter 1, followed by the specific realism of Chapter 2, introduces the reader to the structure of the novel, which is an almost perfect alternation between what Steinbeck called interchapters, or universal chapters, and particular chapters. In the universal chapters, Steinbeck presents the general portrait of migrant workers' lives, as well as portraits of those who would attempt to profit from the misfortune of these displaced people. Also introduced in the interchapters are the machines and corporations responsible for the progress that made the small family farm and the tenant farm, and thus the hope of the farmers, obsolete. The language of the universal chapters remains formal and poetic throughout the novel. Contrasting this diction is the heavy vernacular of the particular chapters that follow one family, the Joads, from their tenant farm in Oklahoma west to California where they hope to find a means of survival. Using the interchapters, Steinbeck hoped to provide musical overtones to the novel. The final effect is symphonic, with the interchapters providing the effect of the full orchestra and those chapters focusing on the Joad family providing the solos.

Of further importance in consideration of the novel's structure is Steinbeck's near equal division of the novel's thirty chapters into three parts, creating the sense of a three-act play and a parallel to the biblical story of the Israelites' exodus from Egypt. Chapters 1 through 10 establish the conditions that make it necessary for the Joads, and others like them, to leave their ancestral homes. In the loss of homes and the possessions that must be either sold or destroyed, the story's characters lose past identities and are thus prepared for the thematically important transformation from self-concern to altruism. Chapters 11 through 19 take the Joads from Oklahoma to California, the migrants' exodus from the bondage of the banks and landowners. They are moving toward their promised land. In Chapters 20 through 30, readers witness the life the Joads face in California, the new form of slavery into which they have been sold by the yellow handbills filled with promises of work.

Both Chapter 1, a universal chapter, and Chapter 2, the reader's first introduction to a member of the Joad family, are key in the expectations they create that are sustained throughout the novel. Chapter 1 first presents the picture of an uncaring nature where the sun continues to rise upon the ravaged land, but where light cannot reach through the clouds of dust. This loss of light establishes a figurative loss of order or direction in the people's lives, and the reader anticipates a resolution to the resulting chaos.

The effect of this darkness upon the novel's men is the second expectation established in this first chapter. The women are shown watching their men because "women and children knew deep in themselves that no misfortune was too great to bear if their men were whole" (7). If the man broke, was unable to hold the center around which the family was ordered, the family would be lost to chaos. For the remainder of the novel, the reader joins the female characters in their constant vigil over the men.

Chapter 2 is the first particular chapter, and here Tom Joad is introduced as he makes his way home after being paroled from prison, where he has served four years for killing a man in self-defense. During his journey back to the family, Tom comes first upon Jim Casey, the preacher whose sins have driven him from the pulpit. Tom is presented as a man of action, while Casey is shown as a man who is led by his thoughts. This first scene with Tom and Jim is important because throughout the novel they will borrow from each other's major personality traits and together come to symbolize the solution Steinbeck envisions for a world torn apart by its own progress.

The remaining chapters in this first section of the novel present the Joads giving over their separate lives to join the extended family's pursuit of a better life. The older Joads must forfeit the land that has been theirs longer than any can remember. The single men no longer have the luxury of time in which to pursue their physical and emotional desires. Connie and Rose of Sharon must delay their hopes of a home for their growing family. Even Winfield and Ruthie must contribute to the needs of the family and thus forfeit the natural freedom of childhood. Whether concrete or abstract, these individual needs and purposes are what Jim Casey claims make people "unholy." "But when they're all workin' together, not one fella for another fella, but one fella kind of harnessed to the whole shebang—that's right, that's holy" (110).

As the Joads make their way to California, they face hardships and setbacks, and the family begins to grow even further beyond its biological limits. While still in Oklahoma, the family dog is hit by a car and killed, and Grandpa Joad dies. The Joads' loss in numbers is made up by the joining with Mr. and Mrs. Wilson, a couple traveling alone to California in search of work. There is an immediate give and take between the Joads and the Wilsons, with the Wilsons offering aid and comfort during Grandpa Joad's death, and the Joads offering mechanical assistance when the Wilson car breaks down. Chapter 14, one of the most significant chapters in the novel, is placed between these two events. This chapter marks the halfway point of the novel and offers the clearest presentation of Steinbeck's theory of the forming of a dynamic group from separate, paralyzed selves. This group, sharing both pain and possessions, begins to consider itself "we" rather than "I," and in doing so poses a greater threat against those who would threaten its survival than the individual driven to gain through increased ownership.

The final chapters of this middle section of the novel concentrate on the Joads' assimilation into the new society of migrants. Chapter 18 takes them into California, where they stop to rest at a river camp before crossing the desert that separates them from the state's agricultural areas. While bathing in the river, Tom and Pa Joad meet a father and son who warn the Joads of the abusive treatment they, as "Okies"—the name universally applied to all the dust bowl migrants—will receive from Californians who are afraid of what a group of hungry people might do. Ma Joad receives a taste of this treatment when a sheriff arrives at the family tent to warn the Joads that they will be arrested if they do not move on by the next morning. Ma's near physical attack of the sheriff with an iron skillet emphasizes the reaction the Californians fear. Chapter 19, an interchapter, looks to history to explain the relationship between those who accumulate property and those who are hungry, warning that those who are pushed down will eventually become strong and unified and strike back against those who push them.

The first two particular chapters of the final section of the novel, Chapters 20 and 22, offer the extreme contrast between two of the Joads' early experiences in California. The first is their short stay in the Hooverville camp, a makeshift, disorderly migrant settlement where the residents are vulnerable to the anger and abuse of the outside, native community. Except for the connection made between Floyd, a young migrant worker, and the young Joad men, the atmosphere of the camp is one of isolation and distrust. The Joads seem to be out of place and bewildered in Hooverville. Ma Joad incurs the wrath of a fellow camp mother for sharing the leftovers of the family's stew with the camp children. Uncle John, startled by the children's hunger, attempts to give his own food to them but is stopped by Tom. Uncle John's inability to help the children makes him feel guilty for holding five dollars of his own money away from the family's funds. These burdens are too much for Uncle John, who goes off on his own to get drunk. The dark possibilities of migrant living are also too much for Connie, Rose of Sharon's husband, whose talk of a radio repair job and a comfortable home continue to show his concern for self. Connie sneaks away from the camp, leaving not only the group, but also his wife and unborn child.

The Hooverville camp is also the setting for a pivotal moment in the novel, one that serves to illustrate Steinbeck's earlier claims about the natural tendencies of the repressed. A farm labor contractor and a sheriff arrive at the camp to announce work opportunities. Floyd, the young man who befriends Tom and his younger brother Al, challenges the contractor about wage guarantees for the work. The sheriff steps in and threatens to jail Floyd as an agitator, and as Floyd runs away, Tom trips the sheriff. Seeing the sheriff on the ground jolts Jim Casey from thought to action. He kicks the sheriff as a way of distracting attention from Tom and later takes the blame for tripping the sheriff. Casey is taken to jail and thus leaves the family, but unlike the earlier losses of groups members, Casey's absence signals a sense of beginning rather than of ending.

Fear of being burned out of the Hooverville camp forces the Joads to seek another place to live, and they become part of the dramatically different Weedpatch government camp community. As tenant farmers and later as migrants, it is clear that they have never been exposed to pure democracy as it is practiced in the government camp. The making and enforcing of the camp rules is carried out by the camp residents, not by the federal government or the camp manager. The residents work together, providing daycare, cleaning communal areas, and organizing entertainment for the good of all the members of the community. By presenting the Joads' near perfect experiences at the government camp, Steinbeck stresses the benefits of self-governance for all people, not just for those who gain power through ownership.

Chapter 24 highlights the control the camp residents can have in upsetting the machinations of the work outside the camp's fences. Tom and other men have been warned that there will be infiltrators at the camp's Saturday night dance. Only if laws are broken inside can the sheriffs enter the camp. Democracy works in the camp, and as a result, few rules, much less laws, are broken. Sending outsiders in to incite the residents is the only way the authorities can get inside. A group of the camp men, including Tom Joad, is able, through organization and planning, to identify and put out the infiltrators before any trouble occurs. Steinbeck shows that a group can protect itself from outside threats.

As rosy as the picture of Weedpatch is, no society or philosophy is perfect. The camp is surrounded by a fence, and while it may work to keep objectionable people out, it also serves as a place of confinement for the residents. Steinbeck calls the camp a reservation, immediately inviting an association with the Native American reservations in which the government cannot interfere with the laws and lives of the people, but also where there is rampant unemployment, poverty, and shame. Those living in Weedpatch face low wages, when they can find work at all, and the children quit attending school because of the shame they are made to feel as "Oakies." The Joads cannot be physically sustained by the philosophy of social democracy; thus, after one month, they must leave the government camp in search of work.

The novel's final five chapters complete the political message Steinbeck has built throughout the novel. In Chapter 26, the Joads unknowingly pass through a group of picketers as they enter a peach farm where they have been promised work. The conditions in which the Joads find themselves are deplorable. The cabin they are given for shelter is filthy with grease, and they are forced to pay inflated prices for food at the farm store. On the first night at the farm, Tom sneaks past the guards, who are intended to keep the workers away from the picketers, in order to investigate the commotion the Joads noticed when they arrived at the camp. He finds a group of labor organizers, apparently headed by Jim Casey.

While serving his jail sentence for assaulting the sheriff at the Hooverville camp, Casey meets labor agitators. Through them, Casey is able to comprehend the significance of people's struggles that his earlier days in the wilderness could not help him fully understand. The difference between the two contemplative experiences is significant. When he wandered the land after leaving the church, Casey was alone. In jail Casey was with others, the people who make up the great soul of which he was only a part. In this communion of souls, knowlege arrived at is greater, more complete. In jail Casey comes to realize that struggle is based on need, and when enough people demand what they need, they will get it. Some may be punished for their demands, but progress will continue. This revelation is what brings Casey to the peach farm strikes, where Tom finds him, and where Tom kills the strikebreaker who attacks and murders Jim Casey. Tom's act of justice forces the Joads to leave the farm and migrate once again in search of work.

Steinbeck's political message does not die with Jim Casey. After Casey's death, the Joads move into a railroad boxcar that they share with another family, the Wainwrights, and Tom spends his own time alone in a cave made of blackberry vines where he must hide from the law as his wounds from the attack heal. When he emerges, almost as if from a womb, he has assumed Casey's role as messenger. He tells Ma he is leaving to take up the fight for working people and that he will be found wherever there are people in need. The effect of Casey's message on Tom ripples throughout the Joad family and into the boxcar community in the final scenes. The torrential rains and the coming of Rose of Sharon's baby move Pa from his frozen state, and he organizes the other men in the boxcar camp to build a levy around the camp to protect it from flooding. The Wainwrights want to flee the flooding but decide to stay when they see others joined together in building the levy. As Casey prophesied, they are punished for the demands they make, this time upon nature. Falling trees tear the bank, and the cars flood. Rose of Sharon's baby is stillborn, and when Uncle John takes the apple box in which the body is laid and places it in the stream, the box turns over and spills the baby into the water. After two days of fighting the flood, they must take a step back from their fight and retreat to higher ground.

The Grapes of Wrath does not end with the negative side of Casey's message; rather, it ends with the promise that progress toward fulfilling need will continue, even after setbacks. This hopefulness is illustrated in the most compelling scene of the novel. Having seemingly lost everything, including her husband and baby, Rose of Sharon performs a totally selfless act. The Joads find a barn safe from the flood, inside of which are a starving father and his frantic son. The father has sacrificed all of his food to keep the son healthy, but now is in danger of dying. Knowing what she must do, Rose of Sharon gives her milk-swollen breast to the dying man. The novel ends with this moment. The impact of the scene requires none of the explication of the universal chapters.

CHARACTERS

The thematic emphasis of *The Grapes of Wrath* is on the importance of the group rather than the individual and is mirrored by Steinbeck's treatment of characters in the novel. There is no one character that is the story's hero. As a result, it is difficult to identify a single protagonist. Of the dynamic characters in the novel, that is, those who develop throughout the plot, Tom Joad's change in character is the most apparent, and as a result, Tom is often identified as the novel's protagonist.

When the reader first encounters Tom on his way back to the Joad farm after being paroled from prison, his goals are personal, even selfish. He tells Jim Casey he wants women and drink, those pleasures denied him in prison. Even when he begins the journey with his family to California, there is no indication that he has joined them in order to help them. Indeed, as a man on parole, leaving the state is a risky choice for Tom and could negatively affect his family if he is caught. But staying in Oklahoma would have meant being alone, and Tom had been alone too long. One of the first indications we have that Tom is beginning to act from a consideration of others is when he fixes the Wilsons' car in New Mexico. Later Tom trips the sheriff at the Hooverville camp so that Floyd can run, and he helps to keep the government camp safe from infiltrators. By the end of the novel, Tom has clearly changed from a man acting on his own needs to a man of altruistic action.

A larger thematic principle is illustrated in Tom's development from selfishness to selflessness. From the beginning, Tom represents justice, but initially it is a justice for self. Tom goes to prison for defending himself against an unjust attack. As the novel progresses, however, Tom's actions are in defense of others, first when he hits the sheriff at the Hooverville camp, and later when he kills Jim Casey's murderer. Until these final pages of the novel, there is never a sense of Tom as a man of thought, like Casey. He will never be a philosopher, but philosophies will not feed people; actions will. When he is hiding from the law for killing Casey's murderer, however, Tom experiences an epiphany; indeed, he comes to understand that fighting against unjust oppressors is the greatest type of justice. Tom's most memorable lines in the novel exemplify his new belief: "Wherever they's a fight so hungry people can eat, I'll be there. Wherever they's a cop beatin' up a guy, I'll be there . . . I'll be in the way guys yell when they're mad an' - I'll be in the way kids laugh when they're hungry an' they know supper's ready" (572).

With Jim Casey, we see a development quite opposite from the changes Tom Joad undergoes. Casey's development illustrates a shift from thought to action. As the novel opens, Jim shares with Tom the incomplete philosophies he has developed through his experiences, first as a preacher, and then as a man who cannot square his ideas about men, the flesh, and humanity with formal religion. Casey has come to believe "there ain't no sin and there ain't no virtue. There's just stuff people do" (32). The true spirit, for Casey, is the love of people, all of whom belong to "one big soul ever'body's a part of" (33).

The other characters initially view Casey purely as a thinker, a view made obvious by their hesitation in having him help prepare the pig for salting as they get ready to leave for California, or in having him help repair the Wilsons' car. In the eyes of the Joads, Casey's job is to pray and preach, which they ask him to do to his own discomfort. Their acceptance of Casey as a man of action comes during the Joad family's short stay in the Hooverville camp, when he takes the blame for Tom's assault on the sheriff and accepts the consequence of arrest and jail. Accepting the blame shows Casey's willingness to sacrifice himself for his fellow humans. Early in the novel, readers question Casey's motivations, especially because of his sexual experiences as a minister. To some degree, however, this doubt is mitigated by Casey's definition of sin. From the moment he saves Tom from the sure return to Oklahoma on a parole violation, however, it is clear that Casey's focus is the welfare of his fellow humans.

Casey is transformed when he comes out of jail. Disconnected theories of souls and sin have congealed into solid ideas about justice and about how collective action is necessary to achieve this justice. Now, even Casey's thoughts are focused on action, the action of organizing workers to protest the abuse of migrants. Eventually, action in the name of justice will be the cause of Casey's death.

Ma Joad's role in the novel is foreshadowed by the description of dust bowl women provided by Steinbeck in Chapter 1. Ma is a woman watching to make sure not only that her man has not broken, but also that her family does not break. As long as these things do not happen, the family will survive. Chapter 1 also prepares the reader to contrast Ma's constant activity with Pa's psychologically frozen condition. Ma's role, then, is to keep people together while always focusing on the practical requirements of survival. She consoles and persuades when family members are frantic, she tends to the dying, and she manages what food there is so her family will not starve. In this role it becomes necessary for Ma to evolve from the traditional female/mother, one who follows the leadership of her man, to a leader herself. This shift begins early in the novel, when Casey asks if he can join the Joads on their trip to California. "Ma looked for Tom to speak, because he was a man, but Tom did not speak. She let him have the chance that was his right" (127). Like Tom, Ma is not driven by thoughts or by philosophies, but by actions. When the question of taking Casey is brought up at the informal family meeting that evening, Pa asks if they can feed an extra mouth. "It ain't kin we? It's will we?" is Ma's response (139). Although she turns the final decision over to the men, the reader sees her filling in for these men who seem to have lost their ability to function traditionally as they lose their land and their livelihoods. It is not without some cost. Pa Joad's "spirit was raw from the whipping" issued by Ma's tongue when he suggested there may not be room for Casey (140). Ma's response is only a whipping, however, and not a breaking of her man's spirit.

Perhaps the clearest indication of Ma's move into the leadership role is her roadside stand in Chapter 16, when she threatens Pa with a jack handle, thereby threatening the entire family with her wrath if they separate because of the Wilsons' broken car. Tom and John attempt to convince her that separating is a practical decision but "she was the power. She had taken control" (231). For the rest of the novel, Ma will be the leader of the Joad family, pardoning them for their weaknesses and, as in the last scene in the novel, blessing them for their goodness.

ROLE OF MINOR CHARACTERS

There is the same temptation to assign religious meaning to Rose of Sharon as there is with Jim Casey. As soon as her name is introduced, connections are inevitably made between the oldest Joad daughter and Christ, to whom the name Rose of Sharon is often applied in traditional Christianity. Such connections are difficult for most of the novel as, except for her pregnant condition, there is little similarity between the immature, often whining, self-centered young wife and Jesus Christ. As with Casey, however, Steinbeck's interest here is not in the Bible's miracles but in the people to whom those miracles are assigned. Rose of Sharon does mature during the course of the novel, perhaps as a result of focusing on the welfare of her unborn child, and this maturing shows a development from a selfish nature to an altruistic nature. By the time the Joads migrate to the peach farm for work, Rose of Sharon has stopped whining and begins to contribute to the family goal of survival and protecting Tom from the law. Even after she loses her baby, we do not see self-pity from Rose of Sharon. Indeed, by sharing her still full breasts with a dying man, Rose of Sharon performs the novel's final and ultimate act of altruism.

After Ma Joad wins the roadside battle over the family splitting up, little is seen of Pa until the end. But because Pa is the Joad family patriarch, the reader watches carefully for the actions and reactions of this once vital and active man. For most of the novel, he is a man who needs to be led by others, not because he cannot take necessary action, but because, outside of the familiarity of the farm and his patriarchal role there, he does not know how to function in the new circumstances of migration and dependence upon others. This inactivity is reversed at the end of the novel when he rallies the other men at the rail car camp to build a levy to stop the approaching flood. Since his first motivation for this act seems to be protecting Rose of Sharon, his daughter and thus part of himself, during childbirth, it is not clear that Pa Joad becomes fully integrated into the altruism highlighted by Steinbeck as the favorable human condition.

The oldest Joads represent the unreclaimable past of the family. While Grandpa Joad fantasizes about a new life in California, he stubbornly refuses to leave when it is time to begin the trip, and the family must drag him to get him into the truck. He dies shortly after the trip begins. Likewise, Grandma Joad does not want to leave her native Oklahoma and dies shortly before the family reaches California. Because these characters are unwilling or unable to adapt to the shifting conditions of the family, they are weak and unable to survive. Their deaths facilitate the expansion of the family beyond the biological. As they die, they are replaced by others outside the biological family, first the Wilsons and then the Wainwrights.

Muley Graves, the displaced farmer who chooses to live an almost animal existence rather than be forced off the land, ironically foreshadows the type of person into which many of the novel's main characters evolve. While Muley lives the most isolated, and thus most individual, life among the characters, he is the natural embodiment of altruistic action. As we later see other characters doing, he shares his food with Tom and Casey not from a sense of guilt, but because he "ain't got no choice" (66). As Casey and Tom do later in the novel, Muley defies the sheriff and others who hunt him as an animal because he must stand up for what is right, for what is his, regardless of the rules established by those with more money and more power.

Like most of the minor characters of *The Grapes of Wrath*, Uncle John's role is driven by theme rather than by plot requirements. His inclusion in the trip to California represents the extension of the biological family, which must occur to allow a natural transition from the emphasis on the biological family to an emphasis on the larger, human family. The Wilsons and the Wainwrights help populate this larger family of which the Joads eventually find themselves a part.

Al Joad is presented as a man of practical action. He is necessary to the group because of his ability to carry out mechanical tasks. His actions, whether repairing the truck or working in the fields, are based on immediate physical need rather than on philosophy. His character does not develop significantly in the novel. He is eager to find a wife, and when Aggie Wainwright agrees to marry him, he is ready to leave the family.

Noah, the afflicted member of the family, seems also to be a man of action, incapable of meaningful thought, but Noah's ultimate action in the novel, ironically, arises out of thought rather than physical need. Noah leaves the family at the California river because he believes his presence will only hold the family back. He feels he is a hindrance to the survival of the larger group; thus, he sacrifices himself in order to ensure their survival. Like Grandpa and Grandma Joad, Noah is less fit and his loss contributes to the strength the family will need as they reach their destination.

Connie, Rose of Sharon's young husband, leaves the group for a less beneficent reason than does Noah. His personal but naive desire to live a comfortable life in a city drives him to desert both his wife and unborn child, as well as the larger Joad family. While his feelings seem justified to the reader, his actions leave the reader unsympathetic.

The youngest Joads, Ruthie and Wainwright, appear only to round out the large family, but, in fact, further contribute to the realism of the novel. Because of their youth, they adapt to each circumstance presented them without think-ing. Thinking causes some members of the family to resist doing what is neces-sary for survival and causes Connie to turn his back on the survival of others.

THEMES

From the opening lines of *The Grapes of Wrath*, deep literary naturalism, dis-cussed in Chapter 2 of this book, is at work, and many of the novel's themes come directly from this tradition, including the hopelessness of humans when confronted with an uncaring universe and the evolutionary processes that have made humans unable to survive against either nature or technology. Literary naturalism embodies the idea that there exists no perfect condition, either so-cial or spiritual, toward which humans progress. No god or other spiritual en-tity leads the people away from their suffering and toward some final paradise. These are only useless dreams of the future that prevent people from taking the actions that make survival possible in the present world, where they are pitted against nature and technology. The Joads and other migrants like them cling to their handbills advertising work in California as if these sheets of paper are messages from heaven, promises of salvation. Readers are tempted to equate the migrants to the ancient Israelites, leaving Oklahoma in a grand exodus that will take them to a promised land. This comparison is problematic, however, because Steinbeck has already presented a portrait of people hopeless in the face of natural and technological forces that have removed from humans con-trol over their own lives.

The dust bowl farmers cannot make rain, and they cannot take nourish-ment from the land in the absence of rain. Where the farmer used to be the cre-ator of life on the land through the planting of seed and the reaping of the harvest, the tractor and seeder now move across the earth, raping it in an im-personal act of reproduction. Those who take their places atop these monster machines become as disconnected from the land as the machines. Once farm-ers themselves, these men are no longer dependent upon the crop's yield for their livelihood, but instead upon the hours spent on the back of the machine. This detachment from the land parallels a detachment from, and thus breaking apart of, the community. The operator cannot consider the traditional com-munity, based on a kinship with those beside whom he worked the land, be-cause he must stay focused on himself and his family and the $3.00 per day that can be earned from the destruction of his neighbors' lives.

This amoral attitude is yet another theme of naturalism and is shown by those outside the migrant community. The attitudes of the bankers and farmers toward the migrants are determined by profits rather than by ideas of right and wrong. The car dealers prey on the desperation of the migrants by over-charging for their product and misrepresenting the condition of the vehicles in order to ensure their own survival. The desperate migrants buy because they must, and the dealers abuse them because they can, and they do it with an atti-tude of "I'll close 'em, I'll deal 'em or I'll kill 'em" (86).

There seems to be no hope left in the face of nature's wrath and the techno-logical progress fueling human greed. Like others who wrote in this tradition, however, Steinbeck does not accept as final the complete helplessness of hu-mans in the face of such an unconcerned universe. If the focus on the individ-ual is a symptom of the degeneration typical of the naturalist view of the world, Steinbeck offers the rebuilding of the community as the treatment. This theme of the power of the group as opposed to the weakness of the individual exem-plifies Steinbeck's phalanx theory, derived from the author's own scientific study of creatures in nature, particularly marine creatures. That grouping is the natural state, making separation from the group thus unnatural, is illustrated by the changes that result in the movement of the characters from "I" to "we." This idea embodies in part the philosophical concept of the oversoul first pre-sented in American literature by nineteenth-century author Ralph Waldo Em-erson. The idea of the oversoul, a spiritual force that embraces all souls, is explicitly introduced in Chapter 4 by Jim Casey, who tells Tom, "Maybe all men got one big soul ever'body's a part of" (33). If there is a promise of survival for these people broken by evolutionary progress, if there is a Darwinian "fit-test," it lies not in individual instinct but in the forming of groups, which, like schools of fish, extend beyond the biology of family.

This extension beyond the family is shown first in the decision by the Joads to allow Casey to travel with them to California, and later by the joining to-gether of the Joads with the Wilsons, and then with the Wainwrights. These larger groups provide both physical and psychological support, and as far as is possible there is a sharing of material goods. Steinbeck intends the reader to see this sharing as a natural act of the group. Muley Graves shares his food with Tom and Casey when they are joined, even temporarily, as a group. Sairy Wil-son provides comfort to the Joads as Grandpa is dying and gives them the quilt that will become his burial shroud. The Joads stop the progress of their journey to repair the Wilsons' car. Later, while living in the boxcar, the Joads share with the Wainwrights the promise of work in the cotton fields, and Mrs. Wain-wright helps Ma Joad care for Rose of Sharon during the delivery of her still-born child.

The most striking example of the strength of the group is provided by the Weedpatch government camp. There, everything but money and food is made equally available to all of the camp's residents, including the sharing of labor, democratic self-governance, and the dignity that is every person's right. This camp is shown in stark contrast to the Hooverville camp, where even though people are physically grouped, few have chosen to join their neighbors in a community.

No group is permanent in *The Grapes of Wrath*, not even the family, because none, not even the government camp, can provide all that is needed for its members' survival. The weakest members die, while others leave the group. The Joads become weak in the government camp because they have no work, and they must leave. Communities break apart when threatened, as when the authorities promise to burn the Hooverville camp, or when the boxcar camp is flooded. But after each of these instances, Steinbeck continues to offer promise that new alliances will be formed, new communities developed, and that this solidarity is the way of hope for those who would seem to have no hope. The novel's final scene seems to return to the beginning, with nature once again ravaging the migrants and with the loss of the family's car, echoing the loss of the home in the story's opening pages. By having Rose of Sharon offer her breast to a starving man, however, Steinbeck closes his story with the promise that as long as humans continue to grow beyond individual needs and desires, there is hope for survival. It is the poor and oppressed in whom Steinbeck places this ability to grow. As Ma Joad tells Tom at the Hooverville camp, "Why Tom, we're the people that live. They ain't gonna wipe us out" (383).

Underlying all the themes in *The Grapes of Wrath* is the idea of justice. For Steinbeck, justice is located in human experience and, therefore, what happens as a result of nature or of God may not be measured as just or unjust. Individuals are responsible for securing justice on their own behalf, as Tom did when he killed a man in self-defense. But Tom's self-defense had a negative outcome. He was sent to prison, itself another unjust act. As Steinbeck shows in the novel, it is when people serve the need of others that the greatest chance for justice exists. When people demand justice for others, the controlling emotion is compassion, which Steinbeck for the rest of his career will claim as the element most necessary to save a declining society. Jim's compassion for others drives him to self-sacrifice. Rose of Sharon's final act of sharing is an act of compassion for a dying man. Both of their actions were made necessary because of the injustice they and their fellow migrants faced.

SYMBOLISM AND LITERARY DEVICES

Woven throughout *The Grapes of Wrath* are various symbols that contribute to the understanding as well as to the richness of the text. The most obvious symbol in the novel is the turtle in Chapter 3. It is a seemingly defenseless animal, struggling to overcome both the natural and human hazards encountered as it makes its way southwest through Oklahoma. The land turtle is described as a creature of singular determination, directing all of its energy and focus in a forward movement across the land. While crossing the highway that cuts across its path, the turtle is spared by a female driver but is then targeted by a light truck that "flipped the turtle like a tiddly-wink, spun it like a coin, and rolled it off the highway" (22). The encounter with the truck leaves the turtle on its back, but it recovers from the momentary setback and returns to the southwest trek. This turtle's obstacle-filled journey foreshadows the Joads' experiences as they make their way southwest to California. Like the turtle, the family meets with roadblocks that impede the progress of their migration, including illness, death, and mechanical failures. Reinforcing this symbolic association, the turtle is described as having yellow toenails, the same color as Tom Joad's prison issue shoes.

In addition to the symbolic connection between the turtle and the Joads, Steinbeck creates a physical connection when Tom finds the turtle and carries it with him as he looks for his family. There is a risk here of making the symbolic meaning too explicit; however, the effect is formally significant. The crossing of the turtle from a universal chapter to a particular chapter establishes the connection between the subjects of the universal chapters, the greedy bankers, cheating car dealers, and benevolent migrants, and the novel's particular characters.

There is a great deal of religious symbolism in *The Grapes of Wrath*. One example of this occurs after the Joads finish preparing for their journey to California. For their final meal, they kill the pigs, eating the bones and preserving the remainder for the trip. This feast in Oklahoma is reminiscent of the Jewish Passover, celebrated to remember the binding together of the family through God's promise that preceded the Israelite's flight from Egypt. A more explicit symbolic element in *The Grapes of Wrath* is water. The book is framed first by the absence of water and then, finally, by its overabundance. Water becomes symbolic in Chapter 18 when the Joads stop at the river before crossing the desert into California's farming country. As the Red Sea did for the ancient Israelites, this river separates the Joads from their known enemy, the drought that has taken their farm. Across the river is the hope of a new life with new opportunities, but like those fleeing Egypt, the Joads are made to wait for their reward, all the while facing the changes, temptations, and trials that would strengthen them for the days ahead. Additionally, the river represents baptism, an experience of initiation and naming. Up to this point, the Joads have been displaced farmers traveling toward a new purpose, but in reaching California, the purpose, migrant labor, becomes a reality, or at least a possibility. In this new role, they are given new names, not by those promising in the presence of God to care for them, but instead by those who detest them. At the river, the Joads formally become "Oakies."

There is also a symbolic connection between Jim Casey and Jesus Christ that is made clearest when Jim sacrifices himself for the others. When first introduced, Casey is a spiritual man who has been wandering in the wilderness in search of answers to life's greatest questions. He offers himself up to punishment to save a fellow man. Like Christ, he excuses his killer with the words, "You don' know what your're a-doin" (527). Even Jim Casey's initials, J. C., tempt a symbolic association. Although it may allude to biblical scenes and characters, *The Grapes of Wrath* is not a religious novel, and it does not attempt to prove a particular religious moral. By drawing symbolic connections between the character Jim Casey and the religious figure of Jesus Christ, however, Steinbeck reminds the reader that Jesus the man was the prototypical organizer of men in the pursuit of justice for unfortunate and oppressed people. Steinbeck is not pointing the reader's attention to what Christ meant, but instead to what Jesus did. This strategy creates sympathy for Casey and his followers, particularly in those readers who were suspicious of the fledgling labor union movement of the 1930s, thereby making the symbolic significance of Jim Casey politically as well as artistically effective.

ALTERNATE READING: MARXIST CRITICISM

Marxist literary criticism is closely linked to the nineteenth-century doctrines of Karl Marx, a German political philosopher and economist, and Frederick Engels, a German philosopher who collaborated with Marx on *Manifesto of the Communist Party* and *Das Kapital*. The ideologies of Marx and Engels became the foundations for both socialism and communism. The ideas of Marx and Engels, known as Marxism, were derived from studying the historical patterns of civilizations. Marx claimed that social history consists of the history of struggles between the ruling classes and the oppressed, working classes. He focused on nineteenth-century capitalism in order to identify cycles of class struggles. From these studies, Marx predicted a revolution of the working classes against capitalism that would eventually lead to a classless society, the Marxist ideal.

A Marxist interpretation of literature is concerned with how a piece of literature is influenced by economic, social, and historical forces. Marxist criticism looks to the social circumstances represented by a literary work, specifically the imbalance existing between the smaller class of capitalists and the larger laboring class, and how the literature addresses those social circumstances, thus focusing on the work's content or theme. The production of the work, the literary style or form, is only important insofar as the author creates new form and style to highlight new structures and relationships within the society. *The Grapes of Wrath* lends itself to a Marxist reading because of its presentation of workers struggling against an economic system that makes survival seemingly impossible in times of crisis and because of the social changes these workers make to endure the economic oppression.

The Marxist critic might begin a study of *The Grapes of Wrath* by focusing on the novel's presentation of social classes. With the droughts and economic depression shown as immediate causes, Steinbeck portrays a society deeply divided between those people possessing property, whether it is land, business, or machinery, and those who have lost everything. Aside from the rare exception, such as the diner, the property owners are depicted as oppressive capitalist machines focused on profit, using any method—no matter how ruthless—to attain it.

The first example of the inhumanity of property owners is presented in Chapter 5, where the land-owning banks are described as monsters, created by men but out of men's control. These monsters are fed by profits, and "when the monster stops growing, it dies. It can't stay one size" (44). Because the tenant farmers restrict the profits, and thus the growth of the monster, they must be removed from the land and replaced by the farm machines, a new type of monster, which can keep up with the bank's steadily increasing appetite for profit. The individual owner of the large farm, like the bank, is incapable of conscience when dispossessing the tenants of their homes. Business owners abuse the financially weak in other ways. The car dealers buy cheap from those who must sell off their possessions for food and sell higher than is fair to those who have chosen to migrate in hopes of finding work.

In much the same way as Marxism analyzes history to determine social patterns and class struggles that would lead to revolution, Chapter 19 of *The Grapes of Wrath* analyzes patterns of land ownership, using for example the taking of Mexican land in California. Steinbeck shows the evolution of farms into industry, a phenomenon caused by the evolution of a love for the land into a love for money. As farms grew larger, ownership was reduced to a few, and the farm industries employed those who would allow themselves to be treated as slaves. Like a philosopher, Steinbeck warns what will happen as these "great owners" ignore the lessons of history that show what repressed workers will do when the repression becomes too great. This foreshadows the acts of rebellion, both large and small, of the last ten chapters of the novel.

Steinbeck's presentation of individualism as weakness is significant as an attack on capitalism. Individualism is a primary and celebrated characteristic of this dominant American economic philosophy and, as such, is in direct conflict with Marxism. For Marx, the individual must be sacrificed to the greater number, the working class as a whole. Those characters who cling to individualism, like Connie, whose grand dreams of becoming a radio repairman are greater even than the needs of his wife and unborn child, are impotent, unable to contribute anything to the well-being of the group. The novel's other characters, such as Tom, who become less focused on individual needs and desires and more altruistic in their actions and ideas, create a challenge to the ideas embodied by capitalism.

While not the primary focus of the Marxist critic, the structure of *The Grapes of Wrath* does draw attention to the many people on both sides of the capitalist divide, the monied and the oppressed, who are the subjects of the novel. The universal chapters convince the readers that all banks function according to an inhuman greed, not just the particular bank that pushed the Joads off their land. Likewise, universal chapters present the enormity of the migrant problem of which the Joads' experiences provide only a microscopic view. Thus, Steinbeck has succeeded in presenting the full scale of a historical circumstance and making it believable through the particular focus on the Joads. Yet another way in which the style of *The Grapes of Wrath* is of interest for the Marxist critic is Steinbeck's combining of various literary genres or traditions to create a product that defies sole definition by any one of them. The novel is part realism, part naturalism, part epic, part historical novel, and part political novel, and Steinbeck draws from each what contributes the most to the political message. As with the characters in the novel, no single style is important; the strength of the whole is what matters.

6

Cannery Row
(1945)

In 1943, during the height of World War II, John Steinbeck left the safety and relative peace of America to visit the European war front as a correspondent for the *New York Herald Tribune*. The devastation he witnessed disturbed Steinbeck greatly and continued to do so long after he returned to the United States. Early in 1944, safe at home with his new wife Gwyn Conger, and with his first child on the way, Steinbeck began writing *Cannery Row*, a project that, because it allowed him to create humor, brought him enjoyment and relief from the memories of war.

With its absurd humor, *Cannery Row* is enjoyable for the reader, just as it was for the author. But it is also a serious book at many levels. It continues the development of Steinbeck's non-teleological idea (see Chapter 2 for futher discussion), and Steinbeck once again attempts a re-creation of the novel form, synthesizing the use of loosely connected episodes, reminiscent of *Tortilla Flat*, with the use of interchapters, a technique Steinbeck used in *The Grapes of Wrath*. The synthesis is not merely a borrowing of early modes, however. Steinbeck uses episodes and interchapters in new ways, showing clearly his continuing evolution as a writer.

SETTING, PLOT, AND STRUCTURE

The ability to create vivid setting is one of John Steinbeck's gifts as a writer, and *Cannery Row* is one of the clearest illustrations of this gift. Steinbeck presents the setting of *Cannery Row* in the novel's preface: "Cannery Row in Monterey in California is a poem, a stink, a grating noise, a quality of light, a tone, a habit, a nostalgia, a dream" (5). This opening sentence combines the sensory reality of Cannery Row with the psychological and emotional effects it has upon those who know it. As Steinbeck moves to a presentation of the people of Cannery Row, the universal quality of his setting becomes clear. Cannery Row is everybody. It is the unemployed, the lowest of laborers, and the highest of bosses. It is the best and the worst of humanity found at all its levels.

When the noise of the canneries stops, and the "people straggle out and drop their way up the hill and into the town," then Cannery Row is in its natural state, "quiet and magical" (6). After describing the journey home of the cannery workers at the end of the day, Steinbeck introduces the novel's cast of characters, the bums, the whores, the merchants, the artist, and Doc, the scientist who runs Western Biological laboratory whose happiness is the purpose behind all of the action in *Cannery Row*. Steinbeck outlines his purpose in the final words of the preface. Like a scientist, Steinbeck proposes to present, "alive" (6) for view, like a specimen, the qualities of Cannery Row. Like the scientist collecting delicate flat worms, he must allow *Cannery Row* to make its own way onto the page, "to open the page and let the stories crawl in by themselves" (7). Here, the reader's purpose is also defined, not just to see the words on the page, but to discover Steinbeck's *Cannery Row*.

The first six chapters of *Cannery Row* present the world in which the controlling action, which begins in Chapter 7, occurs. Chapter 1 tells the birth story of the Palace Flophouse and Grill, the home of Mack and his five fellow bums who are behind all the major action in the story. Lee Chong, to whom most of the town is in debt, accepts as payment for Cannery Row resident Horace Abbeville's huge bill an unused building filled with fish meal. Knowing this exchange has alleviated much of the financial burden from his large family, Horace goes to the building and shoots himself. This is the first of three suicides to occur in *Cannery Row*.

Shortly after the suicide, Mack, the leader of the group of Cannery Row bums, comes to Lee Chong suggesting that he and the boys move into the building to protect it. The building has never needed protection before, but Lee Chong knows if he refuses Mack's offer, protection will surely be needed in the future. When Mack and the boys move in, the building becomes the Palace Flophouse and Grill. This first chapter of *Cannery Row* is Steinbeck's genesis. When the boys looked from the Palace, they could see Western Biological and Doc's actions there, and what they saw was good to them. They know Doc is a good man, and the idea emerges that they should find a way to reward him for his goodness. Thus the idea toward which the rest of the novel moves begins here.

Much of the philosophy of *Cannery Row*, indeed of any place, is introduced in Chapter 2. "The Word" (17) or the name is, according to the narrator, something that takes in the actual facts of the "Thing" (17) the word signifies. In the interchange between Word, which the author has created, and Thing, the facts are altered, the reality weakened, and what is left is vision, interpretation. Lee Chong, the narrator claims, must be more than the greedy capitalist he appears to be, or that his profession implies; he also has a soft side. The narrator then turns to Mack and the boys, who are described as "the Virtues, the Graces, the Beauties" (18). They are known as bums, but they may be the highest among the human species because they have discovered the secret to surviving the world; they want nothing because from the wanting springs the disease that ultimately kills humanity.

Continuing to set his stage, Steinbeck next introduces Dora Flood, the madam of the Bear Flag Restaurant, the local whorehouse. Dora is in the business of selling sex, an illegal act, but she is described as law abiding. Furthermore, she is charitable; Dora truly cares about the welfare of those on Cannery Row. The Bear Flag is "clean" and "honest" (19), offers no hard liquor, and half of its whores are Christian Scientists. As a result, Dora and her business are accepted as part of Cannery Row society. This idea of social acceptance becomes key to the later action, but it is first introduced through the story of William, Dora's first watchman. William is ostracized by Mack and the boys, which leads him to kill himself with an ice pick in front of Dora's Greek cook. This is the second suicide in the novel, an example of the effects of society on the individual.

It is difficult at this early stage of the novel to distinguish clearly between Steinbeck's chapters and interchapters. In *The Grapes of Wrath*, the interchapters provide the universal or general context within which the story of the Joad family story unfolds. The interchapters in *Cannery Row* are much less distinct, although they retain the shift in tone and language found in *The Grapes of Wrath*, usually becoming more objective, poetic, and philosophical. Chapter 2 has these qualities of an interchapter, although it includes specific discussion of the novel's main characters. Chapter 4 is the first interchapter that does not contribute directly to the novel's main plot.

Chapter 4 introduces the old Chinaman who walks downhill to the beach each evening and uphill to an unknown destination in Monterey each morning. No one knows who he really is or why he does what he does, but no one bothers him. When eventually challenged by a young boy visiting Cannery Row, the Chinaman's eyes become one big eye in which the boy sees a desolate landscape, barren but for a variety of small animals. The vision frightens the boy because "there wasn't anybody at all in the world and he was left" (26). Like the interchapters in *The Grapes of Wrath*, the chapter introduces the general theme of friendship, allowing the later action of the novel to develop it for the reader. Unlike *The Grapes of Wrath*, this interchapter presents action occurring in the specific vicinity of the novel's main action through a character known to the main characters.

Chapters 5 and 6 introduce Doc, first by telling who he is and, second, through his actions and words, with Chapter 6 additionally serving as a bridge to the chapters in which the main action will begin. In Chapter 5, the narrator first describes Western Biological, the lab run by Doc. Only after describing the place does the narrator move to the man, already partially known through the description of Western Biological. Over the years, Doc has become a permanent fixture on Cannery Row, and his presence alone has exposed its citizens to art, music, poetry, and philosophy, not to mention science. Because of the greatness of his mind and the fullness of his compassion, everyone in Cannery Row wants to do something nice for Doc.

The novel shifts back to action in Chapter 6 with Doc collecting marine animals from a tide pool. A description of the life in the tide pool is offered, with a clear analogy established between marine life and human life. Hazel, one of the Flophouse boys, is helping Doc collect specimens for the lab. Hazel embodies all of the positive human psychological characteristics, but he is not capable of organizing the information stored in his mind; Hazel can remember but not think. This day Hazel is trying to make sense out of Henri the painter who continues to build a boat but never finishes it. Doc tells Hazel that Henri loves boats but is afraid of the water. Hazel cannot process this information, so he moves to the subject of the stinkbugs—why they always have their tails in the air. Doc's understanding of human-centrism, which accounts for his ability to forgive humans, is found in his answer to Hazel's inquiry. Doc tells Hazel they are praying. He continues to explain that the stinkbugs' habits are not remarkable; it is the human belief that the habit is remarkable that is the truly amazing thing. If humans were to do something as strange as the stinkbugs, they would likely be praying, so humans say the bugs are praying. This ability to analyze and understand humans allows Doc to coexist in a place where he is so obviously different from those around him.

The idea of doing something nice for Doc evolves, in Chapter 7, into a plan to throw him a party. Mack and the boys have no money, want no money, but are resourceful in getting the things they need. The boys quickly decide they will go to Carmel Valley to collect frogs, and then sell the frogs to Doc to finance the party.

The boys' ability to adapt to their environment is not unique, although Steinbeck shows they are the purest example of this gift. That this ability is a human characteristic, whether utilized or ignored, is supported by the interchapter story of Mr. and Mrs. Sam Malloy in Chapter 8. In 1935, during the height of the depression, the Malloys moved into an old, discarded boiler, making it their home. The opportunity for profit arose from the empty pipes just downhill from the boiler, which Mr. Malloy rented out to single men as sleeping quarters. Mrs. Malloy's reaction to having an income from the pipes exemplifies the discussion in Chapter 2 about the diseases, both emotional and physical, caused by wanting. Mrs. Malloy wants curtains for her windowless boiler home. Whether her desire indicates mental imbalance, resulting from general wanting, or whether it indicates adaptation to her environment is ambiguous, forcing the reader to analyze each seemingly crazy action of the novel against the two possibilities.

Chapters 9, 11, 13, and 15 present the preparations for the frog hunt, with the alternate interchapters developing the stories of the minor characters, which will be discussed in the character section of this chapter. In Chapter 9, Mack goes to Doc and tells him he and the boys need money for a good cause. Doc tells Mack he will buy 300 frogs if the boys catch them. Mack then borrows Lee Chong's broken down truck; Lee Chong only agrees because he will profit from Gay, who has joined the boys after being thrown out by his wife, repairing the truck to running condition. The boys head toward Carmel, but the truck develops problems. Gay leaves to get a part but ends up in jail after a long series of coincidences.

After Eddie, another member of Mack's boys, steals the needed carburetor, they drive into the Carmel Valley, stopping at the pool where they believe they will find the frogs. The serendipitousness of the boys' survival is illustrated by the food items the boys put on to cook while they sleep and wait for the frogs to emerge. They have a rooster that was killed by a truck, carrots that fell from another truck, and onions, the only item in the cook pot the boys had to steal.

As they are eating and planning for the hunt, the owner of the land where they have camped comes to run them off. Mack manipulates the man by showing sympathy for the man's injured dog, and the man invites them to his house where there is a better frog pond. The landowner's wife has gone into politics, and his loneliness becomes apparent when they return to his house and, in celebration of their company, he brings out a five-gallon keg of corn whiskey left over from Prohibition. Mack doctors the man's dog and, in return, is offered one of the pointer's puppies. After two hours of drinking, Mack and the boys remember why they are there and prepare for the hunt.

The frog hunt illustrates Mack's unconventional approach to life. Mack's plan, in contrast to any conventional method, involves flashing lights, loud noise, chasing the frogs en masse into the water, wearing them out, then trapping them on the other side of the pond as they weakly attempt to escape. There is no sophistication to Mack's plan, just as there is no sophistication to much that these bums do; but the plan accomplishes the largest possible catch of hundreds of frogs with the least amount of time or effort, which begs the question as to why anyone would use the traditional approach to catching frogs. (This approach requires the hunter to sneak up on the frogs and, if detected, to chase them, hoping the frogs will not escape to the water.)

While the boys are catching frogs, Doc has gone to Los Angeles to collect small octopi. His trip shows that Doc has friends but is always alone. Along the way, he makes frequent stops for food and drink, mostly hamburgers and beer, and it slowly becomes clear that Doc is feeding his loneliness with food, just as he feeds it with music and books back at the lab. The only hope for alleviating Doc's loneliness on the long trip is a hitchhiker he picks up, but the man begins preaching to Doc about the danger of drinking and driving, and Doc throws him out of the car. Once he arrives in Los Angeles, Doc has good success at gathering octopi and other creatures and then stops to observe the brilliance of the shore environment. The peaceful environment is quickly put in contrast against the dead body of a girl Doc discovers. Overwhelmed by finding the dead girl, Doc tells a passing man to contact the police and collect the bounty for himself, and Doc quickly leaves, heading back to Cannery Row.

Plans for his surprise party progress steadily in Doc's absence. The boys use collected frogs as payment for food and decorations for the party and bring the remainder of the frogs to the lab as a surprise for Doc. The party begins and ends before the arrival of the guest of honor; the revelers drink all the liquor, eat all the food, play Doc's music, and get into a fight with strangers who mistake the lab for a whorehouse. The lab is nearly destroyed during this last activity, and the box holding the frogs is broken, allowing the frogs to escape. The party is over and the guilty celebrants gone before Doc even returns to Cannery Row.

When he does return, Doc's anger causes him to hit Mack, who has come to make amends. After striking Mack a second time, Doc realizes Mack is not going to fight back, and he gives up. Mack tells him that apologizing will not do any good, that the party's outcome is typical of the way his good intentions have turned bad throughout his life. Doc, relieved of his anger, cleans up the mess in the lab, salvaging what he can.

The action of Chapter 23 is pivotal to the story. The fact that something bad has happened to Doc disturbs the balance of the entire community, beginning with the Palace Flophouse, over which "a black gloom settled" (131). The boys feel guilty, guilty enough for Hughie and Jones to get jobs at a cannery, and for the otherwise gentle Hazel to get into a fight with a soldier and lose the fight intentionally. The gloom spreads, and the result is the social ostracism of Mack and the boys.

Doc's conversation with Richard Frost, another Cannery Row resident, is the first indication of hope for the bums. He observes that Mack and the boys are the world's "true philosophers" (133); they understand things so well they are able to avoid the pitfalls, such as money and the desire for it, that would certainly ruin their lives. Their souls are intact and their intentions remain good. While Doc is unaware of the ostracism the boys are facing, the discussion between Doc and Frost explains the bad cloud spreading through the town; the boys have no opportunity to give of their kindness and generosity, and the void created is filled with violence and natural disaster. When Darling, Mack's puppy, becomes ill, the boys take her to Doc and she gets well after they follow his advice. This interchange of trust and kindness spreads through the city, and good begins to replace the infecting evil. The opportunity for good leads Mack to Dora for advice, and she tells him to throw another party, this time one Doc can actually attend.

The "benignant influence" (148) now spreading throughout Cannery Row causes everyone to join in the preparation for Doc's party. Mack and the boys decide on a birthday party and go to the lab to learn Doc's birth date, which he lies about. No one was officially invited to the party at Doc's lab, but "everyone was going" (156). People begin making or procuring gifts for Doc. Acceptance and generosity have returned to Cannery Row.

Doc hears about the party from a stranger at a local bar and begins making his own preparations. He locks up his best music and lab equipment to protect them from the fighting that will certainly be part of the celebration. In Chapter 28, the reader is reminded that so much goodness is itself unnatural and the balance of good to bad will always find itself. Frankie, the young, neglected boy who cannot learn and is uncoordinated, is introduced in Chapter 10. At age eleven, Frankie begins coming to the lab because it is safe and peaceful there and because he adores Doc. Doc cares for him and he helps Doc around the lab. Frankie is most happy when Doc gives parties. At one party he excitedly prepares a tray of drinks so he can serve one of the women guests, hoping for a compliment from Doc. His coordination fails and he drops the tray on the woman's lap. Horrified, Frankie runs and hides; Doc follows him but realizes there is nothing he can do to help Frankie. Frankie appears again in Chapter 28. He has heard about Doc's surprise birthday party and wants to give Doc a gift. He is drawn to a clock at Jacob's Jewelry Store, but the clock is $50, so he breaks in at night and steals it. The police catch him and call Doc, who wants to take responsibility for Frankie, to help Frankie now because he could not the last time Frankie needed him. The authorities, however, say it is time for Frankie to go to a state institution. When Doc asks Frankie why he stole the clock, Frankie responds only with the words, "I love you" (165). This time it is Doc's turn to run, and he does.

The readers' expectations for another party disaster, established by Steinbeck in Chapter 30, are foiled and the party is a great success. There is an initial fight that energizes rather than deflates the celebration. Doc feeds the guests and reads them ancient poetry, making everyone sad from remembering lost loves. Just as with the first party, strangers arrive thinking the lab is a whorehouse and another fight breaks out, making everyone happy. Sometime late in the night someone lights a twenty-five-foot string of firecrackers presented to Doc by Lee Chong.

While it is a great, legendary party, it is bittersweet for the guest of honor. The foreshadowing of Doc's emotions at the end of the novel comes through the poem read at the party and from the next chapter's story of a fat gopher living in a vacant lot in Cannery Row. The gopher has found the perfect burrow hole and looks forward to a happy and reproductive life there; the only problem is there is no female with which to reproduce, eventually forcing the gopher to move elsewhere. Like the gopher, Doc has found a seemingly perfect life, complete with satisfying work, friends, and the respect and admiration of his community. But while cleaning up the lab after the party, Doc notices the poem he read to his friends and begins to read again the stanzas recounting remembrances of pure moments of experience, of love and of beauty and of "the whitest pouring of eternal light" (185). Doc's eyes tear as he finishes reading, and the reader is left to determine whether Doc cries because his life, like the gopher's, is not completely satisfied, because his home is not the perfect place friends and respect and parties make it appear, or whether he is weeping for the joy his life truly is. The answer may be in the idea of balance, of good and bad and life and death, found throughout the novel.

CHARACTERS

Those who study John Steinbeck often encounter difficulty when they arrive at character analysis. Scholars most usually look first at character development when doing character analysis, and it is at this first stage that they are often stumped by Steinbeck's work. Larger works, such as *The Grapes of Wrath*, *East of Eden*, and even *The Winter of Our Discontent*, offer rich opportunities for study of character development, but in much of his other work Steinbeck is less interested in what a character may become than in what a character is. Such is the case with the characters in *Cannery Row*; for the most part, they are static, or nondeveloping. This is not to say, however, that they are not interesting or important. Indeed, the characters in *Cannery Row* are vivid and, most important to the observer, they are alive.

Doc is the novel's main character. Steinbeck places him at the nucleus of this community and directs much of the action toward him. While the other characters may have a loose basis in people Steinbeck knew or had heard about in Cannery Row, Doc's character is drawn directly from Ed Ricketts, Steinbeck's dearest friend in Monterey. The facts of Doc's life, his work, and his habits are borrowed closely from Ricketts'. The emotions and words Steinbeck gives to Doc must be considered truth, if not fact, because of the tribute Steinbeck intended for his friend.

Doc is the most complete of the characters in *Cannery Row*. Physically, Doc is small, wiry, strong, and passionately fierce. "He wears a beard and his face is half Christ and half satyr and his face tells the truth" (29). While he is an established and integral part of the community, he is distinct from all the other characters who, while individual in their qualities, seem to flow from similar experience. One thing that sets Doc apart is his intelligent and philosophical understanding of his environment. He observes life like the scientist he is and from that observation can construct theories about his Cannery Row friends. The most significant element of his understanding is that he shares it, instructing his Cannery Row neighbors about life and about each other. The result of Doc's wisdom is that people of Cannery Row, understanding each other through him, are a cohesive, unified community. This unity is only broken in the novel when the community believes Mack and the boys have hurt Doc intentionally, a sin for which forgiveness comes slow and hard.

Additional clues to just how rich Doc's life is may be found in Chapter 12, which also offers helpful information about the other characters populating Cannery Row. Steinbeck claims that Monterey has a long literary tradition and goes on to show this through the satiric story of Josh Billings, a local author and humorist who died in Monterey one night. After embalming Billings, the local doctor threw his organs into a gulch, where they were promptly claimed by a boy and his dog for fishing bait. This enrages the citizens, who consider the treatment an insult to the esteemed author, and they retrieve the body parts so they can be buried in a lead box inside Billings's coffin. The stated moral is that Monterey would not allow such "dishonor" of a "literary man" (70). This idea of honor, however misunderstood or misused, points to a similar consideration toward Doc, Monterey's man of science, who would be held in at least as high a level of esteem as the author Josh Billings. Indeed, if one considers how badly Steinbeck himself was treated by the Monterey community after his last novel about that town, *Tortilla Flat*, when the town figuratively cut Steinbeck's insides out, it would be easy to assume the man of science would garner greater admiration than the author. Because of Steinbeck's experiences with his neighbors, the story works to place in context Doc's standing in the community and to remind those neighbors that Steinbeck had not forgotten their ill treatment of him.

While the people of Cannery Row find it easy to express their respect and adoration for Doc, he has difficulty leaving his unemotional, scientific role and expressing his feelings to his friends. He is able to act out of emotion, but it is difficult for him to put his feelings into words. He is able to easily analyze the things he observes and to share his analysis, but he cannot share what he feels with these people who care so much for him. This is the reason why, as the narrator states in Chapter 17, Doc always has friends but he is always alone.

Doc's isolation in a crowd of friends helps to explain the effect he suffers when finding the dead girl's body on the beach near Los Angeles. But more importantly, this incident shows the deep conflict within Doc between science and human desires and emotions. Doc is accustomed to death; as a scientist he preserves specimens, but he must also take the life of those species in order to do so. There is no indication in the novel that Doc is negatively affected by his work. When he encounters the dead girl's body, however, Doc is unable to face the death in front of him, and he hurries away, suffering from the "terrifying flute" (106) playing loudly in his head and overwhelmed by the vision of the girl's beauty. Only when he leaves the beach does the music begin to subside. Doc cannot handle the emotions that result from the inescapable facts of this species. Humans love, humans inflict pain on one another, and humans die. The novel ends with Doc alone in his lab, playing the music and reading the poetry with which he attempts to fill his loneliness. Alone he can weep, but he weeps because he is alone.

Mack and the boys represent a type of character created in earlier works by John Steinbeck. While they are not *paisanos*, their habits and motivations are very much like those of the characters in *Tortilla Flat*, Steinbeck's other Monterey-based novel. In *Cannery Row*, however, Steinbeck offers explicit definition of his bums both through the narrator's and Doc's observations of the boys. From the beginning, it is clear that these men are special because of the way they have chosen to live their lives, however distasteful that way may be to some. Indeed, that distaste is what Steinbeck asks us to analyze and reconsider.

Chapter 1 introduces the way Mack, leader of the Flophouse gang, operates. He manipulates Lee Chong, almost to the point of extortion, in order to acquire the empty building as a residence for the bums. His manipulation is not limited to those outside of his group; as well as being their leader, he is also "to a small extent the exploiter" of the men he leads (13). But, there is generosity behind the suggestion that he and the boys should do something for Doc. Can Mack, then, be an exploiter and also be good? The question is answered in the discussion of "Word" and "Thing" which immediately follows in Chapter 2. Mack and the boys are described as being "the Virtues, the Graces, the Beauties" (18). They are angels and gods and mortals who protect and give the world charm and beauty. These qualities result from their desire to merely survive. So, if Mack exploits his fellow bums, it would seem he does so for what he believes is their own good and perhaps for the good of Doc.

Doc most clearly explains the purity of Mack and the boys in chapter 23 when he bets Richard Frost that they will not stand up to watch the parade as it passes by them. He tells Frost that as the world's "true philosophers" (133) they have gained the understanding that prevents them from allowing the world and materialism to eat them up. They get what they need to survive, but they do not desire anything beyond their basic needs. Doc identifies the social paradox Mack and the boys exemplify; they are considered failures because they can be open, honest, kind, and generous; the opposite qualities are necessary to accomplish success. Mack and the boys have held on to their souls rather than trading them to achieve material riches.

Mack is the only one of the boys who makes any personal pronouncements, but as the leader of the other men, and as their representative, it is possible to conclude that what Mack says about himself can apply abstractly to the other boys as well. When Mack goes to Doc after the first party, after Doc has expressed his anger by hitting Mack, Mack says it will not help for him to apologize because being sorry will not change how things happen with him. The mistakes he made in trying to do a good thing, throwing Doc a party, are indicative of the way every good thing he has tried to do in life has been wrong or disappeared. He had a wife once who left him because of this. While this evokes sympathy for Mack, and as a consequence for the others with him, it ironically supports the reason already given for their unique and special existence. When they let desire take over, even desire stemming from an impulse for goodness, their lives suffer ruin, if only temporarily.

ROLE OF MINOR CHARACTERS

If Doc and Mack and the other boys are the main attraction in *Cannery Row*, then the minor characters are the sideshow. All life is magic on the row, but these characters are the brightest colors in Steinbeck's landscape. They help to make the picture of life on Cannery Row complete, and they help to clarify the major events occurring in the novel.

While many of the minor characters are presented briefly as subjects of the interchapters, Lee Chong is a constant presence in the novel. Just as the action in small towns once centered around the general store, Lee Chong's grocery is the center of much of what goes on in Cannery Row. Lee Chong illustrates one of the major ideas of the novel, that existence is a mixture of good and bad. Lee Chong is capable of generosity and goodness, but he is also a merchant, clearly representing the materialism presented in the novel as the greatest evil, the greatest destroyer of humans.

Because he has a greater role in the novel, Lee Chong is a serious character. Many of the characters glimpsed only briefly in the interchapters border on the absurd; they seem so impossible that they must surely be pure fantasy. It is important to remember that each of these characters carries part of Steinbeck's message, a message made more palatable by their magical qualities, a magic that Steinbeck integrates with reality just enough to make these characters true.

Dora is in the business of sex. She is larger than life with a big body and loudly colored hair. Like Mack and the boys, she ignores the law, but only when the law stands in the way of her survival. The natural instinct to survive is greater than manmade moral law that makes what she does objectionable to some and illegal to most. The natural instincts of Dora and her girls toward goodness are not affected by her illegal activities. These women are charitable and caring toward the Cannery Row community. Through these women, half of whom are Christian Scientists, Steinbeck shows that honesty and generosity are possible regardless of the choices one makes about surviving in the world, further supporting the characterization of Mack and the boys.

The Malloys' choices of making a home in an abandoned boiler and then wanting to hang curtains where there are no windows seem truly comical. The Malloys, however, show what happens when people move beyond merely attaining what they need to live and begin wanting more. The wanting does not begin until the couple begins earning an income from the rent of the empty pipes. Without money, they are content in their boiler; with money, they desire things that have no use beyond decoration, such as curtains and antique car parts.

There are desires beyond material wanting, each with its own set of problems. Henri the painter desires a beautiful boat, and he is constantly building one that will never be finished, will never see the water because of Henri's fears. Because Henri lives on his unfinished boat with no bathroom, the women who come to live with him always leave. The flagpole skater desires celebrity, and so he sets out to break a record. Richard Frost desires understanding about the world, a desire that causes him to get drunk and to suffer his wife's anger when he cannot figure out how the flagpole skater relieves himself while on the skating platform. Only after he discovers that the skater has a bucket on the platform can Richard go home and make up with his wife, his desire momentarily fulfilled. Mary Talbot desires peace for her husband, Tom, who risks becoming a fourth suicide in *Cannery Row*. Not knowing how to cure his depressions, Mary throws parties, even when there are no resources to do so. At these lean times, Mary rounds up the neighborhood cats and gives them tea parties. When Tom finally hits the deepest regions of depression, Mary goes out to get her feline guests and finds one of the cats in trouble, which makes Mary hysterical. His wife's pain is enough to snap Tom out of his despair. When he focuses on her needs, his needs become bearable, a lesson Mary has exemplified all along.

Those who are unable to adapt life to their desires or to eliminate the wanting from their lives altogether do not survive in Cannery Row. Horace Abbeville cannot live with the debt he has accrued trying to feed his large family, and he cannot live with the idea that the problems will continue, so he kills himself. William the watchman cannot live with the ostracism he suffers from Mack and the boys; he desires their respect and approval, so he kills himself. Joey, one of the young boys in Chapter 26 who is trying to stir up boyish trouble in Cannery Row, lost his father to suicide. Because he could not get a job, Joey's father took rat poison and died, only to have the family visited the next morning by a man with a job offer. Despair is the deadliest of sins, and Steinbeck shows that despair is a result of desire, for social acceptance, or for financial security. These are the things that the novel's true survivors, Mack and the boys, are able to endure and ignore.

THEMES

Many of *Cannery Row's* critics could not see beyond its humor. Since they felt mere humor was not enough from a man who had indicted an entire nation in *The Grapes of Wrath*, many proclaimed *Cannery Row* trivial. Indeed, much of what makes *Cannery Row* popular, even today, are the funny stories about funny characters living in a magical world. Yet, underneath the humor resides the indictment these same critics called for but did not or could not identify. In *Cannery Row,* Steinbeck offers serious commentary about the state of American life that is defined by a decline in American values, a warning Steinbeck continued to sound for the remainder of his career.

Steinbeck makes it clear that it is desire, or wanting, that leads to the degradation of a society. But there is little to support the idea that such degradation has occurred fully on Cannery Row. Lee Chong seems to be a poster child for materialism, but to some degree, Cannery Row itself makes it impossible for him to fully forfeit his humanity for material gain. Likewise, Dora is unable to ignore her neighbors' needs for the sake of profit.

It is in part because those with economic power have not sold their souls to the god of wealth that Cannery Row is a place with intact values, even if those values are inconsistent with larger society. Surviving each day without taking advantage of or harming others is the primary value of Cannery Row, standing in direct contrast to the every-man-for-himself-to-the-top-of-the-money-mountain values Steinbeck identified in much of America. He saw that this second and prevailing philosophy was accompanied by certain side effects. The man on whose land Mack and the boys collect frogs represents these effects. He is clearly successful. He owns enough land to include two ponds, and his wife has entered politics, a true measure of success in America. But he must guard his land by force, arming himself against the nonlanded class to protect what he owns. While his wife's activities enhance his social position, he is left essentially without a wife, a helpmate, partner, friend, and so he is alone and lonely.

With no aspirations, and consequently no residual effects of aspirations, Mack and the boys stand as the emblems of the generosity and goodness Steinbeck sees as slowly disappearing from America. They are as common as men can be, but their commonness is their gift, protecting them from the spread of the American disease, just as they were somehow protected from the influenza virus that raged through Cannery Row.

Surviving the threat of decaying values on the one hand, as well as basic physical survival on the other hand, is a moment-by-moment, day-by-day endeavor. Thus, Steinbeck's theme of non-teleological, or "is," thinking exists easily beside the novel's other main ideas. Life on Cannery Row exemplifies the idea that only what "is" is sure and that what might or could be, the idea behind the longing for material and financial success, is a very risky gamble. To a certain extent, the way Mack and the boys live represents an antithesis of teleological thought. Not only do they not consider the end of life and what might occur after death, the ultimate in teleological thinking, they do not even concern themselves with daily goals. When they leave for the Carmel Valley to search for frogs, they take only two loaves of bread and Eddie's liquor jug. Mack believed they would find what food they needed when they needed it. Mack is not gambling that they will find the food they need. Mack knows they will because that is the way things are, which he knows from experience. True to his knowledge, food is found as well as stolen, and the boys are supplied with what they need.

Only when they make plans toward a hoped-for but unknown outcome do the boys fail, and the failure is painful. They walk into the unknown when they make plans for the first party for Doc. They dream of the party and how Doc will react, and in the dreaming they lose all reality. They are holding on to their hopes when they begin the party without Doc and when they get into a fight that nearly destroys the lab. Thus, when Doc reacts in anger and the town ostracizes them for their failure, Mack and the boys' lives are thrown off balance. The second party succeeds because the boys do not try to affect a planned outcome. Consequently, the boys go back to their normal approach to life—just allowing what is to be.

Steinbeck's non-teleological philosophy has its basis in science, with much of its development occurring through long conversations with his friend Ed

Ricketts. It is natural, then, that his theme finds additional support in his presentation of vivid observations from nature, such as the description of the Great Tidepool in Chapter 6, which form clear connections between humans and the rest of the natural world. There is no judgment in Steinbeck's descriptions, only fact, only what "is." The comparisons may be the only problem with Steinbeck's science; he is looking at the marine creatures through a human lens and assigning human motivations to them, exactly what Doc does when he tells Hazel the stinkbugs are praying. But this does not diminish the importance of the scientific description in the novel. The non-teleological theme will continue to develop in Steinbeck's work until his final pieces of fiction, in which he begins to show concern for teleological possibilities.

SYMBOLS

The characters, specifically the minor characters, are the clearest symbols in *Cannery Row*. Throughout the novel, however, there are other symbols used to reinforce Steinbeck's themes. The place itself is a symbol of the larger world and human experience to which the novel's themes apply. Many of the single elements in the story, such as Doc's music, Lee Chong's store, and the creatures Doc collects, have already been discussed in the context of their symbolic importance to theme or plot. A select group of items, the gifts presented to Doc at his birthday party, invite a separate symbolic analysis.

While much of the thematic analysis has focused on the novel's stated theme of the dangers of wanting, these gifts represent the contrasting human quality of generosity and, thus, along with Mack and the boys, represent the hope for humankind with which Steinbeck makes sure the reader is left. The parties show that even the most profit-driven character, Lee Chong, is capable of giving. But even with the parties, there is buying and selling involved. The food, the decorations, and the liquor must all be purchased, and Lee Chong is happy to profit from the town's generosity toward Doc. But no commerce is involved in any of the gifts selected for Doc. Some are made by the givers; the Bear Flag girls make Doc a quilt from their old dresses, and Henri creates a piece of pincushion art. Others are selected from the givers' own belongings; Lee Chong parts with an impressive string of fireworks, and Sam Malloy presents Doc with a well-shined antique engine part. Finally, Mack and the boys collect their gift to Doc—twenty-one tom cats they have trapped around Cannery Row.

At another level of meaning, each of these gifts represents a different aspect of human existence, a different need. The quilt will bring Doc comfort, and like Henri's pincushion art, will also bring him aesthetic enjoyment. The firecrackers celebrate the triumphs that occur even in the midst of despair. Sam's engine part points to a need to remember the past and to human inventiveness, the drive to make life better and easier. Finally and most ironically, the tom cats Mack and the boys collect symbolize the commerce that is unavoidable in human experience. Doc makes his living and ensures his own survival by the sale of various animal species, and Mack and his boys, however alienated from business themselves, are able to give Doc a gift that will make his own business better.

ALTERNATIVE READING: PSYCHOLOGICAL CRITICISM

In many ways, Doc is both biologist and psychologist in *Cannery Row*. When he explains the limits of human understanding to Hazel, and when he helps Richard Frost to understand Mack and the boys, he is using psychology. Doc's limited psychology suggests the potential for a closer look at the human psyche as it is presented by *Cannery Row*'s characters, which is the purpose of the psychological approach to literature. Contemporary psychological analysis of literature finds its basis in the work of Sigmund Freud, the Austrian physician and father of psychoanalysis who wrote *The Interpretation of Dreams, Totem and Taboo, Ego and Id*, and other works, as well as those who followed him.

Freud's work emphasized the unconscious elements of the human mental processes. What had earlier been designated as unconscious, Freud divided into the "preconscious," which includes those conscious processes that are conscious for only a short time and then become latent but can be recalled to consciousness again. Those processes that can only be recalled with great difficulty, or not at all, Freud classifies as the unconscious. Based on this understanding, Freud also claimed that most mental processes are individual and, more controversially, that human behavior is driven by sexuality, the libido. Finally, Freud argued that social taboos against sexual impulses force a repression of desires and memories, relegating them to the region of the unconscious.

An analysis of unconsciously driven human behavior is useful to the literary critic in that it may offer answers to questions about the motivations and actions of characters. To see how Doc, Mack, and the boys can be better understood through psychological analysis, it is necessary to also examine Freud's claim that the mental processes are assigned to three psychic zones: the id, the ego, and the superego. At the deepest level of unconscious process is the id, where the libido resides, which has as its function the fulfillment of pleasure. Alone, with no conscious order to keep it in check, the id is the most chaotic of psychic processes, seeking only to satisfy instinctual desire. At the level of the id, there is no morality, no values. The ego is one of the levels of consciousness that regulates the drives of the id. It is governed by reality. Finally, there is the superego, which serves to protect society by imposing moral regulation on the id. It is directly opposite the id in purpose and, acting alone, could be as dangerous as an unchecked id. It is the job of the ego to apply reason to the other psychic processes and to create the balance that defines a psychologically healthy individual.

Applying psychological theory to a literary work involves creating a case study of a character or characters. This involves identifying the character's impulses and attempting to explain these through psychoanalytic theory. Much can be learned from *Cannery Row* by examining both Mack and the boys, who function as a unit, and Doc. Doc perceives his Flophouse friends as being the psychologically healthy members of an otherwise sick society. Based on his rationale for health, they do indeed seem to be balanced. However, applying Freudian theory, the boys' rejection of social values, their perpetual unemployment and lack of motivation to improve their social position or even their creature comforts, indicates an unconscious rejection of parental authority that, like society, is characterized by rules and order. Society becomes representative of parental authority, especially that of the father, in the Oedipal stages of development where the father is seen as an obstacle to a boy's sexual desire for his mother. By escaping from society's rules and repression of desires, the boys are able to create a seemingly blissful existence where natural impulses such as drinking, fighting, and celebrating are not suppressed. Doc explains this as healthy functioning; it is representative, however, of an out-of-control id unregulated by either the ego or the superego.

The fact that the boys find their bliss so close to the water, the Monterey Bay, also supports the idea that they are rejecting paternal authority. Water is a female element and represents freedom, distinct from the rules of society associated with the father. When the boys leave the water and go inland to the Carmel Valley, they find loneliness and violence, both presented through the landowner. The landowner, alone because his wife is busy with politics, approaches the boys with a shotgun, and his dog by his side. The shotgun is symbolic of violence, but by its very shape becomes a phallus, an image reinforced by the name of the dog's breed—pointer. This violence and the phallic symbolism show the land to be a male element and is connected to the paternal/parental authority the boys reject, in this case by returning to the water-edged Cannery Row.

While the boys are able to follow Doc's sexual encounters through a window in the Palace Flophouse and Grill, they are not shown to have any sexual experiences of their own. Indeed, there is never any personal discussion of sex by Mack and the boys. This is indicative of repressed sexual impulses and could be explained as Oedipal neurosis resulting from a strong but unfulfilled sexual affection by their mothers. The boys' drinking addresses this neurosis in two ways. First, it physically ensures a decreased sexuality, since alcohol is known to suppress sexual functioning. Secondly, it serves as a substitute for sexual fulfillment.

Doc's psychological characteristics help to explain why Mack and the boys, as well as all of Cannery Row, are drawn to him. Doc is described as being loyal, kind, and mostly patient, which are predominantly maternal characteristics. Doc is also closely related to water through his work, which reinforces his identification with the maternal. While the boys are quick to ignore or rebel against the paternal, they long for the security of the maternal, which is why they suffer such guilt after the first attempt at a party for Doc. That they have, by doing harm to Doc, attacked the maternal also accounts for why the Cannery Row citizens are so complete in their social ostracism of the boys.

It is clear that Doc does have a sexual life, but it is not a healthy one. Women come and go from the lab, and the curtains are drawn and the music plays, but no woman stays, leaving Doc alone, a victim of his own Oedipal problems. The extent to which healthy sexuality is missing from Doc's life is shown by the ways he attempts to compensate for a lack of meaningful human contact. Doc's appetite for food and drink is voracious. He does not even get out of Monterey on his trip to Los Angeles before he must stop for hamburgers and beer. The trip to Los Angeles is not measured in miles, but in the number of times Doc stops to satisfy his hunger, mostly with more hamburgers and beer, but also with complete meals. It is his appetite, his physical desire that grows as he leaves the security of his friends, which ultimately motivates him to order the beer milkshake, which he has previously only fantasized about. As long as Doc has food, and as long as the boys have Doc, there is little reason for any of these characters to seek long-term, committed relationships with women. This leaves the reader to envision only a future for Cannery Row where Doc continues to function unconsciously in the maternal role and where Mack and the boys continue striving to please and appease Doc.

7

The Pearl
(1945)

By 1944, when Steinbeck began writing *The Pearl*, his disillusionment with the American Dream, the promise that individual wealth achieved through self-determination could bring true happiness, was complete. Steinbeck's own financial success had brought him material gains, but also much personal anguish. Four years earlier, Steinbeck had embarked upon a six-week sea journey along the Mexican coast with his close friend, marine biologist Ed Ricketts. They collected marine specimens for Ricketts's work, and they spent a great deal of time with the Mexican people. Out of this experience came Steinbeck's *Sea of Cortez: A Leisurely Journal of Travel and Research*, a journal that included a simpler version of the folk tale Steinbeck tells with *The Pearl*. After his trip with Ricketts, Steinbeck was approached about writing a screenplay that would be produced in Mexico. In the screenplay and later the novella, *The Pearl*, Steinbeck's philosophical concerns come alive in a place and in people about which Steinbeck had come to care deeply.

SETTING, PLOT, AND STRUCTURE

Before he wrote his short novella *The Pearl*, John Steinbeck had already written a screenplay of the story for a movie to be filmed in Mexico. *The Pearl*'s film connection is apparent in the structure and setting of the novel. The action occurs chronologically, with clear distinctions made between the action that occurs at different times of day, especially in the morning and at night, and in different locations. The novella is framed by two mornings, beginning with the morning that leads to the main character Kino's great pearl discovery and ending with the morning Kino and his wife Juana return to the diver village with their dead son. Between these two mornings, representative of birth and death, are the days from which will come discovery and the nights from which will come evil.

Place, or setting, also helps support *The Pearl's* messages. Undisturbed, the diver village is a place of order for the divers. The further they get from their homes, the more they experience chaos and threats to that order. The town represents authority and civilization to the villagers, but in reality, it presents an evil, the cheating and abuse of authority that make it, ironically, uncivilized. As Kino and Juana move even further away from their home into the wild, uninhabited areas separating them from the Mexican capital, the evil takes off its mask and order breaks down altogether.

It is through these elements of time and place that the plot of *The Pearl* moves. *The Pearl* is the story of the journey, both literal and metaphorical, of Kino the pearl diver. In Chapter 1, the journey begins as Kino awakens one morning beside his wife, Juana, with his beloved son, Coyotito, nearby in their simple brush house beside the gulf waters in a pearl diver village. The rituals of Kino's mornings—witnessing the sun rise, eating Juana's simple corn cakes, and hearing the Song of the Family, the inner music that confirms for Kino his true good fortune as a husband and father—establish the starting place for Kino's journey. These are the things with which the rest of the novel's action will conflict. This conflict begins immediately. While eating their breakfast, Kino and Juana see a scorpion moving toward their son on the rope from which his box cradle is hung. The parents are unable to prevent the scorpion from biting Coyotito. Their neighbors gather in and around their house while Juana attempts to suck the poison from Coyotito's wound, but in fear for her son's life, Juana insists that he be taken to the doctor in the adjoining town.

This trip to town is the first of two that Kino and his family will make. With each trip, they are accompanied by their neighbors, and with each, they return home without achieving their desired goal. This first trip to the doctor is fruitless because, since they have no money and only a few valueless seed pearls, the doctor's servant tells them the doctor is out treating a "serious case" (17). In fact, the doctor is lying in his grand bed wearing silk pajamas and eating his breakfast while he daydreams. Kino, angry and frustrated, attempts to find a pearl that will satisfy the doctor's fee. Juana gives Coyotito the more traditional treatment of a seaweed poultice but also prays that Kino will find the pearl that will buy Coyotito the doctor's care. Kino does find "the greatest pearl in the world" (26), and also finds that his son seems to be recovering from the scorpion bite.

Chapter 3 establishes the idea of greed from which arises the story's pivotal message. News of Kino's great pearl travels quickly from the diver community to the town, and everyone there, from the beggars to the priest, considers what will be personally gained from Kino's pearl. Steinbeck offers an almost scientific explanation for this phenomenon of greed: "The essence of pearl mixed with the essence of men, and a curious dark residue was precipitated" (29). The effect on the town is presented in apparent contrast to the scene in Kino's house where his brother, Juan Thomas, and the neighbors have gathered to celebrate his discovery. Kino tells them of the four things he will do with the money from the pearl. On the surface, his plans seem modest enough; a church wedding, new clothing, a rifle, and an education for Coyotito are simple desires compared to the doctor's epicurean daydreams. Kino's desires and those of the doctor are not dissimilar, however. Kino's wants reveal a previously unrealized dissatisfaction with his life as a pearl diver. They uncover his shame, both in his appearance and in his marriage, and a need to cover that shame with an official marriage and new clothing. The rifle, the narrator states, illustrates that humans are never satisfied, that "you give them one thing and they want something more" (31). Lastly, his desire for Coyotito to be educated is not a desire for the means of a good job in the town for his son, but rather a desire for the knowledge that Kino says will free the entire family. Kino holds onto this desire as he holds onto the pearl, refusing to give it up even when the pearl becomes a danger to his family. In his refusal, Kino re-enacts the biblical story of the fall of man; Kino eats from the tree of knowledge, and, as a result, experiences a fall from the innocence he has known as a poor pearl diver.

Kino is not left alone for long with his own dreams of riches. He is visited by the priest, who hopes Kino will remember the church when the pearl is sold. At this point, Kino begins to hear the music of evil that will continue to mix with the Song of the Family as long as he has the pearl. The sounds of evil grow stronger when the doctor visits and tricks Kino and Juana into believing Coyotito is still in danger from the scorpion. The doctor gives the baby poison to make him appear sicker, which is the first act of violence resulting from the promise of the pearl. The reader knows the doctor is only attempting to locate the pearl, which Kino has buried, so that he can steal it. Kino senses the doctor's intent and moves the pearl to a new hiding place. That night brings the second act of violence associated with the pearl. An intruder comes to steal the pearl, and Kino attacks him, drawing blood. Because of her ability to reason, which is the complement to Kino's desires, Juana is now able to see the pearl as evil and, fearing that it will destroy them all, asks Kino to throw it away. Kino is not able to give up his own desire to know and his need for Coyotito to have knowledge,

Kino's own desire to know, and refuses to acknowledge Juana's warnings of the danger.

In Chapter 4, Kino moves further away from the world he knows and into the darkness of the unknown, the world of dealing and deceit, all the effect of owning the pearl. The chapter opens with the second morning of the story, but in contrast to the first morning, this day is filled with nervous excitement. Kino and his family are dressed in their best clothes, the wedding and baptism clothes made and saved for the sacramental rites they could not yet afford. The pearl buyers are also nervous in their anticipation of Kino's visit. The pearl will not make them wealthy, since they all work on salary for the same buyer, but their excitement comes from the idea of the game, the hunt in which Kino is the prey.

The reaction of Kino's neighbors to this day is perhaps the most important. They feel the excitement as they prepare to follow Kino to town to sell the pearl. Their participation does not entirely work to reinforce the communal bond between pearl divers, however. Setting themselves apart from Kino and his declarations about what he will buy once he has sold the pearl, the neighbors proclaim they would give the money to charity and warn that wealth will destroy Kino. This warning is based partly on jealousy on the neighbors' part, but the neighbors function throughout the novel as a combined voice similar to the chorus of Greek drama, and this role has its own significance that must be considered. The words sung by the chorus in Greek drama often expressed the feelings, emotions, and ideas of truth impossible to present through the hoped for realism on the stage. In *The Pearl*, the truth the neighbors present is that charity is good and wealth will destroy, and this truth foreshadows the events to come.

Kino's brother, Juan Thomas, warns Kino that he may be cheated by the buyers. Juan Thomas is correct in his warnings. The first pearl buyer tells Kino that the pearl is too big and offers Kino a low price for the pearl. He arranges for three other buyers, his supposed competition, to confirm his appraisal. As with the doctor and the priest, Kino hears the music of evil and leaves with his pearl, planning to take it instead to the capital for sale. In making this decision, Kino psychologically separates himself from his community and his life with that community. Kino has "lost his old world and must clamber on to a new one" (58). Juan Thomas confirms this defection by telling Kino he has defied the "whole structure, the whole way of life" for their people (58). This way of life is the accepting of the social and economic structures that give pearl buyers, doctors, and priests authority over the poor pearl divers. The rest of the community begins to also question this authority by considering whether they had been cheated by the pearl buyers all of their lives, but they deny this possibility because of the devastating effect such a truth could have on their world. Kino knows his pearl is valuable, and this belief is further confirmed that night when a second intruder comes to steal the pearl. Again Kino must draw blood to protect his great pearl. As with the first attack, Juana tells him the pearl is evil and asks him to throw it back to the sea. Again he refuses, asking her to believe in his decision, his plan to sell the pearl, because he is a man.

Chapter 5, the third morning and day of the novella, presents the physical separation of Kino from his past world. He has already planned to leave this day for the capital but must overcome obstacles placed in his way. The first is Juana, who rises early to sneak out and throw the pearl back to the ocean. Kino stops her, hitting and kicking her, and Juana recognizes murder in Kino's eyes. Next, Kino is attacked by another dark figure whom he kills. Juana, knowing that she cannot stop Kino because he is "half insane and half god" (64), hides the dead man and returns the pearl to Kino. Their brush house is set on fire, and they discover their canoe has been destroyed. Kino's killing of the intruder and the destruction of their house make it impossible for Kino and his family to remain in the diver village, but the way of travel Kino knows best, across the water, is also made impossible. Thus, he and Juana are forced to escape to the wild, uncivilized lands where they hope to hide from those who wish to steal the pearl as well as make it to a city where they can sell it at a fair price.

Chapter 6 presents the completion of Kino's physical journey. He ends up where he began. His psychological journey brings Kino to a new place, but the travel there brings great loss. As they flee the village, Kino and Juana must travel at night so they will not be detected. They are going toward the town of Loretto, a place associated with miracles, indicating there is still hope. However, Kino is becoming more dangerous, more animal, as they leave their known world. As this change happens the music of the pearl becomes stronger, "and it [is] interwoven with the music of evil" (77). Now Kino understands that the pearl is a dangerous thing because he does not have the power, gained through wealth, to keep it and realize its potential benefits. By this time, however, he is forced into "panic flight" from the three hunters tracking his family. In this panic, Kino is reacting still on animal instincts, and only after taking strength from Juana do his movements calm. They go to a pool of water high in the mountains. Juana and Coyotito are hiding in a cave as Kino attacks the three hunters resting by the pool in the darkness of the night. As Kino attacks, the rifle of one of the hunters goes off. Kino is able to kill all three hunters, but the cost is the life of Coyotito, who is killed by the rifle fire.

The final scene of the novella is heavily cinemagraphic. Steinbeck creates a visual image that eliminates the need for characters' speech. The setting is once again the diver village, with the sun setting in the background creating long shadows. Kino and Juana are walking along the road, she carrying the body of Coyotito. They walk side by side rather than in the usual single file. Their position on the road indicates a change that has occurred within Kino. The distinction between male and female has become blurred. In Chapter 4, Kino asked Juana to believe he would be able to protect their good fortune because he was a man. Ironically, Kino's actions as a man without reason or caution are what cost them their greatest fortune, Coyotito. It is not shame that makes Kino walk side by side with Juana, but instead the change in Kino that allows him to accept within himself the female qualities of carefulness and reason, thus creating in Kino a new kind of man. Whereas before he became even more determined to hold onto the pearl after being challenged for it, Kino is now able to see that its cost to him, the life of his son, is too great, so he throws the pearl back to the sea.

CHARACTERS

As a parable, *The Pearl*'s message is universal. Steinbeck communicates the parable's truth, or moral, through Kino and the journey on which his pearl takes him, making Kino the protagonist, or major character of *The Pearl*. Kino's development as a character can best be described as realization. He comes to realize the risks of greed through great loss, but more importantly, he realizes the dark potential resting within all humans. Initially, Kino is a poor but content husband and father. Without the money for an official marriage to Juana and a baptism for Coyotito, he has created a family on his own terms, the terms of a pearl diver whose ability to survive is measured by the number and quality of pearls he finds. The opening lines of the book paint a picture of Kino's happiness with his life. Awakening beside Juana, he hears the Song of the Family, a celebratory music playing within Kino's own soul. He celebrates the sunrise also because it affirms the continuance of life and thus of the family that brings Kino so much pleasure and completeness. Over breakfast, Kino and Juana are able to communicate without speech because their knowing of one another is deeper than the senses.

Kino's contentment with his life is tested by factors that force him away from the comfort of his existence. His temper flares when he is unsuccessful in getting the rich doctor to treat Coyotito's scorpion bite. After finding the great pearl, Kino verbalizes the things he will buy with the money the pearl will bring. In these desires, the reader detects cracks in Kino's earlier, apparent happiness with his life. As the threat of losing the pearl becomes greater, so too does Kino's resolve to keep it because, he states, "This pearl has become my soul. . . . If I give it up I shall lose my soul" (73). Indeed, as the evil associated with the pearl and the wealth it signifies enters Kino's soul, he becomes a bully and a killer, no longer the simple pearl diver made happy by a wife, a son, and a new day.

Juana's thoughts make it clear that Kino's change is not a loss of one man and the creation of a new man, but instead the result of conflicting drives within Kino. After he attacks her for trying to throw the pearl back to the sea, she justifies her lack of anger with the consideration that, as a man, Kino is "half insane and half god" (64). When first introduced, the reader sees Kino the god, a creator of life pleased by an inventory of his creation. The discovery of the pearl brings out, or realizes, the part of Kino that is half insane. Sanity is equated with order—in Kino's case the order of his established world—and the pearl brings disorder or chaos to that world, thus the insanity.

The narrator states in Chapter 4 that "Kino had lost his old world" (58), but the insanity is never complete. Throughout the test of owning the pearl, Kino remains connected to his old world, if only by a precarious tether. After deciding to take the pearl to the capital for sale, he is afraid and hears the dark music of the enemy, but his mind holds onto the "deep participation in all things, the gift he had from his people" (59) that will enable him to face the challenges of a journey to the capital. Later, traveling through the darkness of night as he and his family flee their village, Kino is able to overcome his fears and the unknown through an animal instinct that arises in him, "some ancient thing out of the past of his people" (74). Even though the songs of the pearl and of the enemy grow louder in Kino, the Song of the Family never dies completely. Indeed, the Song of the Family begins competing with the Song of the Enemy when the hunters trap Kino and his family. When Kino and Juana return to their village with their dead son after Kino has killed the three hunters, Kino is returning to the known. By experiencing such great insanity, the god within him may be weakened, but enough remains for him to finally see the evil within the pearl and to cast it back to the sea and out of his life forever. This realization completes Kino's development.

Kino's journey is also the journey of a hero. From American westerns and comic book stories, the term *hero* is often associated with grand actions of goodness and justice; a classical hero, however, is characterized quite differently. One of the major identifying factors of the classic hero is his or her initiation, or passing from immaturity to adulthood through a series of steps: separation, transformation, and return. Kino's journey takes him through each of these stages of development. Finding the pearl separates him from his known world first psychologically and then physically. During the journey to sell the pearl in another city, Kino is finally able to see in the pearl illness and death; thus, he is able to realize that the price to be paid for wealth is too high. After this transformation, Kino returns to his village, an object of an important lesson to all of his people about the dangers of wealth and desire. This lesson is the thing of value Kino brings back to his culture, an action also required for those defined as heroes.

Since the focus of *The Pearl* is on Kino's development, none of the other characters noticeably changes through the course of the novella. For Juana, in fact, it is important that she does not develop. Her role in the story is to provide the reason that Kino lacks as he moves further into the unreasoning, or "insane," part of his psyche. It is Juana who, each time the pearl poses a threat to the family, asks Kino to throw it back. When he refuses, Juana risks Kino's anger by attempting to throw it back to the sea herself. There are moments, however, when Juana's actions are emotional rather than reasoned. Asking for the doctor after the scorpion bites Coyotito would seem an emotional request from a poor diver's wife with no means to pay the doctor, but when medical care is refused, Juana does not become angry as Kino does. Instead she relies upon her own resources to address the problem. She treats Coyotito with a seaweed poultice and, for good measure, prays that Kino might find a pearl big enough to pay the doctor. It also seems Juana has lost her reason when she justifies Kino's violence toward her when she tries to get rid of the pearl herself. Her assessment of what being a man means, however, is less excuse for Kino than it is an astute observation that the reader is able to confirm through Kino's behavior. Though she provides reason in the story, it is clear her reason will not stop Kino from his single-minded goal of realizing the pearl's wealth. Kino must arrive at the truth of the pearl through his own journey.

Juan Thomas provides a voice for his silent, younger brother, verbalizing those thoughts and ideas Kino cannot or will not admit. As they travel to the pearl buyer's offices, Juan Thomas warns Kino about being cheated. He tells their father's story about agents who disappeared after being hired by the divers to take pearls to the capital for a better price. The telling of the story has a number of purposes. First, it foreshadows the dangers of Kino's own attempt to take his pearl to another town for sale. Next, it illustrates the thematic message about what can happen to those for whom wealth becomes a temptation to rebel against the established economic order. Finally, because Kino states he has heard the story many times, Juan Thomas's telling of the story shows that Kino is aware of the physical and moral dangers the pearl represents. Later, after Kino refuses the buyer's offer for the pearl, Juan Thomas tells him he has defied his entire way of life. Again the reader is led to believe Juan Thomas is stating what Kino already knows but cannot acknowledge because to do so would mean giving up the pearl, which has become his "soul."

Like Juana, Juan Thomas cannot stop Kino from taking his journey with the pearl. He acts as another helpmate to Kino, displaying those qualities of women, "the reason, the caution, the sense of preservation" (67), that help Juana save her family from Kino's temper. Juan Thomas hides Kino and his family after Kino has killed the thief. He even lies to the villagers about where Kino and Juana are and borrows from the villagers those things his brother will need after leaving the village, including the large knife that lights up Kino's eyes. By displaying these qualities in Juan Thomas, Steinbeck illustrates the potential for all men, and particularly Kino, to realize them also.

The doctor, the priest, and the pearl buyers represent the evil possibilities of the desire for wealth. The doctor embodies the education, or knowledge, Kino wants for Coyotito, but because of his greed, the doctor does not use his knowledge as it was intended, to minister to physical disease. Instead he denies ministration, using the authority education has given him to acquire more wealth. The priest, who as God's representative is a minister to spiritual disease, also holds his services ransom, denying marriage and baptism to those who cannot afford the price of his greed. While the pearl buyers will not realize any personal wealth through their cheating of the divers, they participate willingly, almost gleefully, in a system created to increase the wealth of one man at the expense of the many.

The dark intruders who come three times to steal Kino's pearl and the three hunters who track Kino and Juana through the wilderness are the explicit manifestations of the implicit evil of the doctor, the priest, and the pearl buyers. They are the death and illness to which greed can lead. Yet, they are also formless. Steinbeck does not identify them by clear description or tell for whom they work because they do not represent any single person's desire for riches, but the potential for all people's desire for riches and the evil that results from such desire.

MAJOR THEMES

John Steinbeck distrusted money. As a child, he witnessed the effects that the loss of money had on his own family when his father lost his job. He also saw how far his mother would go to make sure this loss did not affect the family's social standing in their Salinas, California, community. Later, when Steinbeck's books began to sell, he was uncomfortable with the financial success his work earned. Since he was never quite satisfied with the quality of his own work, he was continually surprised at being monetarily rewarded for it. Additionally, this initial success was accompanied by frequent requests from strangers for financial assistance. These requests haunted Steinbeck when they came from people who seemed truly needy and angered him when they came from those who sought to profit from his success. Steinbeck could do little materially to help those suffering from the economic depression in America that coincided with his early literary success, but he was deeply concerned with the problems and issues it manifested. Money's effect on people is, indeed, a recurring theme in Steinbeck's work. In *The Grapes of Wrath*, the emphasis is on the power those with wealth had to destroy the lives of those without means. In

The Pearl, the thematic focus is once again on wealth, but this time Steinbeck shifts the emphasis to the effects wealth has on those who find it.

When the reader is first introduced to Kino, he is a man satisfied with his life. As the story opens, Kino is waking up beside his wife, with Coyotito in his box beside them, and the sound of the ocean waves in his ears, and "it was very good" (5). These words echo those from Genesis used to describe God's satisfaction with each stage of creation. Thus, Kino's world can be compared to Eden, a place of contentment and innocence. His wife, his son, his canoe, and the energy taken from the rising sun fulfill Kino so that he appears to have no yearnings beyond his simple existence. Finding the great pearl, and in it finding the possibility of wealth, creates in Kino the desires he seemed to lack before. He tells his neighbors he wants to use the money he will surely get from selling the pearl to pay for a church wedding, new clothes, a rifle, and an education for Coyotito. Each of these items could separate the family from the poor community in which Kino seemed to find so much contentment before he found the pearl. Kino knows the effect the pearl has had on him, and after being cheated by the pearl buyers, Kino knows he must go to the capital to sell the pearl because he had "lost his old world and he must clamber on to the new one" (58).

His new world does not give Kino the joy found in his old world, however. In the flight from the pearl thieves, Kino comes to see "only death and illness" in the pearl (77). Since he has already said "this pearl has become my soul" (73), then the darkness seen in the pearl can be reflected on Kino's soul. Not only is his life, as well as the lives of his wife and son, in danger, but Kino's very soul is at risk. In order to protect his pearl, Kino beats his wife, kills four men, and loses his son. The death and illness he sees in the pearl is the darkness that slowly, with each violent act, invades Kino's soul. His fall from innocence is complete.

Because of the ancient connection among all the people of the diver community, there is an expectation that the experiences of its members will affect the community, and Kino's experiences do affect the ancient village of brush houses. The idea of community is established early in the story. When Coyotito is bitten by the scorpion, the villagers follow Kino and Coyotito to town to seek the doctor's help. They are not merely onlookers. If the doctor will treat Coyotito, then the community members can hope for his care in the future. If not, they will have confirmation that, as members of the poor diver community, they will not receive his medical care. Likewise, when Kino discovers the great pearl, the other divers initially celebrate his good fortune because it confirms the possibility of good fortune for themselves. This hope is further displayed in the neighbors accompanying Kino and his family to town to sell the pearl.

This cohesiveness between Kino and his neighbors does not last long after his finding the pearl, however. They begin to set Kino apart from the community.

They foretell that Kino's new wealth will destroy him and claim that if they had found the pearl, they would give the money to charity rather than use it to purchase increased economic security. When the pearl buyers tell Kino his pearl is worthless, the neighbors speculate about whether the buyers are correct. While they originally show awe at the sure value of such a large and beautiful pearl, they now claim they were suspicious from the beginning that there was something wrong with the pearl. And when Kino leaves the buyers, sure that he has been cheated, the neighbors justify the buyers' evaluation of the pearl because to believe as Kino did that he was being cheated would be to confirm that the pearl divers had been cheated all their lives, which would be too much to learn.

Because the pearl brings not wealth to Kino, but instead shows the inevitability of his status as a poor pearl diver, the break between Kino and his community is never complete. As a result, when Kino and Juana return from their failed attempt to sell the pearl at the capital, which results in Coyotito's tragic death, it is "an event that happened to everyone" (92). Kino's loss reveals to the entire community that grand dreams promising a better life can only bring pain. It could easily have been the pain of any member of the community, confirming the "deep participation in things" Kino senses in Chapter 5. Kino's loss of innocence is a loss of innocence for the entire diver community.

Complementary to the theme of wealth's destruction of those who find it is that of the natural hierarchy of life. While wealth does destroy, it also gives power to those who have it and weakens the defenses of those who do not. This social reality is the reason the doctor can manipulate Kino and Juana when he comes to "treat" Coyotito, why the priest looks at the members of the diver community as children, and why the pearl buyers feel sure they can cheat the divers without challenge. Those with money and its resulting power are higher in the natural hierarchy and can feed on those who have none. Steinbeck punctuates this point in Chapter 2 with the opening description of sea life meeting the land life, with the dogs and pigs feeding on the dead of the sea.

A final important literary theme in *The Pearl* is that of appearance versus reality. In Chapter 2, the narrator states that the "people of the Gulf trust things of the spirit and things of the imagination" (19), but they do not trust the things their eyes see. This information foreshadows Kino's initial reaction to the oyster when he catches a glimpse of something in it as he is diving. He is hesitant to open the oyster because "in this gulf of uncertain light there were more illusions than realities" (25). When he does open the oyster and sees the pearl, Kino perceives it as a reality, a real way to get medical care for Coyotito and to improve his family's economic status. But even the reality he envisions will not be real, the reader knows, because when Kino looks "in the surface of the great pearl he could see dream forms" (26). Kino might believe he is looking into a crystal ball, but the use of the word *dream* signals to the reader the illusory quality of these visions and, thus, of the pearl's promise. Later, as the pearl becomes the object of Kino's problems rather than the promise of his future, Kino begins to see only death and illness in the pearl, images that get sharper. Instead of dream visions, the pearl begins to offer clear pictures of reality.

Often, the reader understands the reality that the characters cannot. Long before Kino realizes the pearl's negative potential, the reader knows or senses the danger it represents. Likewise, the reader has witnessed the doctor's greed and professional hypocrisy, and so knows his motivations when he comes to Kino's brush house to treat Coyotito's scorpion bite after the news is spread of Kino's pearl discovery. Coyotito appeared to be cured by Juana's seaweed poultice and her sucking of the wound, but since people "don't trust what they see with their own eyes," Kino and Juana do not trust the seeming cure. In this case, the initial appearance is the reality, but their distrust, stemming from their sense of self-ignorance, prevented them from seeing the reality. Juana's treatment lacked the doctor's authority for them because it was free and simple; thus, they are taken in by the appearance of concern by the doctor for Coyotito's well-being. They allow the doctor to treat the baby, even while the music of evil, a signal of reality, is playing in Kino's head.

Neither do the pearl buyers appear to be what they really are. They seem to be in competition with one another, but in fact, they are all working for the same buyer. The narrator informs the reader of the masquerade, so the reader knows from the moment Kino meets with the first buyer, the master of slight of hand, that Kino will be cheated. Again, Kino senses this reality and refuses to sell the pearl at the low price offered, but because of his position, he is unable to understand the nature of the offense against him.

The return of Kino and Juana to the diver community after their failed attempt to sell the pearl in the capital shows a tragically gained ability to distinguish appearance from reality. When they returned, "the people say that the two seemed to be removed from human experience; that they had gone through pain and had come out on the other side; and there was almost a magical protection about them" (93). Kino now has knowledge. It is not the knowledge that he hoped would take him away from his old life; it is a truer form of knowledge that will allow him to understand the life he has been given.

ALTERNATIVE READING: ARCHETYPAL READING

The term *myth* often invokes thoughts of Homer's *Iliad* and *Odyssey*, or perhaps the stories of England's King Arthur. Indeed, these are classic myths, not because of their scope or their fantastical action, but because they each demonstrate fundamental, inner meanings about humans and about the universe.

They symbolize basic human drives and emotions regardless of time or place and are thus universal in meaning and in message, as well as in the response they elicit.

Jungian theory, which finds its basis in the ideas of C. G. Jung, a Swiss psychoanalyst and a student of Sigmund Freud, who was the father of psychoanalysis, is the particular area of myth criticism concerned with archetypes, the universal symbols that are not specific to time or place. For example, throughout history and in most cultures the circle has signified wholeness or unity, and the snake has symbolized evil. Additionally, Jungian theory is concerned with collective memory, the idea that humans have inherited memories, ideas, and emotions from an ancestral past. From the study of archetypes comes Jung's theory of individuation, which is related to those archetypes that are parts of the inherited human psyche—the shadow, the anima, and the persona. The shadow is the dark side of the unconscious self, the weak aspect of the personality. The anima is that part of the psyche from which come the vital forces, often associated with the soul. According to Jung, the anima is feminine, the woman inside each man. The role of the anima is as intermediary between the male's unconscious self and his ego, the conscious, thinking part of man. Archetypally, strong female characters are symbolic of the anima. The final component of the psyche is the persona, man's social self or the personality that is shown to the world. Working opposite to the anima, the persona mediates between the world and the ego.

The myth critic is concerned with identifying those elements in a piece of literature that bring universal responses. To do so, the critic analyzes a work's archetypes—the motifs, themes, and images that have a common meaning or bring a common response regardless of the differences in age or location among the myths. *The Pearl* is suitable for archetypal reading because it touches a similar nerve, or common understanding, among its readers through the many archetypes in the story.

First among the significant archetypes in *The Pearl* is light. Kino's first action in the story is to greet the sunrise. The sun signifies consciousness and, more specifically, enlightenment. From it, Kino receives his energy and the knowledge of self that allows him to bring order to his day. In contrast to light is darkness and night. Darkness is the absence of light; therefore, it is the absence of knowledge and order. It is during the night hours that Kino makes decisions concerning the pearl, including how he will use the wealth gained from it and how he will protect it. These decisions are suspect because he has made them at night when there is no enlightenment. Additionally, all of the violence in the story is associated with darkness. Kino attacks Juana before the sun rises. Coyotito dies during the night. Kino faces each of the thieves in darkness, stabbing two men and killing four during the hours between sunset and sunrise.

Kino cannot identify these enemies because each is formless in the darkness, thus representing disorder.

Kino's pearl is also archetypally important. The pearl is white, a color with conflicting associations. White can represent light, purity, and innocence, but it can also represent death, terror, and unbearable universal truth. When Kino initially discovers the pearl, its light illuminates a future for Kino and his family that would be impossible without the wealth the pearl can bring. This light is quickly extinguished by the evil of the pearl, the violence and death it brings to Kino's life. Ultimately, the pearl also is responsible for Kino realizing the truth that there is a hierarchy within the human species that is determined by wealth and the power it creates, and those without wealth remain at the mercy of those with it.

The final image created in the story is that of the pearl going back to the sea. In contrast to the colors Steinbeck uses for description throughout *The Pearl*, he highlights the color green in the closing image. The water is a "lovely green." "The lights on its surface were green and lovely," and the surface itself was a "green mirror" (97). The repetition of color in the image, punctuated by the positive adjectives, points the reader to the idea of new life and hope that the color green signifies. Having seemingly lost everything, there is still hope of life and growth for Kino and Juana.

Water also functions archetypally in *The Pearl*. From water comes birth, death, and resurrection. From the gulf waters, Kino takes the pearl that brings him hope for a new life, one that will include greater financial security for his family. Just as Kino's old life must end before he can accept a new one, however, life with the pearl must come to an end. The killings of the intruders and Coyotito can also be related to the pearl, a product of the water. All of Kino's dreams for the future die when he casts the pearl back to the water. Out of this experience of birth and death Kino is resurrected as a man who, along with Juana, "seemed to be removed from human experience" and about whom there "was almost a magical protection" (93).

The songs of the family, the pearl, and evil serve as both affirmation and warning for Kino. These songs are part of Kino's racial memory, a primeval, collective unconscious shared by all humans that lies deeper than the personal unconscious. This memory, coming from the experienced histories of all people, contains the wisdom gained from those experiences and is thus a great predictor. The Song of the Family tells Kino what is truly important. The Song of the Pearl and the Song of Evil attempt to warn Kino about the danger of possessing the pearl. When Kino does not accept the warnings or predictions from these songs, evil comes into his life both internally and externally. When he finds harmony with these primeval instincts by responding to them, Kino gains wisdom.

The shadow and anima are particularly meaningful in an archetypal reading of *The Pearl*. In his obsession with keeping the pearl and in his violent actions that result from this obsesssion, Kino displays his shadow. The dark figures who come in the night are also representative of Kino's own shadow. They may be the agents of the doctor, or perhaps the priest, but they symbolize the evil part of the unconscious that is driven by greed. In fighting these intruders, Kino fights his own shadow and attempts to keep it in check. That the shadow is never able to take full control of Kino is one reason he is finally able to relinquish the pearl and the darkness it carries.

The other reason Kino is saved from his own shadow is Juana, who in *The Pearl* represents Kino's anima. Her reason and her caution are the projections of Kino's own anima that, since his shadow is so strong, Kino is not able to realize until the end of the novella. Juana carries these female attributes to remind the reader of what is missing in Kino. When the shadow becomes too strong, when the Song of Evil begins to drown out the Song of the Family, Kino's anima is realized and, while too late, he is able to see that protecting his family is more important than protecting the pearl.

A final consideration in a myth reading of *The Pearl* must be Steinbeck's use and treatment of the American Dream myth. While his story is archetypally consistent, it subverts rather than affirms this particular myth of American culture. The American Dream is characterized by great expectations and hope of finding a new paradise where moral regeneration is possible. In this new paradise, or new world, hard work and virtue make it possible for people to create their own success and control their own social status. In *The Pearl*, Steinbeck imposes this American Dream myth on his characters not to show truth in the myth, but to display the fraud of the myth. Kino's discovery of the pearl should bring him the material wealth necessary to rise above the poverty of his community to a higher socioeconomic position. Instead, it leads to almost complete loss. Kino loses his home, his means of income, and, most tragically, his son. His community, somewhere in the Americas, is not a new paradise but instead a mirror image of the Old World's feudal society where the poor are at the mercy of the wealthy. While Kino is able to hang onto his moral self, there is no sign of moral regeneration in the world outside his poor village. Myth can provide truth about the human condition, but Steinbeck makes it clear that there is no truth in the myth of the American Dream.

8

East of Eden
(1952)

East of Eden might be considered John Steinbeck's most personal work of fiction. The thematic emphasis on discovering new places and new stories echoes the personal changes going on in Steinbeck's life as he wrote the novel, including a divorce from his second wife, Gwyn Conger, and the tragic death of his closest friend, Ed Ricketts (see Chapter 1). *East of Eden* is also a novel about fathers and sons. Steinbeck's own sons, Thom and John IV, were still quite young when their parents divorced, and the author felt great sadness and guilt about his absence from their lives. In *East of Eden*, he gives his sons much of their family history and much of their father, but mostly he shows that old landscapes and old stories can be replaced, something that he realized, in the end, they must discover for themselves.

SETTING, PLOT, AND STRUCTURE

In his long established style, Steinbeck opens *East of Eden* by presenting the novel's setting. The landscape he describes is California's Salinas Valley, a place to which the author has led his readers in earlier works, most notably in his short stories. The valley is bordered to the east by the happy Gabilan Mountains in whose womb the valley rests, and to the west by the "dark" and "brooding" Santa Lucias Mountains. Also introducing the personal voice of the narrator, a voice indistinguishable from the author's own voice, Steinbeck states, "I always found in myself a dread of West and a love of East" (3). He suggests a connection between the story and his personal history by recounting his father's drilling of a well in the valley floor. When the earth was pulled to the surface, it included seashells, whalebone, and redwood. Like his father, Steinbeck drills for the history of the valley through which flows the Salinas River, the "only one we had" (4). That history is discovered through the stories of the people of the valley, both real and fictional.

The remainder of Part 1 of the novel tells three separate histories of the main characters, both real and fictional, who will merge to form one story in Part 2. The stories of Part 1 are the histories of Samuel Hamilton and his family, Adam Trask and his family, and Cathy Ames. In Chapter 2, Steinbeck writes of the migration of his own grandfather, Samuel Hamilton, from Ireland to America, where he meets his wife Liza and where together they homestead in the Salinas Valley on a piece of dry and barren land. While their land may have been barren, the Hamiltons produced nine children, and because he delivered all of his own children so well, Samuel was called upon to deliver other people's babies as well. Although his own land produced little because it had no water, Samuel was able to meagerly support his large and happy family by boring wells on other people's land and harvesting other people's crops. His gifts as a man were large, but they brought little material profit.

In the second part of Chapter 2, Steinbeck moves the narrative to a commentary. This commentary concerns the settlers' greed for land. Most ended up with property that was unusable or which they did not know how to use. Others came to the valley with money and bought the fertile land and built estates. At this point, Steinbeck introduces the main fictional character of the story, Adam Trask, who migrates to the valley in Part 2 of the novel and forms a friendship with Samuel Hamilton, merging the fact and fiction of *East of Eden*.

Steinbeck offers great detail about the childhood of each of his main characters because this information is background for the story's main theme of childhood rejection and its effects. Chapters 3 and 4 are devoted to the story of Adam Trask's childhood. Adam's story begins on a Connecticut farm where he is born in 1862 while his father, Cyrus, is away fighting in the Civil War. Cyrus returns six weeks following Adam's birth after losing a leg and gaining a case of gonorrhea, which he passes on to Adam's mother, who soon drowns herself. Cyrus quickly takes a new wife, Alice, the quiet, clean, and healthy daughter of a neighbor, and Alice becomes pregnant within two weeks with Cyrus's second son, Charles. As Adam and Charles grow, Cyrus begins to fabricate stories of his war experiences. He studies warfare and publishes articles on the subject, drawing the attention of the Grand Army of the Republic, which grants him a secretaryship and sends him traveling as a consultant and lecturer. When he is home, Cyrus rigidly trains his sons in military skills.

Eventually, Adam withdraws into silence to protect himself emotionally from assaults from both Cyrus and Charles who, like his father, is assertive; but Charles is also violent. Adam has little protection from Charles's rage and begins to understand that unless he is prepared to kill Charles, he must never win against his brother. Cyrus senses the dangerous tension between his sons and begins to talk to Adam of the pride and dignity he will gain by becoming a soldier. Cyrus tells Adam that Charles will not be sent to the army because he is not afraid and, thus, has no need to learn courage. When Adam protests that Charles is never punished and that it is unfair that Charles escape enlistment in the army, Cyrus tells him it is because "I love you better" (28).

Adam's enlistment in the army comes quickly, the result of a fight between the sons that occurs on the same night that Cyrus professes his greater love for Adam. Jealous of Cyrus's clear preference for Adam, Charles beats Adam until he is unconscious and leaves. Adam comes to just in time to hide in a ditch as Charles returns with a hatchet and murderous intent. After Adam returns home and talks with his father, Cyrus leaves the house with his shotgun but returns when he cannot find Charles. While Adam is recovering, Cyrus brings the enlistment officer to the house, and Adam is sworn into the army. Adam's hatred of violence and killing grows while he is in the army. While he is away, Charles begins to write to Adam, passing on news of Alice's death and Cyrus's new job in Washington with the Grand Army of the Republic. While it seems Charles is reaching out to his brother in an attempt to heal the pain between them, one letter refers to unfinished business, which gives Adam a chill.

Adam sees his father only one more time, after his discharge from the army in 1885. He spends time wandering the country, knowing he does not want to go home but unsure why. Before long he re-enlists in the army and receives orders to go to Washington, where he sees his now powerful father and learns Cyrus is arranging a good assignment for him. He defies Cyrus and requests reassignment to his old regiment.

Charles builds up the farm while Adam is away, but he is too timid to find a wife to share his life there, so he visits the town whores when his loneliness becomes too great. He does get excited about Adam's return after his first discharge and hires a woman to clean the house, but when Cyrus writes to tell Charles of Adam's re-enlistment, he becomes resentful and the letters between the brothers slowly stop. Charles returns his focus to the farm, continuing to build it and its profits.

After Adam's final discharge from the army in 1890, he writes Charles that he is coming home but again is unable to return to the farm. He lives as a hobo for a time, and when Adam finally decides to go home, he is arrested twice for vagrancy in Florida. Adam escapes three days before his final release, having served a year in jail. When Adam eventually returns, both brothers realize their relationship has changed. Adam is no longer afraid of Charles, and Charles realizes he can no longer beat Adam. This contributes to the difficulty Charles has in telling Adam their father has died and left them $100,000. The brothers worry about where Cyrus got so much money. Charles is afraid he stole it, but Adam makes a choice not to feel shame about how Cyrus might have gotten the money, claiming "I believe in my father" (70). Because Adam has no love for Cyrus, he has no jealousy or suspicion.

Adam's naive faith will be tested by the character whose history is told in Chapter 9, which begins with the narrator's profession, "I believe there are monsters born in the world" (72). Cathy Ames is one such monster. Physically, Cathy seems to be a picture of innocence, but mentally she is an aberration. Cathy is a loner and a liar who learns at a young age that sex is the best tool for controlling those around her. The only people Cathy cannot manipulate through sex are her parents, but she cannot accept their attempts to control her. At sixteen she is physically punished by her father, apparently for the first time, for deciding to quit school and then running away when her parents try to interfere. Feeling trapped, she burns her home to the ground, killing both parents, and escapes to Boston where she plans to become a whore.

In Boston, Cathy, calling herself Catherine Amesbury, becomes the mistress of Mr. Edwards, the same rich whoremaster who owns the girls working at the inn Charles Trask visits. He soon falls so in love with her that he becomes emotionally and physically ill. Cathy begins to steal from Edwards and hide the money. After having her investigated and followed, Edwards discovers both her deception and her secret about the fire. He takes her and the money on the train, telling her he is going to put her to work as a whore, but when they arrive at a small town he beats her and leaves her for dead.

In Chapter 10, Steinbeck moves the history back in time to the story of Adam and Charles Trask. Adam leaves the farm twice because of tension and anger between himself and Charles. After his second return home, Charles tells him the same irritation and anger will grow again, so Adam should just leave for good. It does grow, until Adam tells Charles about breaking out of jail after leaving the army. Charles gains a new respect for Adam because he now feels Adam is not perfect and, therefore, no longer a threat. It is to this farm with its new atmosphere of understanding between the brothers that Catherine Amesbury, in Chapter 11, drags her savagely beaten body, creating the first instance in the novel where the different story lines converge.

The remainder of Part 1 presents the final split between Charles and Adam Trask, a split that begins the moment they find Cathy's beaten body on their doorstep. Charles resists taking Cathy in, but Adam insists that they send for the doctor, who comes and repairs Cathy's injuries as much as possible. Adam's empathy leads him to become protective of Cathy, which Charles does not understand. When Adam eventually allows the sheriff to question Cathy about the beating, she feigns amnesia and will not even admit to knowing who she is.

Adam is deliriously happy with Cathy in the house, but Charles is very nervous. He tells her she will have a scar on her forehead just as bad as the fingerprint like scar he received during an accident. Charles recognizes something in her that others do not because they share many traits. Adam senses the changes going on around him and asks Cathy to marry him. Charles is becoming more suspicious of Cathy and tells Adam that people are talking about Cathy. Adam promises to do something about her within a week, and he does, by marrying her five days later. Charles explodes and calls Cathy a whore. Adam makes plans to take Cathy to California, even after she tells him she does not want to go. On the evening of their marriage, Adam drinks Cathy's sleeping medicine by mistake, and she goes to Charles' bed and consummates her wedding by sleeping with her husband's brother.

Part 2 begins, in Chapter 12, with discussion about the changes occurring at the turn of the century, which creates a time marker of 1900 for the narrative and also provides a philosophical context within which to consider the changes occurring in the narrative. According to the narration, with the changes of the new century goodness has disappeared. Also, with the westward expansion of the United States, everyone was ready to put the misery of the nineteenth-century behind them and move on to new hopes. This commentary establishes the symbolic nature of the characters. Additionally, Chapter 12 introduces the contrast between collective production and individual creativity, the product of the individual mind which, according to Steinbeck, is the human's only "creative instrument" (132).

Both devils and angels are products of human creativity, according to Steinbeck. The product of Adam Trask's individual creativity was the idea of Cathy as an angel, which existed only in his imagination. Steinbeck's imagination, however, has created Cathy as a devil, one whose qualities are thus far hidden from Adam. Steinbeck resumes his story in Chapter 13 with Adam and Cathy now in California. In Salinas, Adam is looking for land, and Cathy is secretly looking for a way to rid herself of the baby growing in her womb. After a failed attempt at self-abortion, Cathy realizes she will have to bide her time and wait to make her next move after the baby comes.

The final merging of the story's main characters occurs when Adam is sent by the townspeople to talk with Samuel Hamilton about drilling wells on the land he wants to buy. When they meet, Samuel talks about the valley's geology and the promise the land holds, but also about the darkness he senses coming over the valley. The reader knows that his words foreshadow future events resulting from the Trasks, especially Cathy, moving to the valley. While previously the novel has presented the Trask fiction separate from the historical fact of the Hamiltons, with this meeting Steinbeck begins to involve his historical figures in the fiction.

Chapter 14 is the story of Olive Hamilton, Steinbeck's mother and one of Samuel's five daughters. The shift here back to history is a significant one. With the meeting of Samuel and Adam the author has just blurred the lines between fact and fiction. Now he moves the narrative back to fact, to the true accounts of his mother's life and, by doing so, suspends the fiction at a point where suspense is created for the reader waiting to see the fulfillment of Samuel's prophesy. Additionally, the stories offered about Olive Hamilton bring the author into the novel, thus pushing even farther the limits of the novel form.

The reader does not have to wait long to witness the black violence wrought by Cathy Trask. She and Adam are now living on their new land. Lee, the Chinaman who will become an important character in the novel, has been hired as a cook. He makes Cathy uneasy because she can't "read" (161) him. But Samuel Hamilton can; he learns Lee was born in the United States and educated at the University of California, and that he speaks like a Chinese immigrant because that is what people expect. He drops the Chinese accent, telling Samuel "you are one of the rare people who can separate your observations from your preconception" (163). When Samuel finally meets Cathy, he gets a cold feeling of despair and later realizes the feeling came from Cathy's inhuman eyes. He associates her eyes with those of a criminal he saw at a hanging when he was a child.

In Chapter 17, Samuel comes to realize his initial observation of Cathy is true. Samuel is summoned from his drilling at the Trask ranch when Cathy goes into labor. During the birth, her viciousness emerges, and she bites Samuel on the hand, forcing him to slap her and hold her by the throat as if he were fighting a dog. Not one but two children are born, both boys, and Cathy refuses to see them. Samuel tells Lee he feels "a dreadfulness coming" (196), which Lee senses also. The dreadfulness is realized after Cathy is recovered from the birth, at which time she sends Lee to town, shoots Adam in the shoulder, and walks away from her home, leaving behind forever her babies, her strongest connection to any other human beings.

As a result of Cathy's departure, Adam essentially stops living, withdrawing into himself much as he did as a boy when facing the assaults of Charles and Cyrus. Still protecting Cathy, however, Adam refuses to tell Horace Quinn, the deputy sheriff, what really happened, instead creating the lie that he shot himself while cleaning the pistol, a firearm he claims he is not familiar with. Horace knows he is lying because he knows Adam was in the cavalry and would be accustomed to pistols. Horace learns from the sheriff in Salinas that Cathy is now working at Faye's, one of Salinas's three whorehouses. They decide to keep her location secret to protect Adam and the twins and to warn Cathy, now going by the name of Kate, that if she opens her mouth, they will run her out of town. In contrast to Adam's stupor, Kate builds a new life with new aspirations. At Faye's, she becomes the model whore, causing Faye to love her as a daughter and, eventually, to write a will leaving everything to Kate. After Faye tells Kate about the will, Kate slowly and methodically carries out a plan to kill Faye, making it look like a natural death and hiding or destroying all evidence, including burying the stolen medicine bottles that held the substances Kate used to poison her madam. When Faye dies, Kate takes her place at the whorehouse.

After fifteen months, Adam is still emotionally dead and has not even named his sons. When Samuel learns of this, he becomes angry and goes to the Trask ranch. When he arrives at the ranch, the first thing he does is to beat Adam, an act totally out of character for the gentle, laughing Samuel. He beats him out of anger for Adam's refusal to live, but also as a means to bring Adam out of his self-imposed imprisonment. Adam thanks him for this, and the two men discuss Adam's fear of what the twins will become because they hold Cathy's blood. Samuel tells Adam not to look for her blood in the twins, that "not their blood but your suspicion will build evil in them" (262). After Lee joins Adam and Samuel for dinner, the three men discuss the biblical story of Cain and Abel, which is significant to Adam's history with Charles and to the possibility of rejection and the resulting guilt for the two new Trask brothers. After the biblical discussion, the darker twin is named Caleb and his brother is named Aaron. Part 1 of the novel closed with the conception of these brothers; Part 2 now closes with their naming.

Many things come to an end in Part 3 of *East of Eden*. The first of these is the life of Samuel Hamilton. Samuel's journey toward death begins with the death of his daughter Una. Burying one of his children causes a sudden aging in the seemingly ageless Samuel. His remaining children are outraged at the change in their father and develop a plan to have Samuel and Liza visit each of their homes, leaving Tom, the only Hamilton still at home, to run the ranch. When the first invitation comes from Olive Steinbeck, Samuel knows it is part of a conspiracy by his children, but he tells Tom he knows he is leaving the ranch to die and he is "content" (291).

Before he and Liza leave the ranch, Samuel goes to say good-bye to Adam Trask. Samuel tells Adam he is wasting his life and his land, which Adam has never planted. Stirring Adam even further, Samuel asks him if he loves one of his sons, now 11, more than the other, suggesting a perpetuation of the story of Cain and Abel as well as that of Adam's own childhood. But such a perpetuation is not inevitable, according to the discussion Samuel, Adam, and Lee have that same evening. After their discussion of the Genesis story the night Caleb and Aaron were named, Lee was disturbed by the implications of the biblical text and took his questions to the Chinese wise men in San Francisco for help in interpretation. After studying Hebrew, they determined that the word *timshel* means "thou mayest" rather than "thou shalt" or "do thou," as later translations offer. "Thou mayest" triumph over sin gives humans a choice that the translated commands do not. Lee tells Adam and Samuel that facing this difficult choice is what makes a man a man. Samuel exercises such a choice when, as he is preparing to leave, he tells Adam about Cathy's life in Salinas.

Samuel Hamilton's death on March 15, 1912, is accompanied by great rains falling on the Salinas Valley. After Samuel's funeral in Salinas, Adam visits a bar, where he learns the location of Kate's whorehouse. Going there, Adam finds Kate in her office, and he feels nothing; her emotional hold over Adam is now gone. His composure enrages her and, drunk, Kate tells Adam that all the world is evil, and shows him photographs of senators, professors, and ministers engaging in perverse sex acts with her whores. Adam is not affected by her anger. He reminds her that she has not asked about their twin boys, and she continues her assault by telling him about sleeping with Charles on their wedding night, suggesting that the boys are not Adam's. This does not matter to Adam. Adam returns to his ranch a free man, a freedom brought to him through Samuel Hamilton before he died.

Chapter 27 marks the midway point in the novel, and it is here that the story begins of Aaron, who writes his name Aron, and Caleb, who goes by Cal. It is a story that threatens to repeat that of their father and his brother Charles. As Adam is returning from Salinas, the brothers are hunting rabbits and, after one is hit with an arrow, the boys argue about whose arrow hit the rabbit. Aron angers Cal, who retaliates by telling his brother that he heard some men talking about their mother, saying she had run away. Just as Adam once chose to believe that his father was not a thief and that his Civil War stories were true, Aron chooses to ignore this rumor in favor of his own truth, that his mother is dead. Knowing this is another weapon with which he can control Aron, Cal goes on to suggest their mother ran away because she did not like them. Aron's torture is cut short by a storm that forces them to run for the house.

Cal's manipulation of Aron continues after they return to the house and find strangers, Mr. and Mrs. Bacon and their daughter, Abra, who have stopped to take refuge from the storm. When the three children are sent outside to play, Abra begins to make fun of the boys for their social immaturity but stops when she learns their mother is dead. Abra tells them she will help them find the grave and go with them to visit their dead mother. Aron's fascination with Abra and her apparent partiality to him cause Cal to play a cruel joke on them. Afterward, Cal is triumphant because he has won at Aron's expense; Cal loves Aron because he is the reason Cal is able to triumph.

Cal's scheming continues during dinner that evening. The boys realize that something in Adam has changed. He had not seemed to notice them before. Now he is discussing school and rabbits with Aron and Cal. Wanting to manipulate the situation, Cal tells Adam about Abra's questions concerning their mother's burial spot. Adam responds with a lie, telling the boys she is buried in the East, and he quickly changes the subject to the possibility of their moving to Salinas. After the boys have gone to bed, Lee tells Adam he is worried about the possible effects of this lie.

Adam then writes to Charles after more than ten years of silence. He tells Charles about his sons but lies about why Cathy no longer lives in their home. Adam asks Charles to visit them in California and ends his letter with a postscript telling Charles "I never hated you no matter what. I always loved you because you were my brother" (362). As he anxiously awaits an answer from Charles, Adam awkwardly attempts to become a real father to Cal and Aron, but his attempts only irritate the boys. He is saved from a full loss of respect by Will Hamilton's delivery of a new Ford automobile, which Adam ordered after Samuel's funeral and after his meeting with Kate.

After a week, Adam, Lee, and the twins manage to drive the new Ford to King City, where a letter is waiting from attorneys in Adam's Connecticut hometown. The letter was sent to inform Adam of Charles's death and his will, which left Charles's large fortune to be equally divided between Cathy and Adam. Chapter 31 begins with Adam going to Salinas to show Kate the letter. Kate suspects that Adam has some hidden motive in telling her about the will, perhaps to get her run out of town. She becomes angry at his lack of emotion or interest in her claiming the money. He leaves Kate in her rage and goes to visit Liza Hamilton, who is living in her daughter Olive's home. When he tells her he is thinking of moving to Salinas, she tells him to speak to her daughter Dessie, who is selling her house, and she asks Adam to visit Tom, who is now living alone on the Hamilton ranch. Adam runs into Will Hamilton at dinner that same day, and Will also asks him to check on Tom. These meetings shift the focus of the novel back to the Hamiltons for a final time and foreshadow the tragedy that develops over the next two chapters, leaving the rest of the novel, in Part 4, to the Trask story.

Dessie Hamilton, the "warm-beloved" (389) Hamilton daughter who infects the world with her joy and laughter, has lost her joy after the breakup of her first love affair. She decides to sell the business that is also her home and to return to live on the ranch with Tom. Will tries to stop her; he is worried about the loneliness she will find there and about her being alone with Tom, whom Will believes has become strange. But she defies Will and moves back to the ranch where she and Tom, in their mutual sadness, attempt to resurrect the joy of their childhood. They begin to plan for a trip around the world, but physical pains that had struck Dessie in Salinas now become more intense. She refuses to tell Tom about them until she becomes desperately ill. He tries to help her by giving her a traditional remedy of salts, but the pain only increases. Tom goes to a neighbor and calls the doctor, who calls Tom a fool for giving her the salts. The doctor is too late, and Dessie dies. After Dessie's funeral, Tom is assaulted by his own guilt. To his mother, who objects to suicide, Tom writes a letter saying he has bought a wild and unpredictable new horse. He then writes a letter to Will asking him to tell Liza he was thrown by this horse and kicked in the head. After mailing the two letters, Tom returns to the ranch and shoots himself in the head. The two children who carried the most of Samuel, his laughter and his sensitivity, are now gone.

Part 4 of *East of Eden* begins with Chapter 34, a short chapter of commentary concerning the evaluation of good or evil that occurs after a man's death. The first three parts of the novel have presented re-enactments of the myths of Adam and Eve and of their children in the lives of twentieth-century people. Part 4 tells a new story and in doing so frees the characters from the human limitations presented by the old stories. In Chapters 35 and 36, the Trask family moves into the house Adam has bought from Dessie Hamilton. After getting Adam and the boys settled, Lee moves to San Francisco to pursue his dream of owning a bookstore but returns shortly, telling Adam he is "overwhelmingly glad to be home" (419). Truly, this is Lee's home, where he has become a second parent to Aron and Cal and a brother to Adam. Abra becomes Aron's closest friend at school, while Cal, whose cleverness causes apprehension in those around him, has no friends. The Trasks are beginning to function as a real family. Lee sets out to furnish the new home, and Adam finally begins to crave work. He becomes fascinated with the idea of refrigerating produce and talks to Will Hamilton about buying a Salinas ice house and shipping lettuce to New York on a refrigerated rail car. Will advises Adam to take a more conservative route and to buy beans and store them for sale when the price increases. Adam's thinking here is reminiscent of Samuel, who spent his life inventing ways to make life easier and better. The comparison forces the reader to consider the outcome of Samuel's inventiveness. Like Samuel's, Adam's inventiveness will also have an adverse effect on the family fortune as well as on its reputation. He sends a shipment of lettuce bound for New York and, due to railroad delays, the lettuce rots before it reaches the East Coast. Adam is not devastated by the news of his failure, but his now fifteen-year-old sons are. Aron worries that the family is now poor and his plans to go to college are ruined, and he tells Abra he hates Adam for causing this. Abra, knowing the real reason for Aron's frustration, suggests he ask Adam about Cathy. Aron runs away from her and her courage to face the truth.

Cal is not so adversely affected by Adam's failure, but he begins to feel his father's rejection more strongly and, as a result, to crave Adam's love in equal proportion. In his unhappiness, Cal begins to walk the streets of Salinas at night, and there he learns about Kate's whorehouse. He goes to Kate's and the effect of this experience is so intense that he must turn to Lee for help. Cal tells Lee he believes Cathy shot Adam and left them, "because I've got her in me" (449). Lee angrily rejects Cal's ideas and tells him that to excuse his life because of his mother would be taking the easy path. In the meantime, Aron decides to make the ministry his vocation. He becomes obsessed with the religious; he unsuccessfully attempts to convert his brother and informs Abra that he must practice celibacy, crumbling her dreams of the future and causing her to hate the church.

After the police arrest Cal in a raid on a gambling house, Adam and Cal have their first real personal conversation, increasing Cal's love and protective feelings for his father. Learning that Cal has been to Kate's, Adam tells Cal that he trusts him to protect Aron from the truth about their mother. Cal begins to follow Kate and, after awhile, she challenges him and learns that he is her son. The meeting is enlightening for Cal who realizes for himself that he does not have to be like his mother simply because they share the same blood.

Cal's new confidence motivates him to want to earn a large amount of money for two reasons. First, he wants to send Aron to college so he will not learn about Kate. Also, he wants to offer his father a gift of money to pay Adam back for his loss in the lettuce venture. With America drifting toward World War I, Will Hamilton encourages Cal to buy beans and sell them at a profit, and the two become partners in a business plan. Chapter 14 presents a historical explanation of the sale of American commodities to the British during World War I, thus allowing the reader to more clearly understand the business deal between Will Hamilton and Cal Trask. It also foreshadows the large sum of money Cal will later offer as a gift to Adam.

While Cal is busy preparing a gift for his father, Adam is excited about giving Aron a gold watch in recognition of passing his high school exams a year early. Aron is not interested in gifts from his father; he is only interested in leaving Salinas as quickly as possible and beginning college. The owner of a whorehouse in town has begun attending services at the Episcopal church where Aron serves as an apprentice to Mr. Rolf, the minister. Mr. Rolf believes this madam is a lost soul he must save, but Aron is repulsed by the idea of her, and his anger and desire to leave Salinas, which he believes is filthy, only grows.

When he does go away to Stanford, Aron grows lonely, and his letters to Abra are his only real human contact. Abra, on the other hand, begins spending more time at the Trask home and soon finds that she feels closer to Adam and Lee than to her own father. Lee begins to think of Abra as his own daughter, and the two discuss Cal and Aron. Abra believes Aron has created an ideal out of her, someone who is "absolutely pure" (497), and she would rather lose Aron than have to carry this burden. Cal's excitement over the gift for his father causes Abra to see something in Cal she has never seen before, and she begins to like him.

After her visit from Cal, Kate finds new reason for being afraid when Ethel, one of Faye's whores, comes to Kate and tells her that she has the bottles that contained the drugs Kate used to poison Faye and that Kate thought were still buried in the backyard of the whorehouse. Kate arranges for her to be arrested for stealing and thrown out of town. Soon she worries that Ethel will still be able to expose her, so Kate sends Joe, the whorehouse bouncer, to find out where Ethel has gone. Joe learns that Ethel is dead but tells Kate that she seems to have returned to Salinas. Soon Kate becomes suspicious of Joe and sends the sheriff a note suggesting he check Joe's fingerprints for a real identification. Steadily slipping into paranoia, Kate makes a will leaving everything she has to Aron and then commits suicide.

Aron does not live to know that his mother's last vicious act was to leave her fortune to him. Adam, Lee, Cal, and Abra meet Aron at the train when he returns home for Thanksgiving vacation. Aron tells Cal he does not want to return to college, and Cal becomes worried for Adam's sake. Cal is also jealous of the attention Aron once again is receiving from Adam. Cal is sure that his gift of $15,000 to his father will make him as beloved by Adam as Aron is. When Cal offers his gift to Adam, however, his father tells him he must give the money back to the farmers he has robbed. He thanks Cal for the gesture but tells him he would rather be given what Aron has given him, "pride in the thing he's doing, gladness in his progress" (544). The reminder that Adam loves Aron better is too much for Cal, who later that night takes Aron to see his mother. Aron reacts by going to San Jose and joining the army. When Kate dies, he is not in Salinas to learn of her final evil act.

The town of Salinas is spared the shame that Kate's death could have caused. Joe flees arrest and is killed by Deputy Nobel before he can use for blackmail Kate's photographs of the town leaders engaging in perverse sex. Horace Quinn, the same man who questioned Adam after he was shot by Kate, is now sheriff, and he burns the photos and notifies Adam of Kate's suicide and of her will. Adam reacts with tears to the death of Cathy his wife, not to the death of Kate the whore. Adam wants to tell Aron about the will and the money found in Kate's vault, but Aron is nowhere to be found. He soon receives a letter from Aron telling Adam he has joined the army, and the news causes Adam to suffer a mild stroke. Cal punishes himself by burning the $15,000.

Aside from Adam's decline in health, the Trask home seems to heal from the events of Thanksgiving. Abra begins to visit the house again, which pleases Lee for whom Abra is like a daughter. To express this, Lee gives to Abra his mother's jade button, the only object he had from the woman who was killed violently after his birth. Regeneration seems to be occurring with the advent of spring. Adam's health improves, Abra and Cal go to the country to celebrate the blooming of the Alisal azaleas, and Lee selects flowers for the garden. But spring takes a dark turn when a telegram arrives announcing Aron's death in the war.

In Chapter 55, *East of Eden's* final chapter, the major choices of the main characters must be made. Adam suffers a serious stroke after learning about Aron's death. Cal goes to Adam and confesses his responsibility for Aron's death, and Cal believes that Adam's eyes accuse him of murder. He runs to Abra, who makes him return home to face his father's illness and his own guilt. Lee tells him it is stupid to believe that God allows evil to survive while goodness is destroyed, and that is why Cal must not believe he is a product of a disgusted God who has given up on creating a perfect product. Cal must choose to triumph over this belief. They go into Adam's room and Lee makes a choice to demand that Adam look at Cal and to give Cal his blessing. Adam closes his eyes, appearing to fight Lee's demand, but Lee persists. He demands that Adam give Cal an opportunity for freedom. Struggling, Adam is able to raise his hand barely an inch in blessing before it drops again to the bed. Lee thanks Adam and asks if Adam can say Cal's name, a final blessing for the child who was nameless for the first year of his life. The word that comes from Adam's lips is not his son's name, but "Timshel!" When Adam closes his eyes in sleep, Cal is left with the greatest acknowledgment his father could give, permission to triumph over the sin Cal felt he was destined to live.

CHARACTER DEVELOPMENT

While there are a number of major characters in *East of Eden*, Adam Trask must be considered the story's main character or protagonist. The fictional narrative begins with Adam's birth and ends as he is lying near death fifty-six years later. The major themes of the novel are exemplified through the lessons Adam learns in his development from child to parent, from the one most loved to the one who learns that one should not love someone at the expense of another. His lessons are painfully won, but each makes him a stronger character, a stronger man.

The obstacles that Adam must overcome in order to accomplish true growth as a person are obstacles that are built in his childhood. The first of these is a resistance to truth. When he was growing up, Adam knew that his own mother had done a shameful thing and that shameful thing was associated with her death. Adam believed that if he uncovered the truth about his mother's death, he would repeat her sins and die. Hiding from truth becomes the norm for Adam as he matures. He avoids facing the truth of his relationship with his brother Charles. He makes a choice to believe that his father was truthful about his war service and that Cyrus accumulated his wealth from legal means. When Cathy shoots him and deserts him, Adam retreats to a silent world within himself rather than face the truth of the evil she embodies. Only through Samuel Hamilton's sometimes gentle and sometimes forceful guidance does Adam find the strength to face truth in his life and to understand that facing truth will not make him a shameful sinner or bring him death.

The other obstacle preventing Adam from accomplishing real personal growth is his denial of love. As a child, Adam depends on Charles to protect him from Cyrus, but he is unable to feel love or affection for Charles because of the violence Charles inflicts upon him. The beatings are less painful if Adam does not love the one who is beating him. The years between his childhood and the time he meets Cathy are years empty of love for Adam. When Cathy does enter his life, he allows himself to love her because she is, he believes, weak and defenseless; thus, she cannot hurt him.

Together, these obstacles cause Adam to avoid living because living requires being open to both truth and love, even if they might bring pain. The freedom from fear that Adam finds after Samuel's death and after facing Cathy more than ten years after her violent departure allows him to finally love Aron and Caleb, and become a parent. He is also able to tell Charles, too late for Charles to hear, that he loved him regardless of the pain Charles caused. Adam has learned that the only love a person can be sure of is the love that is felt for another person. Adam still must learn, however, that to love one child better, as he himself had been loved, is the root of evil. Adam's full development as a person occurs at the end of the novel when, near death, he offers his blessing to Cal.

While Samuel Hamilton is a historical figure, the author's own grandfather, Steinbeck fictionalizes him in *East of Eden*, thus creating the opportunity for character analysis. Samuel is not a developing character. At the most basic level, the characterization of Samuel makes of him a character type, that of the wise, old man. By so fully representing Samuel's character, both his strengths and his weaknesses, the reader can compare and contrast his character traits to those of the story's other main characters to help understand the novel's main themes.

Much of Adam Trask's story shows him to be a man afraid of life, but Samuel Hamilton, on the other hand, relishes life. The big man with gentle hands and large, laughing eyes loves laughter, poetry, philosophy, inventing, and getting into other people's business when he sees a pain that needs to be healed. Though faced with the adversity of an endlessly dry ranch and nine children to feed, Samuel finds ways to challenge and overcome those circumstances. His gifts and his optimism extend beyond his own family's circumstances into the community, which repays him with friendship and respect. The extent of the community's love for Samuel is shown in fellow rancher Louis Lippo's warning to Adam that the community would not accept an outsider coming in and doing Samuel harm. Samuel is the light of the Salinas Valley, and only when one of his children dies and he is forced to face death as a reality does Samuel's light begin to dim.

Samuel not only teaches Adam to embrace life, he also teaches him how to be a father. Samuel loves each of his children equally even though they are very different people. This is a lesson Adam learns late, almost too late to offer hope for his surviving son, Cal. Like Samuel, the death of his child takes much of the life out of Adam and begins his own crawl toward the end. Had Samuel Hamilton not shown Adam how to love his children, it is not clear that his response to losing Aron would be so tragic.

Before she is even officially introduced, Steinbeck tells his reader that Cathy Ames is a monster. At first her physical description seems to defy such a characterization—she has a face of innocence, golden hair, and a heart-shaped face—but the more particular physical details Steinbeck offers make her appearance less inviting and more suspicious. She has an abnormally small mouth, directly related to her inability to communicate with others but, more importantly, to the secrets she holds and the lies she tells. She has small ears with no lobes, corresponding to her inability to hear what the rest of the world tells. Her deformed nipples are symbolic of her inability to be either physically or emotional maternal. The most explicit physical connection between Cathy and monsters is her hooflike feet, forcing a clear connection to Satan.

The reader is asked throughout the novel to determine whether Cathy represents pure evil. With love as the prevalent characteristic of goodness, Cathy must be considered a true manifestation of evil. She is incapable of love, indeed of any real contact with other humans aside from sexual contact. Her own self is chaotic; she cannot control her own impulses, and the only way she can establish any order in her existence is to control others. In any circumstance where goodness is required, Cathy is like a trapped animal; lies and manipulations are her tools of escape. She uses them to escape from her parents and from her husband and children. Only in a situation where no goodness is expected does Cathy thrive; thus, she becomes a whore.

The truest test of Cathy's evil is when she is under the influence of alcohol. When she drinks, Cathy becomes more vicious, and the evil she attempts to hide to protect herself from society's punishment is made clearer than at any other time. Adam finally sees her evil clearly when he goes to Cathy to tell her about Charles's will. It is Adam who Cathy has most successfully fooled, and it is when Adam finds her out that Cathy's life beings to unravel and spiral into her own chaotic death. Her past acts of evil are found out by Ethel and Joe; she is forced to face goodness when Cal brings Aron to see her; and the traps that Cathy has avoided all of her life become suddenly inescapable, so she takes her own life alone in a gray room of her own making.

Aaron (Aron) and Caleb (Cal) Trask are the significant characters in Parts 3 and 4 of *East of Eden*. It is through them that Steinbeck presents the complicated issues that result from considerations of good and evil. Aron Trask, like his mother, has gold hair, pink skin, and blue eyes, but he has none of her deceptive deformities. Aron desires goodness in his life so strongly that he, like his father, hides from the existence of evil or pain in his life. The more Aron matures, the more difficult it becomes to evade pain and evil, and the more he takes extreme measures to do so, eventually cloistering himself in a theological world of goodness. Also, because Aron, like his father, refuses to believe in the existence of evil in his life, he is incapable of defending himself from it. His vulnerability finally allows Cal to inflict the greatest pain upon Aron by taking him to Kate's to face their whore-mother. When Adam is forced by Samuel to know the truth about Kate, he accepts his choice to rule over sin, to exorcise the evil of Kate from his life forever, and he is afterwards unaffected by her. But Aron does not have the strength to stand and defend himself from the pain of facing his mother's evil, and he runs away to the army, which is his flight to death.

Comparison is also invited when studying the character of Cal Trask. While Adam and Aron's greatest enemies are the evil they must face in others, the physically and emotionally dark Cal, like his Uncle Charles, must battle what he believes to be evil within himself. Neither Cal nor Charles possesses an inherent evil as Cathy does; each wants to be good to his brother, but instead they inflict pain on others because each feels rejected by his father. Cal's anger climaxes when Adam does not acknowledge his gift of money, and this leads to the ultimate crime against his brother, the son for whom Adam shows the greatest love. The human story Cal is playing out is rewritten only after Cal receives the blessing from Adam. While *East of Eden* ends with this blessing, based on the novel's themes, readers can write for themselves the final development of Cal, the ability to share love as a result of no longer feeling rejected by his father.

Lee is in many ways the fictional counterpart to Samuel Hamilton. They are both viewed as foreign outsiders when they come to the Salinas Valley. Samuel gains the acceptance of his neighbors through his storytelling and his intelligence. Lee must work harder to gain acceptance because he is physically different, making the preconceptions he must overcome greater. Samuel is led by his observations rather than preconceptions. This is another quality Lee shares with Samuel. While he plays to others' preconceptions, his own observations are astute. He can discern the strange atmosphere that descends over the Trask house during Cathy's labor, can see that Cathy is engaged in war rather than childbirth, and he feels the same "dreadfulness" (196) as Samuel does following the twins' birth. Lee's wisdom proves to be as great as Samuel's. The entire novel hinges on the translation of the word *timshel* derived from Lee's curiosity about the Genesis story. Just as Samuel demands that Adam at least go through the motions of living when his sorrow becomes too great, Lee demands that Cal pretend to live when he feels responsible for driving Aron to his death. In the final scene of the novel, Lee demands that Adam give his blessing, and therefore his love, to Cal, just as Samuel once demanded that Adam give to this same son a name.

Because of his wisdom, the Trasks begin to rely on Lee to fill the voids in the family; consequently, Lee brings completeness to a broken family. He becomes a beloved brother to Adam, a mother to Aron and Cal from the moment of their birth, and a father figure to Abra. By filling these voids, Lee is able to facilitate the happiness of those who truly become his family, and the voids in Lee's life are also filled. When he is merely a servant, Lee is lonely and dreams of moving to San Francisco to open a bookstore. By the time he actually makes this move, he is no longer a servant; he is a family member and leaving the Trasks brings to Lee a greater loneliness, so he returns to the home where being motherless and Chinese are not factors in being loved and accepted.

Along with Cal, Abra represents the hope for the future generations of *East of Eden* and so must be considered a major character in the novel. She is not a developing character but she is a round character, one who the reader knows well enough to anticipate actions. Abra is independent and spirited. She knows both good and evil and is strong enough to stand up to the latter. Abra is able to love even when badness exists because she knows that humanity includes badness, and she does not want to relinquish her own humanity. Though she never met him, Abra carries many of Samuel's qualities of love and justice that are also found in Lee. Like Lee, Abra fills the voids in the lives of Aron and Cal. As a child, she becomes the mother Aron never knew and his wife. She later becomes the friend Cal never had. In Abra is found the balance represented by the entire Hamilton family.

ROLE OF MINOR CHARACTERS

Both Cyrus and Charles Trask are minor characters with major roles in *East of Eden*. After Part 1, Cyrus and Charles are only background figures, but this is their primary significance in the novel. Cyrus Trask's function is to model the bad husband and father. Left alone with the baby Adam after his mother's suicide, Cyrus spends his three days in mourning sharing his whiskey with his infant son. Adam is saved when Cyrus marries Alice, but Cyrus's treatment of his new wife is no better than his treatment of his son. Cyrus is driven by a need to be important. His family fulfills this need to some extent and what they lack he compensates for by re-creating his own military history to include great battles and feats of heroism that never occurred. His need for power also drives him to express his greater love for Adam over Charles, making life a hell for both Adam and Charles. Cyrus's actions as a father, set in contrast to those of Samuel Hamilton, provide a context for analysis of Adam Trask as a father.

Charles Trask's function in the novel is much the same as Cyrus's. Charles is the product of the paternal rejection that is the hell a child fears and that leads to anger, crime, and resulting guilt. More than anything Charles wants the same love that Cyrus gives to Adam. There is no indication in the novel that he wants the greater share of Cyrus's love. Indeed, his later actions indicate a desire to share life equally with Adam. But Cyrus's rejection makes this impossible for Charles whose anger leads him to nearly murder his brother and, from this, to suffer the guilt that will leave him a considerably wealthy but completely lonely man for the remainder of his life. While Charles does not die until the end of *East of Eden*, after Part 1, he is merely a presence in the reader's mind to which Cal's character can be compared.

The roles of the remaining minor characters are complicated by the fact that they are historical figures that Steinbeck has fictionalized to a greater or lesser degree. As a unit, Liza and the Hamilton children complete the portrait of a happy, well-balanced family headed by Samuel Hamilton. Those to whom Steinbeck gives a greater fictional role, which include Tom, Dessie, Will, and Liza, are used to create the bridge between fact and fiction that allows the novel to have the qualities of a history. Conversely, it is through these characters that Steinbeck takes the known history of the Hamiltons and, by casting his imagination over the facts, creates a Hamilton family mythology.

Finally, Steinbeck himself must be distinguished as a character in *East of Eden*. To the reader unfamiliar with Steinbeck's ancestry, the integration of the narrator into the story through the voice and personal association with characters and events adds depth and richness to *East of Eden*. For the reader who knows the author's history, however, Steinbeck's integration of self into the novel forces deeper considerations of the distinctions between fact and fiction. The inability of the reader to make clear distinctions between the facts of Steinbeck's family and the fiction he creates for that family further blur the lines between history and imagination and enhance the mythological character of *East of Eden*.

THEMES

Steinbeck manages to include two of humanity's grandest themes in *East of Eden*—the nature of love and the battle between good and evil. The theme of good and evil is suggested in the opening description of the Salinas Valley, in the presentation of the two mountain ranges bordering the valley, one happy, light, and maternal and the other mysterious and frightening. The narrator claims a love of the East where the good Gabilan Mountains lie, but the dread he expresses for the West makes it clear that the presence of evil cannot be ignored. True good and evil do not reside for humans in nature, however, but in people, and it is through his characters that Steinbeck develops his philosophy of good and evil. Cathy, Aron, and Samuel represent the various elements that must be understood to grasp Steinbeck's moral. Cathy seems to embody pure evil. She is driven by it. She is part of the world in body only, and even her body, with inhuman eyes and hooflike feet, suggests a distinction from the human world. As Adam points out to her, she is incapable of seeing goodness and beauty. Aron is presented in direct contrast to Cathy. The pain of others only brings Aron sorrow, so he runs from any such pain. Cal tells Lee that Aron "hasn't enough badness in him" to face reality (459). While he has none of the physical imperfections found in Cathy, his physical perfection and the absence of any badness make him as much a human anomaly as his mother is. Because Aron is incapable of seeing evil, he also separates himself from humanity and creates a world in his imagination that is not the world at all, so he is also part of the world in body only. Cathy and Aron are the material from which humans create devils and angels, both equally inhuman because both are incapable of giving real love, which can only occur in human relationships. Because he cannot reach out to others, Aron does not truly live, does not truly love, and, in death, it cannot be said that he was truly good.

Samuel Hamilton stands as the model of true goodness for Steinbeck. He can see both the good and the evil in the world and this allows him to fully live in the world. Too much evil, as with Adam's withholding of names from his children, is dealt with by Samuel courageously, as when he hits Adam. Too great a concentration on purity, as in Liza's objections to fun in any form, is dealt with less aggressively by engaging in fun behind her back. By recognizing the danger of the extremes, Samuel is able to fully engage in life and, thus, to give his love to humanity. This is why Adam, his family, and all who knew Samuel feel a loss of goodness after his death.

The most important moral to come out of Steinbeck's presentation of good and evil is that all people have the power to choose. The phrase "Thou mayest" gives one the ability to choose not to sin and to choose to return love offered rather than rejecting it out of fear and removing oneself from humanity. The choice challenges all the negative motivations for rejecting real love. Aron and Cathy do not make the choice. Neither does Tom Hamilton, and all three, including Aron when he enlists in a wartime army, choose instead to take their own lives, a final and tragic escape from humanity. Cal, on the other hand, does make the choice to triumph over sin when he realizes he does not have to be like his mother, though it is not without struggle. He will sin again—he will hurt Aron by taking him to Cathy—but he will also give love, to Abra and to his father. The novel closes with the promise of great triumph for Cal.

Because good and evil are defined by the giving or withholding of love, love also becomes a major theme in *East of Eden*. Steinbeck makes a clear distinction between love that is given and love that is received. The only love that can really be sure is that which is felt for someone else. It is also from giving love that pain results. Had Charles and Cal not felt such great love for their fathers, their rejections would have been benign. Had Adam not felt such great love for Cathy, her betrayal would not have caused Adam to become emotionally dead for eleven years. Love for another survives even in the face of betrayal and rejection because it is the only thing that is sure. Charles and Cal continue to want their love acknowledged, a gift Cal finally receives from Adam. When he learns of Cathy's suicide, Adam, who felt nothing for the whore Kate, is struck by grief and cries. Abra, perhaps the healthiest fictional example of love in the novel, is able to give love to Cal even though he has hurt Aron, even though he may not be good.

Language finds double importance in *East of Eden*, where what cannot be expressed and the nature of what is expressed are offered as themes. Steinbeck's first mention of the deficiency of language is in his own attempt in Chapter 1 to describe the color of the valley landscape in summer; it was an "indescribable color" (5). The failure of the narrator to describe the land's color is a result of a lack of proper language. While the consequences of such a failure as Steinbeck's are minimal, the absence of language becomes a major factor when applied to Cathy. Cathy could not tell people what she was like because she did not have a "common language" (184), making her trapped state of being unavoidable rather than voluntary. Even in the worst stages of labor, no sound comes from her lips. Her apparent lack of capacity for expressing her feelings does not excuse Cathy. Cathy never finds a common, human language and remains separated from humanity. After Cathy shoots and leaves Adam, he, too, loses his capacity for language, most notably in his withholding names from his sons. Because of this, he also separates himself from humanity, including his own children. When he is forced by Samuel to give them names, Adam begins to reintegrate himself into the world.

Truth is the second thematic treatment of language in *East of Eden*. Truth is relative to need or circumstance for many of the characters. After telling the war stories he has created to magnify his own Civil War experiences for so long, Cyrus Trask eventually becomes convinced of the truth of his own lies. Cyrus needs to do this because his real life offers little for which to feel proud. After Cyrus dies, Adam is left with truths about his father that offer little to be proud of and he, too, chooses to lie, in this case to himself by believing in his father. Aron later follows his father and grandfather in self-deception, rejecting the possibility that his mother is alive and does not want him, and choosing to continue to believe in the lie his father clings to that Cathy is dead.

Aside from the lies characters tell themselves are the falsehoods communicated for the benefit of others. Cathy's life is itself a tangle of deceit made up of lies told for "profit or escape" (74). She knows no truth because truth is rooted in goodness, which is the quality missing from her person. Her lies result in the most immediately apparent damage to other characters, the suicides, murders, and shootings. But for those who can see that she lives by her lies, such as Samuel, the doctor, and the sheriff, Cathy is no threat. Lee, too, is able to detect Cathy's false nature. It is Lee who warns Adam about the danger of the lie Adam continues to tell his sons about their mother's death. True things do suffer because of Adam's continued lie. Had Aron been told the truth about Cathy rather than having it forced upon him by Cal, his flight to the army, accomplished by his own lying about his age, and his eventual death in the war might have been avoided. Perpetuating the lie makes Adam just as responsible as Cal for Aron's death.

SYMBOLS AND LITERARY DEVICES

East of Eden is no exception to the heavy symbolism that characterizes Steinbeck's fiction. The most easily identifiable symbols in the novel are the names of the purely fictional characters. Adam is symbolic of the biblical first man in many ways. He is given the promise of Eden by his father through the inheritance than allows him to purchase his rich and fertile land in the Salinas Valley. But both Adam and his Eden suffer because he is not able to refuse the evil brought by Cathy, Adam's Eve. Together, Adam and his son Aron are representative of the biblical Abel, who suffered the anger of his brother Cain for being rejected by God. Charles and Caleb symbolize Cain and the guilt wrought by the anger of parental rejection. These classifications of the most blessed and of the rejected are supported by the action in the novel, but become symbolic through the designation of names according to the first letters. Any clear distinction is complicated by other characters whose names begins with "C," Cathy and Cyrus. The first impulse is to assign their characters to the same category as Charles and Caleb, but Steinbeck subverts the analysis at this point by providing characters who have not suffered parental rejection and thus are not driven to crime by the feeling of being unloved. Caleb is the central figure in this subversion. If the symbolic categorization does not hold in analysis, then Caleb, the only "C" character alive at the end of the novel, must not be held to the characterizations of the other figures sharing his first initial, so in Caleb may be found the novel's hope.

The association of Adam and Aron and Charles and Caleb with the biblical Abel and Cain is reinforced by the gifts the brothers in *East of Eden* present to their fathers. Like Abel, who gave to God a sheep as offering, Adam and Aron offer to their fathers living creatures, one a dog and the other a rabbit. Charles's gift to Cyrus of a knife and Caleb's gift to Adam of money are similar to Cain's offering of the fruits of his harvest in that each is a material result of the giver's labor.

ALTERNATIVE READING—ARCHETYPAL READING

Like *The Pearl* (see Chapter 7), *East of Eden* lends itself particularly well to archetypal criticism because of the specific myths, archetypal patterns, and individual archetypes included in the novel that present fundamental meanings of human experience and evoke a universal response by the reader. It also allows the reader to go a further step in analysis and identify where Steinbeck subverts the myth in his efforts to create a new mythology for America.

There are several myths and archetypal motifs operating in *East of Eden*. The paradise motif is one of the clearer patterns presented. When Adam takes Cathy to California, he is determined to create for his Eve a garden in paradise. Adam's ranch does indeed fit the characteristics of the archetypal garden; it is green and abundant. There is water, signifying the mystery of creation and making possible the fertility of the garden. Cathy's pregnancy is also representative of fertility associated with the garden. But Adam's paradise, like his namesake's, becomes a place of sin, the location of the fall that occurs when Cathy rejects her offspring and betrays her husband by shooting him.

The paradise or Edenic myth includes the theme of moral regeneration, which in *East of Eden* is presented by the creation of an American Adam, a hero undertaking a new quest to reclaim the innocence of a pre-fall Eden. This hero, *East of Eden*'s Adam, wanders America after leaving the army idealistically searching for a better place than the home he left behind. After he marries Cathy, he happily rejects the burden of his ancestry by leaving his boyhood home and his brother finally to confront a new paradise of his own. But Adam's quest is foiled; instead of finding Eden he is shown evil. If Adam's dream is the American dream, then his awareness of evil must be a recognition that the dream of America rests side by side with the nightmare of sin America cannot escape.

The motif of initiation is one exemplified by both Adam and Cal. In the initiation motif, the hero undergoes a series of ordeals or tests when passing from youthful ignorance into spiritual maturity. Adam's painful experiences include losing his mother, his relationship with his father and brother, facing the evil that is Cathy and his own spiritual death that this causes, and the death of his son, among others. While Adam makes steps toward spiritual maturity throughout the novel, many with the help of Samuel Hamilton, it is not until he is almost an old man and facing his own death that Adam fully comes of age by acknowledging the damage he has done by loving Aron more than Cal and becoming morally reborn by giving Cal his blessing. Cal's life, also, is presented as an initiation. The ordeals Cal experiences, such as facing his mother and taking responsibility for his actions toward Aron, bring Cal to an understanding that he may make the choice to sin or not. This is Cal's moral rebirth, his coming of age that is initiation.

In addition to patterns and motifs, there are specific archetypal images that reinforce the mythic quality of *East of Eden*. Water has already been discussed as one such image. Others are presented through specific characters. Cyrus and Cathy are both Steinbeck's representations of the shadow archetype, the sinister, devil figure that Carl Jung (see *The Pearl*) calls the shadow. Cyrus is a classic, evil seducer attempting to buy his son's love in order to ensure Adam's participation in his manipulations and the pain he inflicts on others. Even when he is no longer physically present, Cyrus continues, as a shadow, to follow Adam and haunt him in his own fatherhood. Cathy, too, is representative of the sinister shadow figure. Aside from the obvious evil she manifests, her physical characteristics also support such an interpretation. She is born with slightly deformed facial features, feet like hoofs, and abnormal nipples. Yet her ability to seduce others into her web of evil is successful in spite of these features. She truly becomes repulsive as she ages; the greater her sins, the more her body is broken and decays. Cathy is a shadow that haunts the lives of all who come into contact with her.

Cathy also represents the archetype of the terrible mother. This figure in literature includes all the negative aspects of the earth mother and is associated with sexual perversions, fear, darkness, emasculation, and death. As Adam tells her, Cathy is unable to see goodness and beauty, and all that is left is darkness and evil. She is afraid, but she also uses fear to control others. She is a murderer, killing her parents, Mr. Edwards, Faye, and anyone else who threatens her. In shooting Adam and deserting him, Cathy has emasculated the man who loves her. Adam has no relationships with women after Cathy leaves. Perhaps the greatest support for designating Cathy as the terrible mother is the perverse nature of her sexual encounters. Cathy is a whore, one of the literary manifestations of the terrible mother. Other manifestations include the sorceress, the witch, and the siren. But Cathy takes prostitution to the lowest level with the sexual acts, including burning and cutting, she facilitates for her clients. As the terrible mother figure, Cathy Ames finds few equals, except perhaps for Euripides' Medea, who murders her own sons out of jealousy of her husband.

Myth also provides positive archetypal figures, those who help the hero navigate the quest or avoid the snares set by the shadow or the terrible mother. This figure is the wise old man, often presented as the redeemer or savior. The wise old man represents knowledge, wisdom, and intuition, as well as moral qualities of goodness and generosity. The wise old man appears to the hero at a time when the hero lacks the facilities to free himself from a seemingly hopeless situation. Jim, in Mark Twain's *Huckleberry Finn*, is just such a figure. Samuel Hamilton and Lee are the figures in *East of Eden* who provide the other characters, most importantly Adam and Cal, with the guidance necessary to reject Cyrus's example and Cathy's evil, Adam and Cal's specific instances of hopelessness, and thus to take the morally superior path.

In *East of Eden*, Steinbeck relies heavily on myth, but he does not simply include archetype in another retelling of ancient myth. In his letters to Pascal Covici, his editor, Steinbeck claimed that *East of Eden* was a story of replacements. He had discovered that there were other places, other rivers than the one that flows through the Salinas Valley, and he wanted his own sons, Thom and John IV, to discover this also. Just as there are other rivers, there are other stories besides the ones that trap humans in a cycle of sin and jealousy, and *East of Eden* is Steinbeck's other story. It includes many of the patterns and figures shared by the recognized stories, the archetypes, but at the end of Adam's quest the story of mankind is rewritten, leaving hope that Adam's son will exemplify a new story to his sons.

9

The Short Stories

Most of Steinbeck's short stories were written in the early part of his career. It was in this form that he found the clarity of voice and the control over form and device that would characterize his later great works. Steinbeck's first publications were short stories appearing in the *Stanford Spectator* while he was a student. After leaving Stanford, Steinbeck concentrated on his first novel, *Cup of Gold*, published in 1929, but after its publication he turned again to short fiction, publishing the story cycle *The Pastures of Heaven* in 1932. Most of the stories that were published in *The Long Valley* in 1938, Steinbeck's next full length collection of short fiction, had previously appeared in various periodicals, including the *North American Review*, which published "The Gift" in 1933 and "The Chrysanthemums" in 1937, and *Argosy*, in which "The Leader of the People" first appeared in 1936. In 1945, the four stories of *The Red Pony* were published together in a separate volume. Citations from *The Red Pony* stories in the following analysis come from the 1945 Viking collection, while those attributions for "The Chrysanthemums" and "Flight" are from *The Long Valley*. Dates of original publication and dates of publication in collections appear in parentheses after each title.

"THE GIFT" (1933, 1937, 1938, 1945)

SETTING AND PLOT

"The Gift," along with all of the stories in *The Red Pony*, is set on a small, family ranch in the Salinas Valley. Steinbeck relied upon his own memories of his maternal grandparents' ranch in this same valley when he created the story's setting, a place to which he returns in his later works *Of Mice and Men* and *East of Eden*, as well as the stories collected in *The Long Valley*. The ranch is bordered to the east by the Gabilan Mountains, and to the west by another mountain range that figures prominently in "The Great Mountains," the second story in *The Red Pony* cycle.

In the opening scene of "The Gift," the ten-year-old main character, Jody, is awakened from his sleep by the ringing of the triangle that signaled breakfast. This action represents the state of awakening for Jody on which all of *The Red Pony* stories focus. Also important is Jody's reaction to the bell. Not only does it awaken him, he observes its call to eat because it is natural to do so. Just as eating is a natural function of human beings, so too is the stage of growth, of maturing, into which Jody will shortly enter.

That same morning, Jody is given a red pony by his father, Carl Tiflin, who purchased the pony and its red saddle at auction from a bankrupt western show. This gift indicates the recognition that Jody is ready for more mature responsibility and that he needs to be taught how to meet that responsibility. Jody will not have the instant gratification of saddling the pony and flying into the sunset because the pony, like Jody, is untrained. Jody will first have to prove himself by caring for and training the pony, with the help of Billy Buck, the ranch's only hand. Proving himself is not new to Jody, whose father has used this training method before by giving his son a rifle but making him wait two years for the cartridges, longer if Jody treated the rifle irresponsibly. "Nearly all of his father's presents were given with reservations which hampered their value somewhat. It was good discipline" (8).

Perched between childhood and adulthood, Jody uses his gift pony to gain a previously missing respect from his young friends who know the power that a horse provides to the one who rides it. His youthful pride is balanced by the growth Jody undergoes after being presented with the pony. He is patient with the training of Gabilan, the name Jody has given the pony, and he follows the instructions given by Billy Buck, who has a reputation as a horse expert. He also becomes more careful with his other responsibilities around the ranch, such as gathering eggs and filling the wood box, jobs he has previously addressed halfheartedly, in the way of children.

The satisfaction of one day having a pony he can proudly ride is contingent upon Jody's success in raising the pony, but also upon factors outside of Jody's control. He is still a child and cannot escape the constraints of childhood. When Gabilan is left in the corral and it begins to rain while Jody is in school, he cannot rush home to stable the pony because he knows the consequences for leaving school would be severe. He is human, which means he cannot control nature in all of its unpredictability.

Jody does not understand his helplessness in the face of nature, so he looks to Billy Buck, whom he trusts most when it comes to Gabilan, for assurance. When Jody is deciding to leave Gabilan in the corral for the day, he worries that the rain will come, but Billy Buck tells him it is not probable. Even if it does rain, Billy assures him that "a little rain don't hurt a horse" (21). That it does rain is the first broken "promise" Jody suffers. The second is Billy's promise that, if he is around and it does rain, he will put the pony in. When Jody returns from school at the end of the day, Gabilan is still in the corral, drenched and trying unsuccessfully to protect himself from the rain. The third promise Billy is unable to keep is that the pony would be all right. Gabilan becomes severely ill, and regardless of Billy Buck's efforts to cure the pony, it wanders into the hills and dies.

Jody's rage at his own inability to control his fate, and the inability of the adults around him to do so, culminates in a final act of cruelty against one of the buzzards attacking the dead pony, which he beats to death. The story ends with tension rather than resolution. To Jody's rage is added the bitterness of Billy Buck, who turns on Jody's father when Carl attempts to use reason to calm Jody. Billy reminds him angrily that the depth of Jody's feelings, the loss he has experienced, cannot be calmed with reason.

CHARACTERS

Jody Tiflin is described as an obedient little boy, "with hair like dusty yellow grass and with shy polite gray eyes, and with a mouth that worked when he thought" (4). Steinbeck emphasizes the description of Jody's eyes by repeating it later in the story. Jody is also very observant. For instance, he determines the men's plans for each day by listening to the noise of their feet on the floor in the morning to determine what kind of shoes or boots they are wearing. While Jody does seemingly mean or cruel things, like smashing a muskmelon in the garden or abusing Doubletree Mutt, one of the family dogs, he is aware that he has done something bad. These are the actions of a small boy who has not learned how to handle either his boredom or his emotions. In the case of Doubletree Mutt, Jody is later repentant for taking his pain about Gabilan out on the dog, hugging him and kissing his nose to make up.

Some of Jody's traits have been learned from his father. He has adopted much of his father's pride. When he thinks about the first time he will ride Gabilan, he worries that he might have trouble staying on the pony and will grab the saddle horn. Jody believes this would be a sign of weakness, something for which he would feel shame, which is unacceptable for the young boy.

In many ways the best understanding of Jody's character is achieved through the observations made about his pony, observations presented through Jody's own eyes, the point of view from which the story is narrated. The pony is described as learning well how to be led by the halter. "It was not long until Gabilan was perfect at it. But in many ways he was a bad pony" (17). Like the pony, Jody is obedient and learns his lessons well, but he is young and will kick against the forces that attempt to constrain or "bridle" him. Jody's own observation about Gabilan's resentment of being bridled answer the questions of whether Jody's misbehaviors indicate true badness or not. Jody "rejoiced" at Gabilan's resentment "for he knew that only a mean-souled horse does not resent training" (18).

Billy Buck is an important character not only because of his part in the action of the story, but because he also contributes to the way the reader reacts to Jody's actions. With Billy Buck, Steinbeck draws a picture of the stereotypical cowboy, down to the walrus mustache and Stetson hat. Steinbeck develops the character of Billy Buck more fully than either Carl Tiflin, who is given very little physical description, or Jody's mother. The reason for the more complete development of Billy Buck may be the similarities between him and Jody. Both have quiet, gray eyes. There is also a connection between the manner with which these characters conduct themselves. Each knows his place at the ranch; Jody is obedient, while Billy Buck observes the propriety of his position as a employee. The similarities between the two function to focus the reader on these characters and to offer an idea of what kind of man Jody will become. By doing this, Steinbeck is able to control, to some extent, the readers' reactions to Jody's seemingly cruel outbursts. The more Jody is identified with Billy Buck, the more the outcome for this boy is considered positive.

Whether Jody is like Billy Buck because of the part the ranch hand has had in raising him or because there is a natural affinity, Billy is clearly the prevalent role model in Jody's life. Jody finds it easier to talk with Billy Buck than either of his parents, and Billy Buck understands Jody's feelings, as is illustrated when Jody wants to name his pony after "the grandest and prettiest things he knew" (11), the Gabilan Mountains. Billy knows the importance of the name for the boy without explanation from Jody and suggests only that Jody shorten the name to Gabilan. It is Billy's understanding of Jody that places him between the boy and his father, and thus against Billy Buck's own boss, in the story's final scene.

When describing Carl Tiflin, Steinbeck writes only that he is tall. The stature corresponds to the other characteristics offered for Jody's father. Throughout the story cycle, he is described as stern, and this is supported by people's reactions to Carl. His stern nature is the result of a sense of pride and demand for dignity that dictate Carl's actions and his expectations for others. He does not want Jody to teach the pony tricks because it will take away the horse's dignity. He hates anything that indicates weakness. Carl's character traits create a distance between himself and his wife and son, and he suffers from this distance. His feelings are hurt when Jody, who is worried about his pony, fails to laugh at a funny story Carl tells to cheer up the boy. Even when he tries to show compassion for Jody after the red pony dies, he attempts to console his son by applying reason rather than understanding, treating his son like a man rather than a boy. The story ends with Billy Buck, not Carl, rescuing Jody from the tragedy of his loss.

Mrs. Tiflin is only referred to once by her given name, Ruth, which reflects the general lack of this character's development. As is typical for Steinbeck, what is presented is the description of her eyes, which are "brooding and kind" (25). She rarely smiles, but she also does not show any other apparent emotion in the story. In a story with so few characters, to have one who is always connected to the action of the story but about whom so little can be known might seem to be a flaw on the author's part; however, the story is about the growth experiences of a male child, occurring at a time when such experiences are considered distinctly male. The underdevelopment of Mrs. Tiflin, then, serves to emphasize how the other characters, Billy Buck and Carl Tiflin, contribute to Jody's growth.

THEMES

Critics debate whether *The Red Pony* stories represent the coming of age of young Jody Tiflin. Regardless of whether there is a moment in the stories when Jody steps across the threshold into maturity, there are many moments that contribute to his growth, his nearing that threshold. In "The Gift," the culminating moment is the death of his red pony. How Jody deals with this loss will determine the degree of growth resulting from the experience. Rather than fully presenting the outcome of the experience, Steinbeck ends the story with conflict. The first is represented by the tension between Billy Buck and Carl Tiflin. Billy Buck is concerned with caring for Jody's broken heart, with acknowledging the way Jody feels after the loss, while Carl tries to calm Jody by showing him how irrational his anger at the buzzards is. The second conflict between Billy Buck and Jody results in an additional loss for the young boy. Because Billy has not saved Jody's pony, and has broken his word to Jody that the pony would be fine, Jody blames Billy Buck; thus, the reverence he holds for his cowboy hero is lost.

However Jody might change after this experience, the fact that he will change is the significant consideration. The dual loss he suffers forces Jody toward an adult reality where what is loved must eventually be lost, and where humans cannot be bigger than life because life, by its nature, includes failure.

"THE LEADER OF THE PEOPLE" (1936, 1938, 1945)

SETTING AND PLOT

The story "The Leader of the People" opens on a still, windless Saturday afternoon in March. The inactivity is too much for the story's major character, young Jody Tiflin, and he breaks the quiet by intentionally scuffing his shoes and using a cat as a target for throwing practice. Learning from Billy Buck, the ranch hand, that the hay baling is finished, Jody anticipates further activity against his boredom in the hunting of mice in the leftover, soggy hay. The overall picture created is that of a young boy with much to do isolated in a world that offers little outlet for his physical and creative energies. This sense of isolation is reinforced by Jody's overeager response to seeing his father ride toward the house with a letter in his hand. The letter is sure to bring news of some kind, and any news will bring something fresh to upset the monotony of Jody's life on the ranch.

The letter is from Jody's maternal grandfather, announcing that he will be arriving for a visit. The mail has been slow, and his grandfather will be arriving that very day. The reactions to the news are conflicting. Jody is glad, and it seems that his mother is also, but her happiness quickly turns to anger when her husband Carl begins to complain about his father-in-law's visit. The problem, Carl tells her, is that her father "[j]ust talks" (80) when he comes, talks about the same thing over and over again, crossing the plains and fighting the Indians.

Leaving the conflict at home, Jody goes to meet his grandfather on the road. While he waits, Jody's boyishness takes over, but he stops his play when he sees his grandfather and comes to the older man "at a dignified walk" (82). It is clear that Jody has great respect for his grandfather. Jody invites him to join the upcoming mouse hunt but admits it would not be as exciting as hunting Indians.

It also becomes apparent that Billy Buck holds the old man in high esteem. The ranch hand has shaved on a nonshaving day to honor the grandfather's visit. Jody's grandfather expresses the same reverence for Billy Buck because he knew and respected Billy Buck's father and because he knows Billy Buck's abilities as a horse man. The growing number of people who revere the grandfather serves to distinguish Carl Tiflin as the antagonist because of his different attitude about his father-in-law.

Carl's contrariness is made evident when, after dinner, the old man begins telling his stories about crossing the plains, bringing the people west through the double threats of nature and natives. Carl cruelly insults him by reminding him that the story has been told many times before. Jody is empathetic; he knows how Carl can make a person feel, how his grandfather's "insides were collapsed and empty" (87), because this is the way Carl often speaks to Jody. As a gesture of understanding, Jody invites his grandfather to continue with the story.

As he later lies in bed, Jody's thoughts provide another reason the young boy wants to continue to hear his grandfather's stories. These stories are about an "impossible world," "a world that had ceased to be forever" (89). With the possible exception of Billy Buck, Jody believes heroes ceased to exist when the world his grandfather tells of ceased to exist, and he longs for such a world again.

The next morning, Carl complains to his wife again about the grandfather's stories, and the old man overhears the insult. Carl tries to apologize, but the gesture is not enough to erase the grandfather's hurt feelings. When Jody later assures him that he would still like to hear the story, his grandfather is hesitant. He says he cannot communicate what he really wants to say when he tells the stories, that he cannot make people feel what he wants them to feel. None of the adventures, not even the goal, was as important as the western movement itself, how all of the people became "one big crawling beast" (93).

Jody tries to offer hope to his grandfather by saying that maybe he could become a leader of the people just as his grandfather was. When his suggestion is met with the response that people no longer desire "westering" and, therefore, have no need of leaders, Jody is left with little to give his grandfather to ease the sadness. The best he can do is to make his grandfather another glass of lemonade.

CHARACTERS

Billy Buck is not a major character presence in this short story; rather, one of his roles here is as a counter to Carl Tiflin. The more significant function of Billy Buck is to illustrate the type of man Jody's grandfather once was. Jody believes that heroes have ceased to exist, except for Billy Buck. The grandfather, too, associates Billy Buck with the old heroes, admiring him both for his lineage and his own special abilities as a cowboy. Billy Buck's inactivity in the story serves to create of him more a mythic character than a real person.

Billy Buck's warning to Jody that he must get Carl's permission before hunting the mice continues to show Carl as a stern and controlling character. Yet

Carl's more complex emotional qualities, presented elsewhere in *The Red Pony* stories, are more fully developed in "The Leader of the People." His anger about the grandfather's visit seems irrational to the reader. What harm could there be in having to listen, again, to the worn out stories of an old man? The answer lies in what his father-in-law represents, the ability to lead, to be the "the head" (93) of a group of people traveling through an "impossible world" (89). That Carl himself is not a leader is illustrated by Jody's challenge to his position when Jody asks his grandfather to continue his story after Carl's initial insult. Jody clearly does not believe Carl is capable of heroism. Previously Carl has at least represented manly pride for Jody, but when Carl apologizes for his second cruel insult, Jody sees even that diminishing. "It was a terrible thing to him to retract a word, but to retract it in shame was infinitely worse" (92).

In "The Leader of the People," Mrs. Tiflin is a flat, nondeveloping character. Her anger at Carl for not wanting her father to visit establishes the major conflict of the story, and her explanation of why her father tells his stories provides a meaningful introduction of the father's character, more gracefully than if it had come through the narrator. Her importance, then, is as a vehicle for Steinbeck's storytelling.

An understanding of self as responsible to and for other people is important to the promise of Jody's maturity. Jody is still a boy. Steinbeck introduces him as a "little boy" (76), just as he does in each of *The Red Pony* stories. Therefore, it seems natural for him to test adult authority by scuffing his shoes and using the cat for target practice, just as it is quite natural when he tests the use of grown-up profanity on Billy Buck. It is clear, however, that Jody is making steps toward adulthood. He sees beyond his own needs to the needs of others and beyond his own pain to the pain in others. The major step that occurs toward his growth is Jody's reaching outside of himself to address what he sees, as when he asks his grandfather to continue his story after being criticized by Carl, or bringing his grandfather lemonade after he tells Jody that people no longer desire the movement that brought him west to the Salinas Valley.

It is difficult to discuss Jody's grandfather in the normal terms used for character analysis. He does not develop in the story but rather is the impetus for the story. While he elicits an emotional response from the reader, his more important function is symbolic. He is a nameless character whose description conjures a mythic picture for the reader. His fully black clothing is set in contrast to his white beard and eyebrows. His eyes are blue. Alone these details are only slightly meaningful, but considered against the lack of physical description given throughout *The Red Pony* stories for the major characters in the cycle, greater meaning is invited. Indeed, those characters for whom eye color is given all have gray eyes, so in providing color for the grandfather's picture, Steinbeck creates a sense that the grandfather is somehow greater than the life of the

Tiflin ranch. The grandfather is the bearer of myth, the myth that Jody yearns for and that Carl disdains.

THEME

"The Leader of the People" is different from the other stories in *The Red Pony* cycle for various reasons. First, while the major theme of maturation is the same, the lessons presented to young Jody Tiflin do not come directly through the mysteries or tragedies of nature, but rather through the example of human experience, specifically that of Jody's maternal grandfather. Additionally, while the major conflicts remain between humans and their environments, they materialize as conflicts between humans. Finally, the thematic emphasis of the story is on loss suffered; however, the primary loss in "The Leader of the People" is not presented solely as Jody's loss, but as a more universal loss in which Jody participates.

There is less literary naturalism in "The Leader of the People" than in the other *Red Pony* stories. The story's themes are more consistent with those of modernism, specifically the death of myth as dealt with in much of the poetry of those authors, such as T. S. Eliot and Ezra Pound, who defined literary modernism in the early twentieth century. The importance of myth is presented in the character of Jody's grandfather. (See the discussion of myth and archetypes in Chapters 7 and 8.) Like the mythological figures of old, the most significant action of the grandfather's life, leading the "westering," was something his daughter says "he was born to do" (80). It was chosen for him. His physical appearance reinforces this special, almost superhuman quality.

The grandfather is also the storyteller, the one who carries the myth and keeps it alive. Like the oral historians of old, when telling his story, "his voice dropped to a curious low sing-song, dropped into a tonal groove the story had worn for itself" (86). He continues to tell his story; he must, even when he knows no one wants to hear, because to tell is to keep the myth alive, and it is myth that gives meaning to human existence by explaining human existence. The myth is no longer working, however. The world of the grandfather's story no longer exists, and few people are worthy, according to Jody, of the heroic actions of that world. It is difficult to determine whether the world has changed and the people are no longer hungry for heroic experience because the myth that defines that world has died, or whether myth has died because the people have changed. What is sure is that the new world suggested by "The Leader of the People" is a bleak and sad one.

Directly connected to the importance of myth presented in the story is the importance of language. Carl uses his language irresponsibly and shamefully and must take back his words. But the word is more powerful than its sound, and the damage done to Carl's pride and to the grandfather's feelings cannot be repaired simply by retracting the word. The potential of language, and therefore of myth, is great. The grandfather believes he has failed as a storyteller, that he cannot find the right language to make the people feel what the story should make them feel, so on some level he feels responsible for the reaction of people like Carl to his story and, thus, for the death of the story itself.

One final theme of "The Leader of the People" must be discussed here because, even though it is embedded in the grandfather's pain over a changing world and is not fully developed, it is one of Steinbeck's most prevalent themes and is the major theme of his greatest work, *The Grapes of Wrath*. Through discussions with his friend Ed Ricketts, a marine biologist, and through observation of creatures in nature, Steinbeck developed his philosophy of the phalanx. This idea claims that individuals forced to act as part of a group must shift from a focus on the self, the "I," to a focus on the group, or "we." Thus, the nature of the individual in the group changes. As a result of this shift, the goal of the group becomes less important than the experience of being a part of the group. When Jody's grandfather expresses his regret that he couldn't seem to make people feel anything when he told his story, he is expressing Steinbeck's idea of the phalanx. Including this idea at the end of the story, indeed at the end of the entire story cycle, can result in a negative reading of the possibilities facing young Jody Tiflin. If his grandfather is correct and people do not have the desire for "westering," then they will never have the good fortune to experience the "we" thinking that takes over under such circumstances. Jody will not have such possibility. On the other hand, Jody can be considered proof that his grandfather is not correct, that people do still have the hunger for heroic experience that can only occur when groups of people driven by a common goal become one in meeting that goal. If this is the case, Steinbeck leaves us with a larger outcome than simply a hopefulness about young Jody Tiflin finally reaching maturity.

"THE CHRYSANTHEMUMS" (1937, 1938)

The first story of John Steinbeck's collection *The Long Valley*, "The Chrysanthemums" is set on a ranch in the Salinas Valley belonging to Henry Allen and his wife Elisa, who is the story's protagonist. The description of the landscape provided in the first paragraph of the story establishes the isolation Elisa experiences on the ranch. The Salinas Valley, and thus the ranch, is separated from the rest of the world by the "high grey-flannel fog of winter" (1) that allows no sunshine to penetrate. In this darkness, the valley is in a state of anticipation, which foreshadows the coming action of the story. As the narration moves its focus to the Allen ranch, the state of waiting exists in the preparation of the orchards to receive the anticipated rain, and in Elisa's preparation of her chrysanthemums for a new year's growth. Her flower garden, where Elisa is first introduced, is the setting for the first scene of four in the short story.

Henry is speaking with two strangers while Elisa is cutting and thinning her chrysanthemums. In her garden, Elisa is strong and sure, deftly removing the old growth with scissors. In her work, described as "over-eager, over-powerful" (2), Elisa is clearly releasing frustrated energy, but the source of her frustration is not clear until Henry comes to the garden to tell her he has sold thirty of their cattle for a good price and suggests they celebrate by going to town for dinner. When Elisa talks to Henry, her body becomes straight and sharp, almost like her scissors, and her tone with Henry is short, almost curt. She reacts suspiciously when Henry acknowledges her gift for growing flowers, and there is no indication that Elisa is excited about going out that evening.

Elisa returns to her work after Henry leaves to do other work on the ranch. Her garden is now further described, with the emphasis on the complete order that is found there. The planting trenches are parallel, and the dead leaves are placed in a neat pile after Elisa cuts them. While she is working, a wagon traveling down the road turns onto the road leading to the Allen house. An immediate contrast between Elisa's garden and the wagon is established. The wagon is "curious," with "clumsy, crooked letters" painted haphazardly on its side (4). The items listed on the side of the wagon are misspelled, and the offer of repairs being advertised is presented in the single word "Fixed" (4). Even the man driving the wagon is in disarray, with an unshaved face, worn out clothing, and calloused, dirty hands. The wagon stops as it comes to the fence surrounding Elisa's garden. His horse and donkey are in a similar condition as their owner; they "drooped like unwatered flowers" (4), a description that intensifies the attention Elisa gives to her own flowers.

Within the fenced-in garden, Elisa is quick to laugh at the stranger's warning about the ferocity of his dog. Elisa's laughter is unexpected after the tone of her earlier exchange with Henry. As the tinker begins asking directions from Elisa, she puts her scissors into her pocket and removes her gloves, as if she is shedding her protective armor. When the tinker begins his sales pitch, however, Elisa's "eyes hardened with resistance" (5). She becomes short with him and tells him she has no work, maintaining her hardness even after he attempts to gain her sympathy by whining about his lack of work that day.

When the tinker, obviously looking for something to help his case, asks about Elisa's chrysanthemums, she softens once again and begins to drop her defenses, allowing the tinker to lean over the fence to speak to her, now actively penetrating her protective area. He tells her he has a customer who is looking for chrysanthemum seeds. The opportunity to share her expertise continues the transformation of Elisa, whose "eyes shone" (7), and she takes off her hat, freeing her hair and herself for whatever will happen next with the stranger.

As Elisa is preparing some chrysanthemum shoots in a red pot for the tinker and giving him instructions for their proper care, her ability to communicate with him becomes full, almost to the point of intimacy. She is trying to tell him about the proper time to trim the buds, but this is something natural, instinctive for Elisa, something for which she has never before had to find words. She does find words, however, but instead of giving instructions she tells him about the feel of the earth and the plants on her fingers, and the emotion that she derives from such an experience. Sharing this with the tinker causes Elisa to become passionate. The two are now talking in figurative language about the intensity of feeling itself. This is the first moment in the story when Elisa is shown to make real emotional contact with another human, and her fingers come close to making physical contact, but she stops short of touching his leg, she restrains herself from the touching, and the contact is broken. He is uncomfortable, and she is ashamed and guilty.

Out of her guilt, Elisa finds two old and dented pans for the tinker to repair, and the scene changes from her garden to the tinker's wagon. Elisa was the one in control while they were speaking at the garden, but control shifts to the tinker when they move to his space. She asks about his sleeping in the wagon, but when she tells him it would be nice if women could live as he does, he tells her it is the wrong way for a woman to live. Elisa becomes defensive and challenges him. Rather than answering her, the tinker backs down, knowing by now that she is not only strong willed and determined, but also passionate, which is more than the tinker can handle. After she pays him and reveals that she knows how to sharpen her own scissors and beat the dents out of her own pans, the tinker readies to leave, but not before offering a final comment that his life would be very lonely for a woman.

As Elisa watches the tinker leave, it is clear that she has undergone change. No longer seeking the protection of her garden, she stands fully open to the world. She mouths the words "Good-bye—good-bye," then whispers, "That's a bright direction. There's a glowing there" (10). Elisa is shocked by her own words. In baring herself to the world, she has also become open to herself and for the first time she is truly communicating with herself.

The scene now changes to the Allen house. Elisa strips off her dirty clothing and cleans her body harshly and thoroughly. The first inclination is to interpret this as Elisa cleaning the dirt of her experience with the tinker away, as if she is now ashamed and wants to cleanse herself of the memories, but that would be incorrect. After she is finished, Elisa slowly dresses herself in her finest clothes. She is in no hurry to cover herself again because she has just experienced the joy of being uncovered, both literally and figuratively. The bathing is a complete washing away of the old Elisa, the Elisa that could not communicate with herself or with others, the Elisa that kept herself fully covered in heavy clothing to protect herself from herself and others.

When Henry comes into the house, Elisa slips back into her earlier defensiveness. He asks where she is, and she says she is in her room. Her claim to the couple's bedroom indicates that she is not quite ready to open herself to Henry. While he prepares for their evening out, Elisa sits "primly and stiffly" on the front porch, still uncomfortable (11). When he comes onto the porch and compliments Elisa's appearance, she is suspicious and attacks him verbally. He notes that she looks changed, "strong and happy," which finally disarms Elisa (11). Elisa is "complete again," (11) but this is not a complete Elisa whom Henry has ever known before.

As Elisa and Henry are driving to town, the final scene in the short story, she sees on the road the chrysanthemum shoots and the dirt in which they were planted. She is saddened until she realizes that the tinker threw them on the road so that he could keep the red pot in which the young flowers were planted. As their car passes the tinker's wagon, she looks at Henry, avoiding the sight of the tinker. After they have passed, the tinker becomes a part of the past, only a memory. "She did not look back" (12).

Now Henry notes that Elisa is different again. She makes a positive statement about their upcoming dinner and asks if they may have wine. She then inquires about the prizefights that Henry had earlier suggested in jest they attend. Elisa's questions indicate her openness to an evening at the fights, and Henry says he will take her. As if too much new-found freedom in one day might be too much, Elisa says that she really does not want to go. "It will be enough if we have wine. It will be plenty" (13). As the story closes, Elisa is trying to hide her tears from her husband.

CHARACTERS

When "The Chrysanthemums" opens, Elisa, the story's main character, is trapped in emotional isolation. She stays protected behind the fence of her garden, armored by her heavy clothing, and armed with her scissors, ready to defend herself against anyone who might try to get too close. From inside her self-imposed prison, Elisa watches her husband talk with the cattle buyers, just as she watches the rest of the world from this garden where she establishes the order and is in full control. She is good at gardening, but she is not good at people.

What allows Elisa to free herself from the isolation is a stranger. He does not know her, and thus, she has nothing to fear from his judgment. But even with the stranger, with whom she was quick to laugh, Elisa remains guarded. It is not until she is convinced that he is truly interested in her chrysanthemums that

Elisa takes off her hat and allows her hair and herself the freedom to communicate with this tinker. Once given permission, Elisa opens up completely, and the passion that seems to have been directed only to her chrysanthemums before now flows out toward another human being. Her isolation is broken.

Elisa is not isolated because someone else has imprisoned her. It is her own self-image that caused Elisa to construct barriers that protect her from other people. Once she tastes the freedom of connecting with someone else, it is Elisa who makes the even more difficult choice to connect with her own husband. Fortunately, her worst fears are not realized in this choice. Even when she allows others into her experience, Elisa still has control over her own life, for example, choosing just to have the bottle of wine.

Both Henry Allen and the tinker are minor characters in "The Chrysanthemums." There is clear proof that the relationship between Elisa and Henry is not satisfying, but there is no indication that Henry has any negative intentions that cause the problems in the marriage. Indeed, Henry is a character type. In this case, Henry is a typical American husband of the early twentieth century. It is what is characteristic of the type that helps to, in part, explain Elisa's emotional isolation. As the husband, Henry assumes responsibility for the management of the ranch, selling the thirty head of cattle without consulting his wife. It is his price that Henry almost gets for the cattle, not their price. Even though he asks for confirmation from Elisa, it is also Henry who decides how they will celebrate the sale and at what time they will do so. Henry is the world that Elisa believes allows her no control; thus, he is the world from which she separates herself. When Elisa undergoes a change at the end of the story, Henry changes also. His attention is now fully on what Elisa is feeling and what Elisa wishes to do. Because she is more open and less of a mystery, Henry is less afraid.

The tinker also represents a character type in "The Chrysanthemums." He is the dark stranger who arrives to upset the established order. The tinker's darkness goes beyond the color of his clothing and his eyes to his actions. He deceives Elisa by making her think he is a good man doing a favor for another customer by taking her the chrysanthemum shoots. His motive is simply to get Elisa to give him some pots to mend or scissors to sharpen, not to seduce her. But she is seduced into showing her raw emotions to this man, which is more than he is capable of handling. He is like Elisa; he has constructed a solitary world that he controls. But he is different from Elisa; when the opportunity for a human connection arises, the tinker retreats to his anvil and hammer.

THEMES

"The Chrysanthemums" is one of Steinbeck's earlier works of fiction, but it presents the social themes that would mark the author's work for many years.

At a broad level, all of these themes present the difficulties faced by individuals in the social context. Within this general theme is the more specific theme presented in "The Chrysanthemums" of the conflict between the needs of the individual and the needs of others. Elisa needs to feel safe, and she only knows how to ensure her safety by withdrawing into a solitary world where she maintains control. But this world is real only for Elisa, and those who exist outside of her reality must suffer exclusion. The conflict results from those others who do not seek the safety of isolation but instead need and desire companionship and community. Henry makes clear attempts to penetrate Elisa's emotions but is met with coldness, which forces Henry into his own isolated world. When she breaks out of her self-imposed imprisonment and makes steps toward true social connection, Elisa finds true freedom, which Steinbeck would have us know cannot be found by an individual living in isolation.

Issues of gender and sexual roles are also of thematic concern in "The Chrysanthemums." In many respects, Elisa has isolated herself because as a female there already exists an exclusion from the larger, male-dominated society. Henry's business dealings illustrate this truth. When the tinker arrives, he is shown to be almost an outcast from the larger society. He has no home, he lives with animals, and there is no order to his life. Elisa, then, does not perceive in the tinker the same threat based on gender difference as she does from Henry. With the traditional gender roles eliminated, Elisa is free to also assume different sexual responses with the tinker than she would with Henry. While her responses to Henry are described as sharp and cold, with the tinker she melts into an emotionally passionate state. He represents no gender oppression, and similarly, he represents no sexual oppression, allowing Elisa to become empowered sexually.

SYMBOLS

"The Chrysanthemums" serves as a good example of Steinbeck's use of multiple symbols in his short stories, especially those that are not part of a story cycle. The presentation of symbols begins in the first paragraph of the story with Steinbeck's description of the Salinas Valley. The isolation of the valley is symbolic of Elisa's isolation. There is no sunshine in the valley, just as there is no light in Elisa's life, and just like Elisa, the vegetation along the river is sharp. While the valley sits in anticipation, so too does Elisa. Another layer of representation is found in the symbolic connection between the valley and Elisa's garden. As such, the valley is not only Elisa's isolation, but also the physical means of that isolation. The valley becomes isolated because it is surrounded by mountains; the garden is a place of isolation because it is surrounded by a fence.

Her scissors also have a symbolic connection to Elisa. They are powerful scissors used to cut down the "small and easy" (2) chrysanthemum stems to make room for new ones. Elisa deals with Henry in much the same way that the scissors deal with the flower stems, sharply and with ease. That she quickly puts the scissors away when the tinker arrives indicates the difference between Henry, who is related to her solitude, and the stranger, with whom Elisa does not foresee a need for the same harshness she shows to her husband. The tinker comes from outside of the closed-in valley and, thus, brings with him the promise of human contact.

The prizefights and the wine also represent experience outside of Elisa's isolation. Elisa's limited experience focuses on the natural habits of flowers as they occur inside a fenced-in garden, and Elisa knows everything about the chrysanthemums' habits. But what goes on in the fighting ring, also a fenced in area, is a mystery to Elisa, and it is a mystery that involves humans rather than plants. Once Elisa frees herself to the possibilities of experience outside of her protected environment, she becomes curious and thus asks Henry about the prizefights. The wine, too, represents an element of the unknown that Elisa, through her experience with the tinker, finds the courage to discover.

"FLIGHT" (1938)

"Flight" opens with a description of a family farm near Monterey, California, owned by the widowed Mama Torres and her three children. Their farm exists precariously on a slope of land between cliffs dropping steeply to the ocean and sharp mountains looming in the sky, a description that figuratively characterizes the life of the family living on this land. Mama Torres has raised her livestock and her children alone for ten years since her husband was killed by a rattlesnake bite. Emilio and Rosy are the young and more industrious children, while Pepe, 19, is described as congenial but lazy.

The action begins when Mama Torres, searching for Pepe so she can send him on his first adult errand to Monterey, finds her oldest child throwing a knife, his inheritance from his father, at a post serving as a target. While he may be generally unmotivated, Pepe is diligent in his knife throwing, and his accuracy is important to later events in the short story. When Mama tells him she is sending him alone to Monterey for medicine and salt, Pepe understands the symbolic importance of the errand as his first adult responsibility. The occasion is almost ceremonial; Pepe will be allowed to wear his father's hatband and green handkerchief. When his mother admonishes him to take care of these prized family possessions, Pepe proclaims that he is a man, a determination on which the entire story rests.

Mama Torres verbally denies Pepe's manhood, telling him instead that he is a "foolish chicken" (31), but to herself confirms that he is close to manhood. When the other children question her about Pepe becoming a man on that day, since he was given such an adult responsibility, Mama Torres tells them "a boy gets to be a man when a man is needed" (32). The question for the reader becomes whether at any point in the story Pepe faces the need and truly becomes a man. The next action presents the first opportunity for such a consideration.

While at the home of a family friend in Monterey, Pepe, who was drinking wine, quarreled with a man who called him names and then threw his knife, killing the man. After hurrying home, Pepe's explanation to his mother rings with childishness. He tells her the knife "went almost by itself. It flew, it darted before [he] knew it" (33). With no time to concern herself with what has already happened, Mama quickly organizes Pepe's flight from those who will surely come after him looking for revenge or for justice. She gathers a water bag, a blanket, meat jerky, a rifle and the only ten cartridges the family has, and Pepe's father's black coat. Now fully equipped for adulthood, Pepe must flee into the dark mountains. Mama Torres's last preparations are to warn Pepe not to speak to the "dark watching men" (35) in the mountains and to remember his prayers. As he says good-bye to his family, Pepe reminds his mother, "I am a man" (35).

The possibility of Pepe's death during his flight is introduced by the formal death wail his mother cries after his departure, and by his sister's claim to Emilio that Pepe is not dead, "not yet" (36). The reader is not sure whether these responses are a foreshadowing of later action, whether they are introduced by Steinbeck to heighten the suspense of Pepe's flight, or whether they indicate that while Pepe is not literally dead, he is dead to his family. Whatever the true meaning, at this point in the story, Steinbeck succeeds in increasing the readers' level of anticipation.

Pepe's journey into the mountains begins easily enough. The path is worn and recognizable, and there is water and lush vegetation along the trial. As he enters the forest of redwoods, his journey becomes darker, and Pepe becomes more cautious. Farther along the trail, the landscape becomes sharper and wilder; water becomes scarcer, and the vegetation begins to disappear. As if to signal his entrance into a place of death, Pepe sees the dark watchers his mother had warned about observing him from the mountain ridge. He is allowed to continue undisturbed because he ignores the watchers. Additional emphasis is placed on death as Steinbeck soon begins to describe the landscape as "dead" and "starving" (39). Pepe soon notices the silhouette of a man in the distance, the first evidence that he is being followed. Needing rest and water, Pepe rides to a small grassy area where he waters his horse and eats jerky, realizing for the first time he no longer has a knife with which to cut it. He says his prayers and sleeps.

Pepe's judgment in stopping at the grassy area should be questioned here. The reader suspects it would be the first place his followers would search for a young man inexperienced at evading capture. Indeed, his horse whinnies, waking Pepe and alerting him to the presence of others. Pepe quickly saddles his horse and flees, leaving behind his hat, the first important piece of equipment Pepe will lose from being quicker to act than to think.

When morning comes, Pepe believes he has evaded the followers and relaxes his guard, only to have his horse shot out from under him. Now he must crawl like an animal to find protection. From the vantage point where he is hiding, Pepe sees movement and fires his rifle, which is immediately answered by the pursuers. This shot shatters the granite next to Pepe and a piece of the rock cuts its way into his hand. It is not clear whether the followers would have detected Pepe in his hiding place. His decision to fire the first shot gave away his location, resulting in the injury to his hand, and must be called into question in a final analysis of cause and effect that becomes necessary when finally considering the state of Pepe's manhood.

As Pepe continues to crawl through the rocks seeking protection, the pain spreads to his arm from blood poisoning that is traveling from his hand. His father's coat is irritating his swollen arm, and Pepe removes it, leaving it behind as he crawls on. He now has no hat to protect him from the sun and no coat to protect him from the cold of night. Furthermore, he is leaving behind those things of his father's, the hatband and the coat, that represent his move into manhood.

A lion watches Pepe as he makes a hole in the muddy earth to collect water. The lion is waiting patiently for the death it can sense. But Pepe continues to struggle against death and finds the energy to evade the followers once again when he hears the close sounds of horses and dogs. In this moment of flight, Pepe forgets his rifle, without which he will be completely defenseless. Night comes shortly, and Pepe experiences a moment when his "brain spun in a big spiral up and away from him" (47). With morning, however, "his eyes were sane again" (47). But it is clear sanity cannot stop the gangrene that is now filling the wound in his hand or the death the gangrene promises.

In the full light of day, Pepe makes a final decision about his life. With the buzzards circling above him, Pepe says a final prayer and climbs to the top of the ridge where he stands fully exposed to his chasers. The first bullet misses him, but the second finds its target, throwing Pepe off the ridge to his final burial spot on the side of the mountain.

CHARACTERS

Pepe Torres is the main character in "Flight." It is through Pepe that Steinbeck raises the central thematic question of the short story: When does a boy become a man? Pepe is introduced as an indolent nineteen–year old whose laziness makes life more difficult for his widowed mother. Indeed, because he is the oldest male in the home, his seeming irresponsibility makes him a less than sympathetic character from the start. When his mother gives him the grown-up responsibility of going alone to Monterey, there is less a sense that he is truly eager to be an adult helper to his mother than that he wants the opportunity to display the material signs of manhood, his father's hat band and green handkerchief. So, when Pepe kills the man in Monterey because his manhood was questioned by the calling of names, the reader is not convinced by Pepe's explanation to his mother.

Ultimately, Pepe does become a man, but this occurs only in the final action of the short story. He exercises poor judgment through much of his flight, succumbing to the temptation of grass and water at the risk to his safety, losing the very tools he will need for survival, and impetuously giving away his location by shooting first at his followers, the action that begins the process of disease to which Pepe succumbs. Finally, it is in his giving in to the reality of his situation, realizing he is dying from the poison in his body and has no further chance of escape, that Pepe makes the fully adult decision to give himself over to death, to accept the consequences of all of his actions. Then he makes his death as quick and painless as possible by standing as a ready target for his hunters.

The function of Mama Torres and her other children in the story is to introduce the question of Pepe's manhood. It remains a question even after he has left home because of Mama's claim to the children that "A boy gets to be a man when a man is needed" (32). This is the standard against which all of Pepe's actions are be gauged. Additionally, Mama and the children provide the initial consideration of Pepe meeting his death during his flight. The reader will be waiting for the death that Mama laments and Rosy predicts.

THEME

"Flight" is often used by scholars as a near perfect example of literary naturalism, the idea that humans can do nothing to control natural forces, such as biology and heredity. Authors were hesitant to portray naturalism in its purest form because the outcome of such a presentation would be so bleak, so lacking in possible hope for humanity. In most of his work even Steinbeck gave his characters the ability to survive environmental and hereditary forces by adaptation. But "Flight" does not leave the reader with any such hope. Because of his cultural heredity, over which Pepe has not control, he kills another man in a macho attempt to protect his manhood. Society and culture dictate accountability for the crime, and the instinct for survival dictates flight on Pepe's part. The environment to which he flees is too brutal for an inexperienced young man to overcome, and his inexperience also makes him vulnerable to his pursuers. There is little chance from the beginning of Pepe surviving his circumstances, and Steinbeck does not disappoint any hopes for a purely naturalistic resolution to the conflict between man and nature—nature wins.

What happens to Pepe as he progresses in his flight is also thematically important. The further he gets from his home, his society, and the longer he is alone, the more Steinbeck describes Pepe in terms of animal behavior. His crawling is like that of a rattlesnake. As he gets thirstier, the sounds coming from his mouth are hisses. He sheds all the equipment of human survival and faces his situation like an animal. There is little hope Pepe would have survived the consequence of his crime if he did not run away, but in fleeing society, he suffers a loss of personhood, which emphasizes the inevitability of his death.

SYMBOLS

As is characteristic of Steinbeck's work, he begins "Flight" with a vivid description of the setting, which itself stands as representation of the Torres family's existence, vulnerable to the elements that threaten it from all directions. The mountains continue to take on symbolic meaning as Pepe journeys into them, when they begin to represent the power and danger of nature. The mountains contribute greatly to Pepe's eventual death. In this environment, human rules do not ultimately control experience, and human tools, even if Pepe had not lost most of his equipment, are of little use. At the literal level, the sliver of granite that leads to Pepe's death comes directly from the mountains.

Pepe's knife is another important symbol in the story. A knife can be an item of everyday usefulness, or it can be a weapon. Pepe chooses to use the knife as a weapon when he believes his manhood is threatened. As a result, he does not have the knife when there is a clear threat against his very life. In many ways, Pepe acts childishly with the knife, which prevents him from living into manhood. The knife becomes the initial cause of the events leading to Pepe's death. Other items of symbolic significance are the hatband, handkerchief, and coat, all of which belonged to Pepe's father. They are explicitly offered as symbols of maturation, but Pepe's subsequent actions force the reader into an understanding that material items cannot stand as proof of adulthood; it is how material items are used that determines a person's maturity. In the end, the hat and the coat, along with the rifle, water bag, and even the horse, are all important because they contribute to Pepe's ability to survive, which is weakened considerably when he loses them.

The most abstract symbol in "Flight" is the dark watchers. Most clearly they are unexplained figures that the people knew to avoid. But because they are unexplained, they take on other meanings to the reader. Because they are described as "dark," it is necessary to consider the watchers as belonging to a society different from that of Mama Torres.' Therefore, they represent a different set of codes, and because their society is in the mountains, they symbolize the foreignness of the world into which Pepe is traveling. Additionally, the description given forces the reader to also consider the dark watchers as symbolic of death. The narrator states that if the dark watchers are ignored, they will not bother someone who is minding his own business. Death, like the dark watchers, can be evaded if you ignore it, but it cannot ultimately be escaped. Pepe ignores death as long as he can, but when faced with its inevitability, he no longer ignores the dark, watching death, and it must take heed and claim Pepe for itself.

Bibliography

WORKS BY JOHN STEINBECK

Note: Page numbers referred to in the text are to the following Penguin editions.

Cannery Row. New York, 1994.
East of Eden. New York, 1992.
The Grapes of Wrath. New York, 1992.
The Long Valley. New York, 1995.
Of Mice and Men. New York, 1994.
The Pearl. New York, 1994.
The Red Pony. New York, 1994.
Tortilla Flat. New York, 1997.

FICTIONAL WORKS BY JOHN STEINBECK

Cup of Gold (1929)
The Pastures of Heaven (1932)
To a God Unknown (1933)
Tortilla Flat (1935)
In Dubious Battle (1936)
Of Mice and Men (novella; 1937)
The Long Valley (1938)
The Grapes of Wrath (1939)

The Moon Is Down (novella; 1942)
Cannery Row (1945)
The Pearl (novella; 1947)
The Wayward Bus (1947)
Burning Bright (novella; 1950)
East of Eden (1952)
Sweet Thursday (1954)
The Short Reign of Pippin IV (1957)
The Winter of Our Discontent (1961)

NONFICTION WORKS BY JOHN STEINBECK

Their Blood Is Strong (1938)
Sea of Cortez (1941)
Bombs Away (1942)
A Russian Journal (1948)
The Log from the Sea of Cortez (1951)
Once There Was a War (1958)
Travels with Charley in Search of America (1962)
America and Americans (1966)

POSTHUMOUS PUBLICATIONS

Journal of a Novel: The "East of Eden" Letters (1969)
Steinbeck: A Life in Letters (1952, 1969, 1975)
Viva Zapata! (1975)
The Acts of King Arthur and His Noble Knights (1976)
Working Days: The Journals of the Grapes of Wrath (1989)

WORKS ABOUT JOHN STEINBECK

BIOGRAPHIES

Benson, Jackson J. *The True Adventures of John Steinbeck, Writer.* New York: Viking, 1984.
Parini, Jay. *John Steinbeck: A Biography.* New York: Henry Holt, 1995.
Watt, F. W. *John Steinbeck.* New York: Grove Publishing, 1962.

GENERAL CRITICAL STUDIES OF STEINBECK'S WORK

Astro, Richard. *John Steinbeck and Edward F. Ricketts: The Shaping of a Novelist.* Minneapolis: University of Minnesota Press, 1973.

Astro, Richard, and Tetsumaro Hayashi, eds. *Steinbeck: The Man and His Work.* Corvallis, OR: Oregon State University Press, 1971.

Beach, Warren Joseph. "John Steinbeck: Art and Propaganda." In *American Fiction 1920–1940.* New York: Russell & Russell, 1960. 327–47.

Beegel, Susan F., Susan Shillinglaw, and Wesley N. Tiffney, Jr., eds. *Steinbeck and the Environment: Interdisciplinary Approaches.* Tuscaloosa: University of Alabama Press, 1997.

Coers, Donald V., Paul D. Ruffin, and Robert J. DeMott, eds. *After the Grapes of Wrath: Essays on John Steinbeck in Honor of Testsumaro Hayashi.* Athens: Ohio University Press, 1995.

Cook, Sylvia Jenkins. "Steinbeck, the People, and the Party." *American Fiction: 1914–1945,* Harold Bloom, ed. New York: Chelsea House Publishers, 1987. 347–59.

Ditsky, John. *John Steinbeck: Life, Work, and Criticism.* Fredericton, NB: York Press, 1985.

———. *John Steinbeck and the Critics.* Rochester, NY: Camden House, 2000.

Fensch, Thomas. *Conversations with John Steinbeck.* Jackson: University Press of Mississippi, 1988.

Fontenrose, Joseph. *John Steinbeck: An Introduction and Interpretation.* New York: Barnes & Noble, 1963.

French, Warren. *John Steinbeck.* New York: Grossett & Dunlap, 1961.

———. "John Steinbeck." In *The Politics of Twentieth-Century Novelists,* George A. Panichas, ed. New York: Hawthorn Books, 1971. 296–306.

———. *John Steinbeck's Fiction Revisted.* New York: Twayne Publishers, 1994.

Frohock, W. M. "John Steinbeck: The Utility of Wrath." In *The Novel of Violence in America.* Dallas: Southern Methodist University Press, 1950. 147–62.

Gannet, Lewis. *John Steinbeck: Personal and Bibliographical Notes.* New York: Viking, 1939.

Gladstein, Mimi Reisel. *The Indestructible Woman in Faulkner, Hemingway, and Steinbeck.* Ann Arbor, MI: UMI Research Press, 1986.

Hayashi, Tetsumaro, ed. *Steinbeck's Literary Dimension: A Guide to Comparative Studies.* Metuchen, NJ: Scarecrow Press, 1973.

———. *John Steinbeck: The Years of Greatness, 1936–1939.* Tuscaloosa: University of Alabama Press, 1993.

Jain, Sunita. *John Steinbeck's Concept of Man.* New Delhi: New Statesman Publishing, 1979.

Johnson, Claudia D. *Understanding* Of Mice and Men, The Red Pony, *and* The Pearl: *A Student Casebook to Issues, Sources, and Historical Documents.* Westport, CT: Greenwood Press, 1997.

Levant, Howard. *The Novels of John Steinbeck: A Critical Study.* Columbia: University of Missouri Press, 1974.

Lisca, Peter. *The Wide World of John Steinbeck.* New Brunswick, NJ: Rutgers University Press, 1958.

———. *John Steinbeck: Nature and Myth.* New York: Thomas Y. Crowell, 1978.

Marks, Lester Jay. *Thematic Design in the Novels of John Steinbeck*. The Hague: Mouton, 1969.

Millichap, Joseph R. *Steinbeck and Film*. New York: Frederick Ungar, 1983.

Noble, Donald R., ed. *The Steinbeck Question: New Essays in Criticism*. New York: Whitson Publishing, l993.

Simmonds, Roy. *John Steinbeck: The War Years, 1939–1945*. Lewisburg: Bucknell University Press, 1996.

St. Pierre, Brian. *John Steinbeck: The California Years*. The Literary West Series. San Francisco: Chronicle Books, 1983.

Tedlock, E. W., Jr., and C. V. Wickers, eds. *Steinbeck and His Critics: A Record of Twenty-five Years*. Albuquerque: University of New Mexico Press, 1957.

Timmerman, John H. *John Steinbeck's Fiction: The Aesthetics of the Road Taken*. Norman: University of Oklahoma Press, 1986.

———. "John Steinbeck's Use of the Bible: A Descriptive Bibliography of the Critical Tradition." *Steinbeck Quarterly* 21 (1988): 24–39.

Yano, Shigeharu, Tetsumaro Hayashi, Richard F. Peterson, and Yasuo Hashiguchi. *John Steinbeck: From Salinas to the World*. Tokyo: Gaku Shobo Press, 1986.

CONTEMPORARY REVIEWS OF STEINBECK'S SHORT FICTION

THE LONG VALLEY (1938)

Booklist, 1 Oct. 1938: 48.

Davis, Elmer. *Saturday Review of Literature*, 24 Sept. 1938: 11.

New Yorker, 24 Sept. 1938: 92.

Soskin, William. *New York Herald Tribune Books,* 18 Sept. 1938: 7.

Thompson, Ralph. *New York Times*, 21 Sept. 1938: 29.

———. *Yale Review*, Winter 1939: X.

Young, Stanley. *New York Times Book Review,* 25 Sept. 1938: 7.

THE RED PONY (1945): "THE GIFT" (1933, 1937, 1938, 1945), "THE GREAT MOUNTAINS" (1937, 1945), "THE PROMISE" (1937, 1938, 1945), "THE LEADER OF THE PEOPLE" (1936, 1938, 1945)

Chicago Sun Book Week, 16 Sept. 1945: 2.

New York Herald Tribune Books, 4 Nov. 1945: 6.

Thompson, Ralph. *New York Times,* 29 Sept. 1937: 21.

Time, 11 Oct. 1937: 79.

Walton, Edith H. *New York Times Book Review,* 10 Oct. 1937: 7.

CRITICISM OF STEINBECK'S SHORT FICTION

Davison, Richard Allan. "Hemingway, Steinbeck, and the Art of the Short Story." *Steinbeck Quarterly* 21.3–4 (1988): 73–84.

Hughes, Robert S., Jr. *Beyond* The Red Pony: *A Reader's Companion to Steinbeck's Complete Short Stories.* Metuchen, NJ: Scarecrow, 1987.

———. "Steinbeck, The Short Story Writer." In *Steinbeck's Short Stories in* The Long Valley: *Essays in Criticism,* Tetsumaro Hayashi, ed. Muncie, IN: Ball State University, 1991. 78–91.

Timmerman, John H. *The Dramatic Landscape of Steinbeck's Short Stories.* Norman: University of Oklahoma Press, 1990.

"THE CHRYSANTHEMUMS" (1937, 1938)

Osborne, William R. "The Texts of Steinbeck's 'The Chrysanthemums.'" *Modern Fiction Studies* 12 (Winter 1966–67): 479–84.

Petite, Joseph. "The Invisible Woman in Steinbeck's 'The Chrysanthemums.'" *Journal of Evolutionary Psychology* 16 (1995): 285–91.

Piwinski, David J. "Floral Gold in Steinbeck's 'The Chrysanthemums.'" *Notes on Contemporary Literature* 27.5 (1997): 4–5.

Shillinglaw, Susan. "'The Chrysanthemums': Steinbeck's Pygmalion." In *Steinbeck's Short Stories in* The Long Valley: *Essays in Criticism*, Tetsumaro Hayashi, ed. Muncie, IN: Ball State University, 1991. 1–9.

"FLIGHT" (1938)

Antico, John. "A Reading of Steinbeck's Flight." *Modern Fiction Studies* 11 (Spring 1965): 45–53.

Benton, Robert M. "A Search for Meaning in 'Flight.'" *Steinbeck's Short Stories in* The Long Valley: *Essays in Criticism,* Tetsumaro Hayashi, ed. Muncie, IN: Steinbeck Society of America, Ball State University, 1991. 18–31.

Jones, William M. "Steinbeck's 'Flight.'" *Explicator* 18 (1959): 11.

Vogel, Dann. "Steinbeck's 'Flight': The Myth of Manhood." *College English* 23 (1961): 225–26.

THE RED PONY (1945)

Goldsmith, Arnold L. "Thematic Rhythm in *The Red Pony.*" *College English* 26 (1965): 391–94.

Hayashi, Tetsumaro, and Thomas J. Moore, eds. *Steinbeck's* The Red Pony: *Essays in Criticism.* Steinbeck Monograph Series, no. 13. Muncie, IN: Ball State University Press, 1988.

Simmonds, Roy S. "The First Publication of Steinbeck's 'The Leader of the People.'" *Steinbeck Quarterly* 7 (Winter 1975): 13–18.

TORTILLA FLAT (1935)

CONTEMPORARY REVIEWS

Benet, William Rose. *Saturday Review of Literature*, 1 June 1935: 12.
Chamberlain, John. *Current History* XLII (July 1935): 7.
Chicago Daily Tribune, 1 June 1935: 14.
Colby, Harriet. *New York Herald Tribune Books,* 2 June 1935: 4.
Mangione, Jerre. *New Republic*, 13 July 1935: 285.
Marsh, Fred T. *New York Times*, 2 June 1935: 6.
Neville, Helen. *Nation*, 19 June 1935: 720.
Saturday Review (London), 23 Nov. 1935: 501.
Spectator, 6 Dec. 1935: 960.

CRITICISM

Alexander, Stanley. "The Conflict of Form in *Tortilla Flat*." *American Literature* 40
    (1968): 58–66.
Hayashi, Tetsumaro. *Steinbeck and the Arthurian Theme.* Steinbeck Monograph Series,
    no. 5. Muncie, IN: Steinbeck Society of America, Ball State University, 1975.
Justus, James H. "The Transient World of *Tortilla Flat*." *Western Review: A Journal
    of the Humanities* 7 (1970): 55–60.
Kinney, Arthur F. "The Arthurian Cycle in *Tortilla Flat*." *Modern Fiction Studies* 11
    (1965): 11–20.
Uchida, Shigeharu. "Sentimental Steinbeck and His *Tortilla Flat*." *Kyushu American
    Literature* 7 (1964): 8–12.

OF MICE AND MEN (1937)

CONTEMPORARY REVIEWS

Canby, Henry S. *Saturday Review of Literature*, 27 Feb. 1937: 7.
Commonweal, 10 Dec. 1937: 191.
Literary Digest, 18 Dec. 1937: 34.
Newsweek, 27 Feb. 1937: 39.
Paul, Louis. *New York Herald Tribune Books*, 28 Feb. 1937.
Thompson, Ralph. *New York Times*, 27 Feb. 1937: 15.
———. *New York Times,* 2 Mar. 1937: 19.
Time, 1 Mar. 1937: 69.
Van Doren, Mark. *Nation*, 6 Mar. 1937: 275.
Walton, Eda Lou. *New York Times Book Review*, 28 Feb. 1937: 7, 20.
Weeks, Donald. *Atlantic Monthly*, Apr. 1937: 384–85.
Wyatt, Euphemia. *Catholic World*, Jan. 1938, 468–69.
Young, Stark. *New Republic*, 15 Dec. 1937: 170–71.

CRITICISM

Ganapathy, R. "Steinbeck's *Of Mice and Men*: A Study of Lyricism Through Primitivism." *Literary Criterion* 5 (1962): 101–104.

Goldhurst, William. "*Of Mice and Men*: John Steinbeck's Parable of the Curse of Cain." *Western American Literature* 6 (Summer 1971): 123–35.

Hadella, Charlotte Cook. Of Mice and Men: *A Kinship of Powerlessness*. New York: Twayne Publishers, 1995.

Lisca, Peter. "Motif and Pattern in *Of Mice and Men*." *Modern Fiction Studies* 2 (Winter 1956): 228–34.

Marsden, John L. "California Dreamin': The Significance of 'A Coupla Acres' in Steinbeck's *Of Mice and Men*." *Western American Literature* 29 (1995): 291–97.

Owens, Louis. "*Of Mice and Men*: The Dream of Commitment." In *John Steinbeck's Re-Vision of America*. Athens: Unversity of Georgia Press, 1985. 100–106.

Scheer, Ronald. "*Of Mice and Men*: Novel, Play, Movie." *The American Examiner* VI (Fall/Winter 1978–79): 6–39.

Spilka, Mark. "Of George and Lennie and Curley's Wife: Sweet Violence in Steinbeck's Eden." *Modern Fiction Studies* 20 (Summer 1974): 169–79.

THE GRAPES OF WRATH (1939)

CONTEMPORARY REVIEWS

Angoff, Charles. *North American Review*, Summer 1939: 387.

Birney, Earl. *Canadian Forum*, June 1939: 94–95.

Booklist, 15 Apr. 1939: 271.

Caskey, J. Homer. *Saturday Review of Literature*, 20 May 1939: 9.

Christian Science Monitor, 6 May 1939: 13.

Cowley, Malcolm. *New Republic*, 3 May 1939: 382–83.

Fadiman, Clifton. *New Yorker*, 15 Apr. 1939: 81.

Jack, Peter Monro. *New York Times Book Review*, 16 Apr. 1939: 2.

Jackson, Joseph Henry. *New York Herald Tribune Books*, 16 Apr. 1939: 3.

Kronenberger, Louis. *Nation*, 15 Apr. 1939: 440–41.

Kuhl, Art. *Catholic World*, Nov. 1939: 160–65.

Stevens, George. *Saturday Review of Literature*, 15 Apr. 1939: 3.

Thompson, Ralph. *Yale Review*, Summer 1939: viii.

Time, 17 Apr. 1939: 87.

Times (London) Literary Supplement, 9 Sept. 1939: 525.

Vaughan, James N. *Commonweal*, 28 July 1939: 341–42.

Weeks, Edward. *Atlantic*, Apr. 1939: 591.

———. *Atlantic*, May 1939: 734.

West, Anthony. *New Statesman & Nation*, 16 Sept. 1939: 404–5.

CRITICISM

Bloom, Harold, ed. *Modern Critical Interpretations of* The Grapes of Wrath. New York: Chelsea House, 1988.

Bowron, Bernard. "*The Grapes of Wrath*: A 'Wagons West' Romance." *Colorado Quarterly* 3 (1954): 84–91.

Carpenter, Frederick. "John Steinbeck: The Philosophical Joads." *College English* 2 (1941): 315–25.

Davis, Robert Con, ed. *Twentieth-Century Interpretations of* The Grapes of Wrath. Englewood Cliffs, NJ: Prentice Hall, 1982.

Ditsky, John. *Critical Essays on Steinbeck's* The Grapes of Wrath. Boston: G. K. Hall, 1989.

———. " 'Pu-raise Gawd fur Vittory!': Gramma as Prophet." *Steinbeck Newsletter* 6.2 (1993): 4–5.

———, ed. "*The Grapes of Wrath*: A Reconsideration." *Southern Humanities Review* 13 (Summer 1979): 215–220.

Donohue, Agnes McNeill, ed. *A Casebook on* The Grapes of Wrath. New York: Thomas Y. Crowell, 1968.

French, Warren, ed. *A Companion to* The Grapes of Wrath. New York: The Viking Press, 1963.

Hayashi, Tetsumaro. "Women and the Principle of Continuity in *The Grapes of Wrath.*" *Kyushu American Literature* 10 (1967): 75–80.

———, ed. *Steinbeck's* The Grapes of Wrath: *Essays in Criticism*. Steinbeck Essay Series, no. 3. Muncie, IN: Steinbeck Research Institute, Ball State Univesity, 1990.

Heavilin, Barbara A., ed. *The Critical Response to John Steinbeck's* The Grapes of Wrath. Westport, CT: Greenwood, 2000.

Johnson, Claudia D. *Understanding* The Grapes of Wrath: *A Student Casebook to Issues, Sources, and Historical Documents*. Westport, CT: Greenwood Press, 1999.

McCarthy, Paul. "House and Shelter as Symbol in *The Grapes of Wrath.*" *South Dakota Review* 5 (Winter 1967): 48–67.

Motley, Warren. "From Patriarchy to Matriarchy: Ma Joad's Role in *The Grapes of Wrath.*" *American Literature* 54 (October 1982): 397–412.

Owens, Louis. The Grapes of Wrath: *Trouble in the Promised Land*. Boston: Twayne, 1989.

Pollock, Theodore. "On the Ending of *The Grapes of Wrath.*" *Modern Fiction Studies* 4 (1958): 177–78.

Shillinglaw, Susan, ed. "*The Grapes of Wrath*: A Special Issue." *San Jose Studies* XVI (Winter 1990).

Shockley, Martin Staples. "Christian Symbolism in *The Grapes of Wrath.*" *College English* 18 (1956): 87–90.

———. "The Reception of *The Grapes of Wrath* in Oklahoma." *American Literature* 15 (1944): 351–61.

Timmerman, John. "The Squatter's Circle in *The Grapes of Wrath.*" *Studies in American Fiction* 17 (Autumn 1989): 203–11.

Visser, Nicholas. "Audience and Closure in *The Grapes of Wrath.*" *Studies in American Fiction* 22 (1994): 19–36.

Wyatt, David, ed. *New Essays on* The Grapes of Wrath. New York: Cambridge University Press, 1990.

CANNERY ROW (1945)

CONTEMPORARY REVIEWS

Adams, J. Donald. *New York Times Book Review*, 14 Jan. 1945: 2.

Booklist, 1 Jan. 1945: 140.

Chicago Sun Book Week, 7 Jan. 1945: 6.

Commonweal, 26 Jan. 1945: 378.

Cousins, Norman. *Saturday Review of Literature*, 17 Mar. 1945: 14.

Longaker, Mark. *Catholic World*, Mar. 1945: 570–71.

Manchester Guardian, 9 Nov. 1945: 3.

Marshall, Margaret. *Nation*, 20 Jan. 1945: 75–76.

Matthiessen, F. O. Review of *Cannery Row. New York Times Book Review*, 31 Dec. 1944: 1.

Mayberry, George. *New Republic*, 15 Jan. 1945: 89–90.

Prescott, Orville. *New York Times* 2 Jan. 1945: 17.

Rothman, Nathan L. "A Small Miracle." *Saturday Review of Literature*, 30 Dec. 1944: 5.

Time, 1 Jan. 1945: 62.

Times (London) Literary Supplement, 3 Nov. 1945: 521.

Toynbee, Philip. *New Statesman & Nation*, 24 Nov. 1945: 356–57.

Wilson, Edmund. *The New Yorker*, 6 Jan. 1945: 62.

Wooster, Harold A. *Library Journal*, 1 Jan. 1945: 32.

CRITICISM

Ariss, Bruce. *Inside Cannery Row*. San Francisco: Lexikos, 1988.

Benson, Jackson J. "John Steinbeck's *Cannery Row*: A Reconsideration." *Western American Literature* 12 (1977): 11–40.

Hedgpeth, Joel. W. "Philosophy on Cannery Row." In *Steinbeck: The Man and His Work*, Richard Astro and Tetsumaro Hayashi, eds. Corvallis: Oregon State Univesity Press, 1971. 89–129.

Lundy, Scrap. "The Unknown Heroes of *Cannery Row.*" *Steinbeck Newsletter* 9 (1995): 29–31.

McKibben, Carol. "Monterey's Cannery Women." *Steinbeck Newsletter* 9 (1995): 26–28.

Owens, Lewis. "*Cannery Row*: 'An Essay in Loneliness.'" In *John Steinbeck's Re-Vision of America*. Athens: Unversity of Georgia Press, 1985.

THE PEARL (1947)

CONTEMPORARY REVIEWS

Baker, Carlos. *New York Times Book Review*, 30 Nov. 1947: 4.
Booklist, 15 Dec. 1947: 152.
Chicago Sun Book Week, 23 Nov. 1947: 7.
Farrelly, John. *New Republic*, 23 Dec. 1947: 28.
Geismar, Maxwell. *Saturday Review of Literature*, 22 Nov. 1947: 14.
Hunter, Anne. *Commonweal*, 23 Janl 1948: 377.
Kingery, Robert E. *Library Journal*, 1 Nov. 1947: 1540.
New Yorker, 27 Dec. 1947: 59.
Newsweek, 8 Mar. 1948: 83–84.
Prescott, Orville. *New York Times*, 24 Nov. 1947: 21.
San Francisco Chronicle, 14 Dec. 1947: 16.
Sugrue, Thomas. *New York Herald Tribune*, 7 Dec. 1947: 4.
Time, 22 Dec. 1947: 90.
Weeks, Edward. *Atlantic*, Dec. 1947: 138–39.

CRITICISM

Karson, Jill, ed. *Readings on* The Pearl. San Diego, CA: Greenhaven, 1999.
Karsten, Ernest E., Jr. "Thematic Structure in *The Pearl*." *English Journal* 54 (1965): 1–7.
Morris, Harry. "*The Pearl*: Realism and Allegory." *English Journal* 52 (1963): 487–95, 503. Rptd. in *Steinbeck: A Collection of Critical Essays*. Robert Murray Davis, ed. Englewood Cliffs, NJ: Prentice-Hall, 1972. 149–162.
Simmonds, Roy S. "Steinbeck's *The Pearl*: Legend, Film, Novel." In *The Short Novels of John Steinbeck*. Jackson J. Benson, ed. Durham, NC: Duke University Press, 1990.
Timmerman, John H. "The Shadow and the Pearl: Jungian Patterns in *The Pearl*." In *The Short Novels of John Steinbeck*. Jackson J. Benson, ed. Durham, NC: Duke University Press, 1990. 143–61.

EAST OF EDEN (1952)

CONTEMPORARY REVIEWS

Booklist, 15 Jul. 1952: 369.
————, 19 Sept. 1952: 33.
Bookmark Oct. 1952: 10.
Brunn, Robert R. *Christian Science Monitor*, 25 Sept. 1952: 11.
Chargnes, R. D. *Spectator*, 28 Nov. 1952: 744.
Gurko, Leo. *Nation*, 20 Sept. 1952: 235–36.
Hughes, Riley. *Catholic World*, Nov. 1952: 150–51.
Jackson, Joseph Henry. *San Francisco Chronicle*, 21 Sept. 1952: 20.
Krutch, Joseph Wood. *New York Herald Tribune Books*, 21 Sept. 1952: 1.
Mizener, Arthur. *New Republic*, 6 Oct. 1952: 22–23.
Prescott, Orville. *New York Times,* 19 Sept. 1952: 21.
Rolo, Charles. *Atlantic,* Oct. 1952: 94.
Schorer, Mark. *New York Times Book Review*, 21 Sept. 1952: 1.
Smith, Eleanor Trouhey. *Library Journal,* Aug. 1952: 1303.
Time 22, Sept. 1952: 110.
Times (London) Literary Supplement, 5 Dec. 1952: 789.
Webster, Harvey Curtis, and Bernard Kolb. *Saturday Review,* 20 Sept. 1952: 11–12.
West, Anthony. *New Yorker*, 20 Sept. 1952: 111–13.
Yale Review, Autumn 1962: 8.

CRITICISM

Buerger, Daniel. "'History' and Fiction in *East of Eden* Criticism." *Steinbeck Quarterly* 14 (1981): 6–14.
Cox, Martha Heasley. "Steinbeck's Family Portraits: The Hamiltons." *Steinbeck Quarterly* 14 (1981): 23–32.
Ditsky, John. *Essays on* East of Eden. Steinbeck Monograph Series. Muncie, IN: Ball State University Press, 1977.
————. "'I Kind of Like Caleb': Naming in *East of Eden*." *Steinbeck Newsletter* 10:1 (1997): 7–9.
Everest, Beth, and Judy Wedeles. "The Neglected Rib: Women in *East of Eden*." *Steinbeck Quarterly* 21:1–2 (1988): 13–23.
Gribben, John. "Steinbeck's *East of Eden* and Milton's *Paradise Lost*: A Discussion of 'Timshel.'" In *Steinbeck's Literary Dimension: A Guide to Comparative Studies*. Tetsumaro Hayashi, ed. Metuchen, NJ: Scarecrow Press, 1973.
Lore, Craig M. "Abracadabra in Steinbeck's *East of Eden*." *Steinbeck Newsletter* 10.1 (1997): 11.
Owens, Louis. "The Story of a Writing. Narrative Structure in *East of Eden*." In *Rediscovering Steinbeck: Revisionist Views of His Art, Politics, and Intellect*, Cliff

Lewis and Carol Britch, eds. Lewiston, NY: The Edwin Mellon Press, 1989.

Wright, Terence R. "*East of Eden* as Western Midrash: Steinbeck's Re-Marking of Cain." *Religion and the Arts* 2 (1998): 488–518.

Index

About the Author

CYNTHIA BURKHEAD is an Instructor of English at the University of North Alabama in Florence. Her major area of literary interest is twentieth-century poetry and fiction.